# BILL VEECK, LOU BOUDREAU, BOB FELLER, AND THE 1948 CLEVELAND INDIANS

## LEW FREEDMAN

SPORTS
PUBLISHING

# To long-suffering Indians fans

Sports Publishing books may be purchased in bulk at special discounts for sales promotion, corporate gifts, fund-raising, or educational purposes. Special editions can also be created to specifications. For details, contact the Special Sales Department, Sports Publishing, 307 West 36th Street, 11th Floor, New York, NY 10018 or sportspubbooks@skyhorsepublishing.com.

Sports Publishing® is a registered trademark of Skyhorse Publishing, Inc.®, a Delaware corporation.

Visit our website at www.sportspubbooks.com.

10 9 8 7 6 5 4 3 2 1

Library of Congress Cataloging-in-Publication Data

Freedman, Lew.
 A summer to remember : Bill Veeck, Lou Boudreau, Bob Feller, and the 1948 Cleveland Indians / Lew Freedman.
    pages cm
 Summary: "A Summer to Remember is a fantastic look at one of the greatest teams ever to play the game, and at how everyone involved in this extraordinary season--from the players to management--made 1948 a memorable year for baseball and the city of Cleveland"-- Provided by publisher.
 ISBN 978-1-61321-647-7 (hardback)
 1. Cleveland Indians (Baseball team)--History. I. Title.
 GV875.C7F74 2014
 796.357'640977132--dc23
                        2014002141

Printed in the United States of America

# TABLE OF CONTENTS

# INTRODUCTION

**T**HE GREATEST BASEBALL summer in Cleveland history was brought to Indians fans by The Maverick, The Boy Wonder, The Pioneer, The Ageless Marvel, and The Good Kid.

The greatest baseball summer in Cleveland history culminated in the early autumn with one of two World Series championships in franchise history.

The greatest baseball summer in Cleveland history was a season-long festival of joy more than sixty-five years ago, yet it seems as fresh and real to fans of today as it was then. Not only was it the last time the Indians won the world championship, the 1948 team was special not only for its achievement, but for the baseball personalities that dominated the roster. It was the stuff of dreams coming true—not just for the delirious observers, but for the people who made it happen.

Since 1948 was also the last year the Cleveland Indians won the World Series, the achievement is all that much fresher because there is no more recent competing memory of equivalent pleasure. Only one other time, in 1920, have the Indians won it all. Given the passage of the better part of a century, there can be few living witnesses to recall the glory of that team. The accomplishment of the 1920 team was also marred by an incident of incredible sadness. During the course of the campaign, shortstop Ray Chapman was struck in the head by a pitched ball and died the next day. He is the only Major League player to be killed as a direct result of a play on the field.

Beyond that, the Indians who made 1948 so sweet, who crafted such a brilliant season, stand out far more as a group than the 1920 bunch. The '48 squad was a once-in-a-lifetime achiever; a confluence of circumstances never to be repeated. Some of the most colorful and popular individuals in baseball history— and certainly Cleveland Indians history—were collected on the shore of Lake Erie that summer and turned loose to create a story as dramatic and exciting as any novel.

* * *

Bill Veeck was the new owner of the Tribe; the soon-to-be labeled "Maverick" who had been waiting a lifetime for a chance to run a big-league ball club the way he saw fit. He had a shoebox full of ideas and when his agile mind was turned loose, he helped make the Indians the most popular team in the sport's history. Playing in Cleveland's gargantuan Municipal Stadium, Veeck gave the fans not only a winner, but better entertainment than could be found on Broadway or in the movies. They flocked to the stadium at a record pace.

The most beloved player in team history was no longer a "Boy Wonder" in 1948, but a seasoned pro. Bob Feller had proven himself to be one of the best pitchers of all time, and he was still throwing hard enough that if a batter blinked, he'd missed his fastball.

Overshadowed by the explosive debut of Jackie Robinson with the Brooklyn Dodgers, Indians outfielder Larry Doby was the first African American to play in the American League, the circuit's "Pioneer" and the second to take a Major League field during the twentieth century. Veeck believed in integrating the game and he put his wallet where his heart was in hiring Doby from the Newark Eagles.

When Veeck needed bullpen help as the season wore on and the Indians scratched to hold onto first place and fight off other contenders for the pennant, Veeck went shopping again, this time reaching out to "The Ageless Marvel." That was Satchel Paige, who had been wowing batters in the Negro Leagues and against barnstorming white teams for more than twenty years already. One of the mysteries that trailed the crowd-pleasing, fireball-throwing hurler was just how old he really was: in his forties, that's for sure. It was too late for true Major League justice to be administered in the case of a past-his-prime Paige, but it was not too late, as many contended, for him to still have moments in the sun.

The manager of this extraordinary team was the extraordinary Lou Boudreau. In a position that went extinct roughly a quarter of a century ago, Boudreau was the squad's player-manager. During the first half of the twentieth century, player-managers, combining the role of full-time field boss and active player, were quite common in the big leagues. "The Good Kid" was both the shortstop and the buck-stops-here leader of the Indians in the dugout and clubhouse. Rarely, if ever, has any single man ever combined the two demanding roles so successfully in the sport's history.

Even more remarkably, despite the supreme talents of those players led by a visionary owner, one other fresh face whom almost no one in Cleveland had ever heard of before the first pitch of the '48 season in April was an even more important contributor than any of them. Rookie Gene Bearden was a supernova who would have a superb season.

And those were just the biggest names. It was a season when newcomers showing their face for the first time played cameo roles. There was drama throughout the long pennant chase as the always-dangerous and usually triumphant New York Yankees lingered on the Indians' shoulders and the resurgent Boston Red Sox, riding the broad back of Ted Williams, would not fade away, either. The result was the first regular-season standings tie in American League history, necessitating a playoff game to determine the opponent for the National League champion Boston Braves.

Along the way Veeck orchestrated special fan nights, just in case a winner on the field was not enough by itself to fill the cavernous stadium. Veeck might as well have had the phrase "A Good Time Was Had By All" tattooed on his chest because he thought it was a sin for anyone to enter a ballpark and not leave it with a smile on his face.

There was only so much in Veeck's control, however. He could not regulate the drama on the field, but if it produced a no-hitter (which it did), so be it. And if the season produced, frighteningly, almost a repeat death of an Indians player while he was at the plate, not so different from 1920, that was horrifying, but that was in God's hands. Yes, there were times in

1948 when the Indians had to come together and rise above adversity.

Nearly everyone connected with the Cleveland Indians of 1948 has passed away, certainly including the majority of their fans. But the Cleveland Indians play on in a new ballpark called Progressive Field. Outside of one of the main gates stands a bigger-than-life statue of Bob Feller in the midst of his wind-up. Rapid Robert watches over the club from this perch.

The team has three times since competed in the World Series, losing in 1954, losing in 1995, and losing in 1997. There have been good times to savor and depressing times to wallow in. The franchise seems to be on the upswing again. The fans of Cleveland have waited a long time to enjoy another championship run.

When the day comes that the Indians win another World Series, the city will rejoice. But any new championship bauble for the trophy case will never replace the drama, suspense, excitement and sheer pleasure of 1948. The Indians can never "top this." The saga of Bill Veeck, Bob Feller, Larry Doby, Satchel Paige, Lou Boudreau, and Gene Bearden is unique.

—**Lew Freedman**
January, 2014

# 1

## 1946–1947

**B**ILL VEECK WAS thirty-three years old when he wheeled and dealed, smooth-talked and cajoled, lobbied and painted a Picasso of word pictures in conjunction with enough guys with deep pockets to buy the Cleveland Indians and become president of the fabled American League franchise.

By then, Veeck was a seasoned front-office man, having been a minor-league team operative and a U.S. Marine veteran hobbled by a serious leg wound suffered during World War II. Unfortunately for him, the leg would give him grief for years and require multiple surgeries.

Putting the best possible light on what some might term a disability that would haunt them for a lifetime, Veeck chose the wooden-leg option and indicative of his adaptability as a man who viewed life as a glass half-full—provided the liquid was scotch—had his faux limb outfitted with an ashtray.

Just in case anyone wondered about the pronunciation of his last name, Veeck later titled an autobiography, *Veeck—As In Wreck*. While his conservative fellow owners, known more for their grouchiness and looking out for No. 1, indeed viewed him as an out-of-control wreck, Veeck actually spread baseball joy wherever he tread and took his franchises on flavorful, but not reckless, romps.

It might be said that Veeck was born to become a baseball entrepreneur. His father, the first Bill Veeck, was a Chicago sports columnist whose acerbic views of the mishandling of the workings of the Chicago Cubs led the exasperated Wrigley family to offer him a job and see if he could do better than current management. He could, and the Cubs won pennants in 1929 and 1932 before his death.

The younger Veeck grew up in the Cubs' offices, working behind the scenes from the time he was thirteen. He took tickets, sold tickets, and watched his father dream up ways to sell more tickets. His father invented Ladies Day, a promotion where women could get into games for free, in hopes of widening the team's audience. Bill stayed with the team after his father passed away, eventually becoming the team's treasurer, but even more famously the guy who installed the famous ivy on Wrigley Field's outfield fencing.

Bill Veeck Jr. had a gift for mingling with the masses, pleasing the everyman, and a knack for filling the house that through the years drew comparisons to P. T. Barnum for brazen hucksterism. While other owners believed he was running his own circus, Veeck never lost sight of the fact that he was selling baseball. Like other owners, Veeck believed that the best way to sell his product was to put a winner on the field. However, his outlook was of this ilk: Why take chances? So he employed his creativity to woo fans to the park with varied entertainment, giveaways, and special nights. That way even if the team did not fulfill its mission by winning that particular game the fan would go home happy anyway. The idea was to make sure that when a spectator went home he was a satisfied customer; whether the team won or lost, and that the next free moment he had he would think favorably about the old town team and come out for another game.

While Veeck was weaned on the Cubs, by the time he was twenty-seven, he was in charge of the Milwaukee Brewers AAA team, in partnership with "Jolly Cholly," otherwise known as Charlie Grimm, the Cub lifer as a player, manager, and broadcaster. This enabled Veeck to try out his promotional schemes off-Broadway. Veeck was the co-owner of record for five years, but he spent three of those years in the Marines. While he was away, his co-owner Grimm telegraphed him the news that he had hired Casey Stengel as manager. It was exactly the type of personnel move Veeck would have made on his own.

During combat in the South Pacific, his right foot was mashed by an artillery unit on its recoil. From there on, Veeck would endure thirty-six operations on the foot and leg. Although the grievousness of the impact put a crimp in Veeck's running ability, it never dented his disposition. Veeck was a night crawler, a carouser, a man who loved a good joke, who enjoyed a good gag, and he very much believed that smiles were in short supply in Major League front offices. He had put in an apprenticeship with the Cubs and when he walked away from Milwaukee ownership, he left with a $275,000 profit—the original cost of the franchise to Veeck's group was $100,000. It was Veeck's dream to apply his theories to the big leagues and if it couldn't be in his native Chicago, Cleveland would do.

In 1946, wealthy Cleveland businessman Alva Bradley, whose sources of income included coal and real estate, put the Indians up for sale. He had been the head of the group that owned the team since 1927. Unlike Bradley and other magnates that served as presidents of their teams, Veeck was not independently wealthy; he just knew people with money who liked baseball. When he learned the Indians were for sale, Veeck raised his eyebrows, but also his guard. Was Cleveland a hopeless case for a baseball city?

Veeck traveled to Cleveland to find out. He spent four days touring the city alone, so as to avoid city fathers putting a smiley face on things. Instead, he spent his time jawing with men on the street and saloon frequenters, gabbing about baseball. He estimated he made between 100 and 150 stops. "I talk[ed] to cab drivers and bartenders, because these are the people who deal in conversation," Veeck said, "the way a butcher deals in veal chops."[1]

From this less-than-scientific sampling, Veeck determined that the people of Cleveland had "enthusiasm with the team and utter disillusionment about the operation."[2]

Veeck was not a money bags and although he was friendly with people who rented penthouses and whose pockets were deeper than the Dead Sea, he did not even dress the part of a tycoon. Veeck was famous for never wearing a sport coat or tie. Along with the curly hair that earned him one nickname of "burrhead," he was also commonly referred to in the press as "Sportshirt Bill." He did not breach his sartorial rules for any reason, including appointments with bank presidents when seeking loans. This meant that occasionally those high poobahs viewed him as someone who stumbled off the street from the beach.

Being the possessor of a nimble mind, as well as a facile tongue, Veeck pulled together the $2.2 million purchase price and became president of the Cleveland Indians. One of Veeck's minority shareholders was comedian and actor Bob Hope, who was originally from Cleveland. If things went horribly wrong, Hope could always tell jokes on a microphone at home plate to amuse the crowd.

After a lengthy negotiation and approval process by the American League owners, the deal was consummated on June 22, 1946. This was well into what would be a lost season for the Indians, but Veeck immediately put his personal stamp on the team by announcing that all games henceforth would be broadcast on the radio, instead of just some. He was also prepared to abandon rickety League Park, which opened in 1891 and had no lights for night games. The park was closed in September of '46, and from then, on the Indians called Municipal Stadium home.

It was too late to salvage the '46 season, and the shaky Indians finished 68–86 in sixth place in the eight-team American League. Bob Feller was the ace of the staff (26–15) with Lou Boudreau anchoring the infield. Veeck was pretty much an unknown quantity at the Major League level at that point in his career. What fans would soon learn was that he wasn't shy about making trades. In an era decades before cell phones, Veeck lived with a phone pressed against one ear. He showed no respect for the clock if he wanted to track down another team's boss and he could be short on sentiment when it came to dealing a local favorite if he thought it would help his team win more games. Almost three decades later, Veeck sought to rebuild one of his teams (the Chicago White Sox) by setting up a desk in the lobby of the main hotel at baseball's winter meetings with an "Open for Business" sign posted on it. However, the philosophy was deeply ingrained and dated to his first days in charge of the Indians.

Making baseball trades can be a little bit like gambling in Las Vegas. You might get lucky and have it work out, but you might also get clobbered by the house. And once in a while you just break even. In the time when Veeck took over the Indians halfway through the '46 season to '48, he shuffled the deck frequently. One trade that was a win-win was his swap of pitcher Allie Reynolds to the New York Yankees for second baseman Joe Gordon and utility fielder Eddie Bockman on October 19, 1946. Reynolds and Gordon were terrific players, but Cleveland needed a second sacker.

The Indians and Yankees did not stop there. They traded a few less prominent players, but one of the pitchers Veeck obtained as a throw-in was a minor-league twirler named Gene Bearden. Bearden could as easily have never been heard from again, and he spent all of 1947 in the minors except for one Indians appearance.[3]

"I'm not going to say that I thought Bearden was going to be anything special," Veeck said. "He was the biggest surprise I've ever had in baseball."[4]

In 1947, Bill Veeck was the biggest surprise Lou Boudreau had in baseball. Boudreau was the best position player on the Indians, and in 1941, at the age of twenty-five, was promoted to player-manager by then-Indians president, Alva Bradley. Veeck loved Boudreau as a shortstop, but did not admire his managing acumen. Veeck was tight with Casey Stengel, who hadn't coached professionally since 1943.[5] Boudreau was a valuable commodity and Veeck felt he could pick up a couple of starting players for him in a trade.

Boudreau had been somewhat of a legendary figure as a high school athlete growing up in the Chicago area—as a basketball player. He led his high school to the Illinois State Championship and two runner-up finishes, and was captain of the basketball and baseball teams in college at the University of Illinois. Renowned Indians scout and later general manager Cy Slapnicka, who also signed Bob Feller, spotted Boudreau on the college diamond. Later, Boudreau earned the nickname "The Good Kid," because he had trouble remembering people's names and called them "Good Kid."

Almost immediately after taking control of the Indians, Veeck, with his close friend and assistant Harry Grabiner, invited Boudreau to dinner in the new boss' hotel suite. Grabiner was going to push for Jimmy Dykes as the new manager, thus beginning an uneasy partnership. Veeck had watched Boudreau operate in '46, and still wasn't wedded to the dual role.

Veeck was not easily intimidated, but he did believe that having the fans on his side was crucial to running a successful franchise. When it leaked that Veeck was going to trade Boudreau to the St. Louis Browns for Vern Stephens, a power-hitting shortstop, and others, he faced a fan mutiny that was nearly as momentous as the crew backlash against William Bligh on the *Bounty*. This was one time Veeck retreated, and Boudreau stayed; not just in Cleveland, but as player-manager.

Boudreau was wary of the boss' intentions as soon as he heard Veeck was going to be the new owner, but the trade rumors

still blindsided him. There had been no reports of an imminent change at the top until three days before the bombshell hit
that Bradley was out. Boudreau said Veeck promptly told him
he was the best shortstop in the game, but made it clear that he
was lukewarm about his managing. After their initial meeting
Boudreau knew where he stood.

"I concentrated on proving to Veeck the things I felt I
had already proved—that I could handle both jobs well,"
Boudreau said.[6]

At mid-season a surprising occurrence gave Veeck an opportunity to show his loyalty to Boudreau as a player. Boudreau
had been on the American League All-Star team every season
from 1940 through '45, but was left off the team in '46 when
managers chose the roster. Veeck protested loudly to AL President Will Harridge, announcing that everyone knew Boudreau
was the best shortstop in the league. Veeck seized on the sour
moment to make Boudreau feel better about being overlooked.

"He gave me a night," Boudreau said. "He also presented
me with a huge trophy that was inscribed, 'To The Greatest
Shortstop Ever Left Off The All-Star Team.'"[7] It was one way
to mend fences and close the distance between the two strong-
willed men.

* * *

Veeck had been waiting a long time to implement his ideas for
fan entertainment at the big-league level. One of the first things
he did was hire a comic named Jackie Price. Price was a character with a bizarre assortment of skills. He could hang upside
down and take batting practice for fifteen minutes. He could
hit two balls thrown to him simultaneously. And in a maneuver

that never failed to astonish, Price could throw baseballs simultaneously to three different bases. While his antics were usually beloved, Price once went too far when he let two boa constrictors out of their cages while traveling with the Indians on a train and Boudreau had him deported, so to speak, at the next station. Veeck later alleged that Joe Gordon was the instigator behind Price's ill-advised prank.

Another baseball clown who gained more notoriety than Price was Max Patkin. Nicknamed the "Clown Prince of Baseball," Patkin was a rubber-faced comedian who acted out his shtick on hundreds of ball fields for decades and even appeared as himself in the movie *Bull Durham*. Famously, Patkin said of Crash Davis (Kevin Costner), the career minor league character in the film, that "He's played in more parks then I have." Veeck helped propel Patkin on his way when he initially hired him as a coach for the Indians before he retreated to the leading comedian role.

\* \* \*

One thing that had to sway Veeck in his decision to go after the Indians was the fact that in 1946, with a losing club, the team was in the midst of drawing 1,057,289 fans.[8] Veeck had long scoffed at the prevailing ownership belief that if a town had a big-league team all it had to do was throw open the gates and people would flow in. As a natural salesman with a sense of showmanship, Veeck thought that was a misguided and haughty approach.

"A baseball team can do more for a city than lift its morale," Veeck said. "Not only doesn't the city owe the operator of the franchise anything, but the ball club, as an organization which depends in many ways on the facilities of the city and is totally dependent on the good will of its citizens, has certain responsibilities toward the city."[9]

On the last day of the '46 season, Veeck actually did throw open the gates of the ballpark—letting fans in for free. Those customers, of course, bought hot dogs and soft drinks and other nutritional supplements so that after the game, Veeck turned over $100,633 to the Community Fund as a donation. Also, in an era when there was no inter-league play, Veeck scheduled popular home-and-home exhibition games with the Brooklyn Dodgers. He gave the proceeds from the exhibitions ($149,534) to the city's sandlot baseball program.

After the '46 season, Veeck had an entire winter to plan his special nights, giveaways, and attractions, and the '47 campaign was where his reputation as a "Barnum" was first established. Among one of the highlights was the day that minority owner Bob Hope showed up unannounced for a game, received a five-minute standing ovation, and then did a fifteen-minute monologue. The Indians sponsored a night for long-time trainer Larry Weisman—and gave him $5,000 worth of silver dollars in a wheelbarrow. The booty had to be taken off the field by a tow truck because it was so heavy. In what would prove to be foreshadowing since Veeck infamously later sent midget (the term at the time) Eddie Gaedel to bat for the St. Louis Browns in 1951, Veeck staged an all-midget, six-person race in Cleveland. Taking a page from his father's playbook, Veeck also worked hard to attract women, once presenting an orchid to the first 20,000 women who showed up for a game. Veeck described that season, saying "Every day was Mardi Gras."[10]

In 1947 the Indians moved up to fourth place with an 80–74 record and drew 1,521,978 fans, a gain of almost 500,000 from the previous year. Veeck kept building, talking of an Indians pennant . . . and soon. In sticking with the point of building, Veeck probed the free-agent market when there was no free-agent market, per se. While looking for unsigned players wasn't the same as it is now, Veeck understood that there was a large pool of talented ball players unaffiliated with any Major League team because of the color of their skin. That was the season Branch Rickey promoted Jackie Robinson from the AAA Montreal Royals to the Brooklyn Dodgers, making Robinson the first African American player in the majors in the twentieth century.

Bill Veeck was an egalitarian man working in a racist sport. He had never before been in a position of authority with a big-league club to put African American players in uniform, although he was aware of their talents. Veeck knew that Satchel Paige, "Cool Papa Bell," Buck Leonard, and Josh Gibson were supremely talented players who could start for any team. But baseball lived by an unwritten rule banning black players.

Commissioner Kenesaw Mountain Landis, the white-maned, stern-faced law of the game, carried out policies with an iron fist. The owners begged Landis, a federal judge, to take the job as commissioner in the wake of the "Black Sox" scandal—when the Chicago White Sox fixed the 1919 World Series. For the owners, it was a raw, open wound and they wanted the game healed fast. And so they yielded to all demands for absolute power from Landis. One of the side effects was having a man in charge that was close-minded about racial integration.

Prominent sportswriters in the black press agitated for change. So did the *Daily Worker*, the Communist newspaper, in an odd alliance favoring social justice. The *Daily Worker* spoke

up so often in favor of integrating baseball and so enthusiasti-
cally endorsed the abilities of Satchel Paige that FBI director
J. Edgar Hoover eventually opened a file on Paige and he was
often kept under surveillance. Satchel Paige, the good-time man
of the game and ultimate contract-jumping capitalist, made for
strange bedfellows with the Communist Party, even by proxy.

During the thirties and first half of the forties, the Philadelphia Phillies were awful. They were one of the worst teams of
all time during that stretch. Between 1933 and 1945, the Phillies lost at least 89 games and broke triple digits in losses seven
times.[11] The worst of the worst was in 1941 when they went
43–111, and 1942, when they improved slightly to 42–109,
benefiting from a couple of rainouts. The team was worse than
a withered pretzel or a cold cheese steak sandwich. It was also
hemorrhaging money and the owners were desperate to sell.

Along came Bill Veeck, hungry to own his first Major League
team and with plans to convert the Phillies into an instant winner.
By stocking the roster with the best available players from the
Negro Leagues, he knew that he could easily turn the struggling
franchise around. This would have been a monumental departure from standard baseball policy and Veeck's big mistake was
in yapping too loudly about his plans. One minute he thought
he had a team and the next minute he was informed by Commissioner Landis that the franchise was sold to someone else.

No attention was paid to this behind-the-scenes maneuver at
the time and Veeck did not talk about it until years later. Besides the
African American newspapers such as the *Chicago Defender*, the
*Pittsburgh Courier*, and the *Daily Worker*, there was limited
lobbying for transformation of the National Pastime as long as
World War II raged. But the war led to the integration of the

Armed Forces and gave those campaigning for more reform a stronger platform.

Branch Rickey pulled the trigger with the signing of Jackie Robinson, and Rickey fully expected that the success of Robinson would immediately lead other teams to follow and sign additional black ball players. The response was a little slower coming than he hoped, but it was Veeck who next stood tall.

Just eleven weeks after Robinson began his high-profile and tumultuous barrier-breaking play with the Dodgers, Veeck signed Larry Doby, the first African American for the Indians and in the American League. Unlike Robinson, who had attended a predominantly white college in UCLA, served in the military, and fiercely fought for his rights, Doby was a native of New Jersey and had not encountered anywhere near the amount of discrimination Robinson contended with before leaving the Kansas City Monarchs for the Dodgers.

Doby was twenty-three when he inked his contract with Cleveland, and had been previously playing second base for the Newark Eagles. Although most big-league clubs, when they began seeking black talent, signed the players without regard for their former affiliation, Veeck reimbursed Newark with a $20,000 payment.

From almost the moment he took over the Indians, Veeck put into motion a plan to integrate the team. He was friendly with Harlem Globetrotters owner and promoter Abe Saperstein. Saperstein not only handled the world famous basketball team, he promoted baseball games in big-city stadiums involving Negro League teams. It was Saperstein who was going to be the conduit of players to Veeck and the Phillies before that sale imploded. This time Veeck cast a wider net and hired his own scout, Bill

Killefer, with the assignment of finding a player who could be a pioneer. Also, Veeck reached out to the black community in Cleveland and began making his idea known.

On July 3, 1947, the *United Press* reported an announcement from the Cleveland Indians front office that the club had signed Larry Doby. It was a very straight-forward and short story, and in the second paragraph it said, "Doby is the second Negro in history to be brought up by a Major League team." It was unclear just what Doby's position would be with the Indians. However, manager Lou Boudreau said, "Doby will be given every chance to prove that he has the ability to make good with us. The reports we have received on his ability are outstanding. I hope he can succeed as he has with other teams."[12]

The next day's account was a bit more dramatic. The *United Press* lead read, "Following Brooklyn's precedent-shattering example with Jackie Robinson, the Cleveland Indians announced today the signing of Negro infielder Larry Doby and predicted that within 10 years Negro players will be in regular service with big-league teams."[13]

That prediction came out of Bill Veeck's mouth, and he added that there would be an open-season scramble by Major League teams to sign the best African American players. Whether that was Veeck's normal optimism in high gear, wishful thinking, or a political viewpoint to let the public know the Indians were not going in alone, is uncertain.

"Robinson has proved to be a real big leaguer," Veeck said two months after his debut. "So I wanted to get the best of the available Negro boys while the grabbing was good. Why wait? . . . there are many colored players with sufficient capabilities to make the majors."[14]

One of the first people sought for comment on Veeck's action was Branch Rickey, who naturally heartily endorsed the Indians' move, saying, "The Cleveland ball club is showing signs that it wants to win."[15]

Veeck was willing to add black players to his roster, although most of the other teams in the majors trailed. Rickey pretty much had the inside track on the best African American players because of his foresight in giving Robinson a chance. That made American blacks into Dodger fans wherever they lived. He already had other African Americans in his farm system on their way up, but Rickey didn't want to remain "The Lone Ranger." He wanted other teams to sign black players, too.

Harold Parrott, who was the Brooklyn Dodgers' traveling secretary, and one of Rickey's chief assistants in the front office, said the Dodgers could have plucked all of the best African American talent for themselves. He noted that he had been on a barnstorming trip to Havana, Cuba, and one of the players was Larry Doby. "We could have had Larry Doby," Parrott said. "Junior Gilliam introduced me to Hank Aaron . . . and that was long before the Braves got a string on him."[16]

Just one day after Doby was introduced to the Cleveland press, somewhat fittingly on July 4, the nation's Independence Day, he made his Major League debut.

For Doby it was a life-altering experience. For Veeck, it was not only a matter of doing the right thing, but of being true to his beliefs in demonstrating a willingness to do anything to help his team win. For the Indians, the addition of Doby would prove critical for the 1948 pennant run.

The time had come to kick down walls. However, for neither Doby nor Veeck was the breaching of the color barrier in the American League in 1947 a path strewn with roses.

Wars are fought because freedoms must be protected. Sometimes it takes guns and ammunition. Sometimes it takes individual courage waging a more subtle battle.

Chapter One notes on pages 277–278.

# 2

## SPRING TRAINING

**B**ILL VEECK WAS thinking big during spring training of 1948 in Tucson, Arizona. He wanted an American League pennant, and he thought the Indians could contend and perhaps had a solid shot at winning their first World Series title since 1920.

Not many experts agreed, as the Indians were not pre-season favorites to capture the flag. Only two seasons before they finished 18 games under .500 and yes, they had produced a winning record in 1947, but skeptics did not envision the Indians making the last leap. The talent seemed too thin and the competition too formidable.

The New York Yankees ran away with the crowd in 1947, finishing 97–57. That was 12 games ahead of second-place Detroit (85–69) and 16 games ahead of third-place Boston (83–71). The Indians placed fourth, 25 games arrears of the Yankees (80–74). Those who sniffed around spring training camps trying to decipher tea-leaf indicators for the upcoming season saw little evidence that the Indians had undergone a

significant upgrade. The Yankees, led as always by the indomi-
table Joe DiMaggio, and the Red Sox, led by Ted Williams, the
last man to bat .400, still had their major artillery intact. The
Tigers? Well, maybe they were a bit more vulnerable.

As spring training began, the Indians roster was by no means
complete, as guys were still playing for jobs in the desert sun.
Cleveland needed another starting pitcher to emerge, and young
players in camp with promise were given every chance to show
their stuff during the exhibition games. Maybe they would
stick with the big club and maybe they would be demoted for
another year of seasoning. What took place in March in Arizona
was going to affect what took place in Cleveland between April
and October.

The most intriguing scenario of the days in camp swirled
around Hank Greenberg and just what role he would play with
the club. The former Detroit slugger was thirty-seven and had
announced his retirement pretty much two years running, but
there he was in the flesh. Greenberg was one of the greatest
power hitters of his era. He won four American League home-
run titles and four American League RBI titles, was a four-time
All-Star and won two Most Valuable Player awards. Greenberg
was also a hero to American Jews because he was public about
his faith and he coped with and brushed off slurs directed his
way in order to succeed.

Greenberg had spent significant time in the service during
World War II, and showed signs of slippage after 1946 due to
his lost years. After the '46 season ended, Greenberg figured
he was finished as a player. Still, he gave it one more try with
the Pittsburgh Pirates in 1947, teaming with that club's devas-
tating slugger, Ralph Kiner. That was it, he decided; no more.

Greenberg was determined to start a career in front office work and Veeck hired him with that in mind, giving him the title of vice president.

However, the Indians' first-base situation was unsettled, and as the team headed to Los Angeles for some exhibition games in the third week of March, the newspaper beat writers were reporting that Greenberg was going to play against the University of Southern California with the Indians' second team. At the time the leading candidate for regular first base duty was Eddie Robinson and he was sidelined with a knee injury.

"I've got to earn my varsity letter," Greenberg said while joking with the sportswriters.[1]

Greenberg was ambivalent. His body told him he should retire, but his mind resisted. He was almost like a married man flirting with a doll he had no business chatting up. Manager Lou Boudreau wanted the matter settled before the end of the short jaunt to LA.

"I certainly would like to have a decision from Hank one way or the other before we go back to Tucson," Boudreau said.[2]

Greenberg slipped on an Indians uniform against USC and in a 6–4 victory he powdered a long double and flawlessly handled fourteen chances at first. He still looked like a player who could contribute and that still didn't finalize matters. Few people in the United States had a more intriguing choice of jobs— big-league first baseman or team vice president? A week later the debate continued. By the end of the month, though, Eddie Robinson was healed and in an exhibition against the Chicago Cubs, he struck a homer and drove in four runs.

When Robinson was growing up in Paris, Texas, his favorite player was Hank Greenberg. He later went so far as to call him "my boyhood hero."[3] There was no room for sentiment in Robinson's challenge, though. He was already twenty-seven and he had never played more than 95 games in a Major League season. It was time for him to grasp opportunity or else risk his career being no more than a blip on a radar screen. Robinson admired Greenberg from afar for years, but did not meet him until that spring training competition occurred.

Robinson won the first-base job and Greenberg retired, staying with the Indians in a front-office capacity.[4] It turned out to be an important decision: Robinson emerged as a key regular for the Indians and it was not clear if Greenberg would have had enough left in his tank to help the team. Certainly, neither he nor Veeck wanted to see Greenberg hang around as a back-up after his Hall of Fame career, although he might well have been a better-than-serviceable pinch hitter. In the end it did not matter; what was hot news in March was a forgotten topic by October.

Unlike Greenberg, who was tossing a coin about which job to do for the Indians, Boudreau was entrenched in two positions. He was the starting shortstop and the manager. What was unknown for sure was who was going to fill out the rest of the infield. Robinson made his case for first and Joe Gordon was going to be the second baseman, but there was another second baseman on the team who was also a recent acquisition; another Veeck catch.

Johnny Berardino broke into the majors in 1939 and was property of the St. Louis Browns when Veeck snared him. Berardino was still another fellow with two jobs on his mind. When he wasn't fielding grounders, Berardino was a Hollywood actor. The Los Angeles native worked in two of the most glamorous jobs any red-blooded American male could want. By

1948, though, he was getting fed up with his limited playing time and losing most of the time while on the Browns payroll.[5] When he signed a seven-year acting contract, he announced his retirement from baseball.

"When they start moving you around like a piece of furniture, it's time to get out," Berardino said in '47.[6] But when he was shuffled to Cleveland, he changed his mind. Veeck said it was okay with him if Berardino wanted to make movies in the winter. After all, in those days, most ball players needed a second income anyway.

Berardino's dual careers were on opposite tracks. He stayed in baseball through 1952, but never played in more than 54 games during a season again. However, while appearing in a number of films, Berardino's chief fame came playing the television character Steve Hardy on *General Hospital* for thirty-three years. He didn't come close to being selected for the Baseball Hall of Fame, but Berardino did obtain a star on the Hollywood Walk of Fame.

Veeck and Berardino evolved into close friends after Veeck rescued the player from the Browns' ineptitude and the experience of regularly losing 100 games in a season. When they were negotiating his contract, Berardino, who was either clairvoyant or buoyantly optimistic, asked Veeck to add a bonus clause to his deal. For every thousand fans over two million that the Indians drew, he would get a $100. Veeck thought Berardino was nuts for even thinking of the proposition.

"Johnny, that's crazy," he told Berardino. "We'll never draw two million."[7] So he put the clause in the contract and sure enough, the Indians set baseball's all-time attendance record and made Berardino $6,200 wealthier.

While the initially reluctant Berardino signed with Cleveland instead of scampering to Hollywood, no one apparently informed him that just because he was an Indian for the moment, he might not be one for long. Veeck did not believe in untouchables on his roster. So on the first day of March in 1948, the *Plain Dealer* had a headline that suggested Berardino was trade bait, though no such deal came off.

The bigger news in the early days of training camp revolved around just what Boudreau was going to do for his outfield. The candidates included few marquee names. Hank Edwards, Walt Judnich, Dale Mitchell, Allie Clark, Thurman Tucker, Pat Seerey, Hal Peck, and Larry Doby were listed as the prospects. Three would start and three would probably be kept on board as back-ups, depending on who stayed healthy.

For all of the fanfare surrounding his arrival in Cleveland, Doby, the first African American in the American League, was not a lock to remain with the big club. Doby was used sparingly by Boudreau in '47 after his July debut. In all, Doby appeared in just 29 games with 33 plate appearances. He did not hit a home run and drove in just two runs while hitting an anemic .156. Starting fresh in training camp in '48 was exactly what he needed. The initial shock of his unusual situation had worn off somewhat, even though he was still the only black player on an otherwise all-white team.

Dale Mitchell could be counted on. He was a sure thing. Mitchell's credentials were the sturdiest in the group. He was the foundation of the outfield for the moment. Mitchell was a 6-foot-1, 195-pound left-handed hitter and thrower. What he was not, however, was a power hitter. He batted a team-leading .316 in 123 games in 1947, but clouted exactly one homer and drove in just 34 runs. Cleveland needed to find some home-run oomph from those that kept Mitchell company in the outfield.

Once again, Greenberg was floated as a potential outfielder, but the big man came closer to suiting up as a first baseman than as an outfielder; a position he had only a passing acquaintanceship with from his days with Detroit. For that matter, Greenberg had only a passing acquaintanceship with Dale Mitchell. The story goes that they encountered one another in left field in Tucson one fine March day and Greenberg asked, "You're a pitcher, aren't you?" Mitchell said, "No, I'm Mitchell." Greenberg replied, "Mitchell what?" in search of the player's last name.[8]

Given that he had been the club's leading hitter the season before, Mitchell might have hoped for more recognition. Things weren't going his way in general in Tucson, at least at first. When he opened his new box of what were supposed to be his 36-inch bats, he discovered they were the wrong length. At least Mitchell knew that as long as he stayed healthy he would own one of the outfield slots.

Hank Edwards, known as "The Red Head," first took a turn in the Indians' batting order in 1941 and except for two missed seasons due to World War II, had been a mainstay on the roster; sometimes used as a right fielder and sometimes as a pinch-hitter. He was coming off a .260 season with 15 home runs in '47, so he knew that he had a place on the roster, even if it wasn't as a starter. Edwards' career had been interfered with several times by major injuries. When he was healthy he was a solid player, but four times he had crumpled with serious bodily breakdowns—a broken leg, a broken wrist, a broken collarbone, and a dislocated right shoulder. In one of the sport's greatest understatements of all time, Edwards once said rather plaintively, "I've had tough luck with injuries."[9]

Walt Judnich offered promise. In five seasons for the St. Louis Browns, he'd hit between 14 and 24 home runs each season, and if he showed that kind of pop in Tucson, there was a fair chance he could claim one of the outfield slots. Veeck had picked him up in a trade with Bob Muncrief during one of the owner's frequent phone calls to the failing Browns, in exchange for Dick Kokos, Bryan Stephens, Joe Frazier, and $25,000. While Veeck had high hopes for Judnich, it wasn't clear if he could play center for a contender.

Thurman Tucker was a dark horse in the field. Veeck acquired him for Ralph Weigel in a trade with the Chicago White Sox during the off-season. Tucker's credentials were the opposite of Judnich's. To Tucker, hitting home runs came as naturally as speaking Swahili.[10] And it wasn't just his bat that interested Veeck; he was covered as much ground in the outfield as an antelope. Facially, Tucker was a dead ringer for the comedian Joe E. Brown (which explains his nickname, "Joe E."), but in the field, those who sensed poetry in the way he wielded his glove compared Tucker to Tris Speaker. Speaker was considered the best outfielder in Indians history and one of the best in the sport. In fact, the *Telegraph Herald* quoted the Indians as saying Tucker was "the finest defensive player in baseball."[11]

Much later, when he analyzed why his home runs came around only slightly more often than Haley's Comet, Tucker said, "I didn't weigh much (165 pounds), and I had to furnish my own power. I didn't have enough weight to hit the junk pitchers."[12]

Hal Peck, another double-lefty, was an unpredictable entry in the outfield sweepstakes, as he was frequently injured and his skills were still roughly unknown. In the fall of 1942, when Peck's future was bright in the Brooklyn Dodgers organization, a mishap nearly derailed his baseball life for good. While at home in Wisconsin, Peck shot himself in the foot—literally—blowing off two toes with a shotgun.

At first doctors were negative about the likelihood of Peck resuming his baseball career, but a creative approach to the problem resulted in him being built a special shoe that compensated for the lost digits. He got another shot at the big leagues with the Philadelphia Athletics, but hurt his throwing arm in another fluke accident, this one involving twisting the handle of a car door.

By the time Peck reached Cleveland's 1948 spring training camp, he was in good health and had adapted to his special shoe.

"I used to feel bad about my foot, but I know I'm lucky to have it," Peck said. "If it had happened a quarter of an inch farther back it would have been in the arch and I'd have only a heel to walk on."[13]

In December of 1947, Veeck traded pitcher Red Embree to the New York Yankees for Allie Clark. New York had too much talent and Clark was unlikely to ever make a regular dent in the perennial world champions' lineup. He had appeared in 24 games in '47, though, batting .373 and collecting a ring. Before that, Clark batted .334 at AAA Newark, so he seemed like a guy who could put his stick on the ball. Clark was billed as an outfielder, and hence in the mix for one of those green pastures positions Boudreau was attempting to sort out.

As the spring wore on, Boudreau was pleased to note Clark's versatility. He might not fill an outfield opening, but he could play other positions, which could prove to be very valuable in a long season.

Also amongst those trying to make a case for a full-time job in the Indians' outfield was Pat Seerey. Seerey had been with the Indians since 1943 and the chief attribute he brought to the table was power. Seerey could hit home runs with some regularity, hitting 26 in 1946 for the Tribe. However, he was more likely to flail at the breeze then make solid contact. He had been good for 100-something games in the outfield in recent seasons, but he was also good for about 100 strikeouts a year.[14] When he connected, Seerey could propel a ball out of the largest of ballparks—which Municipal Stadium was. The only problem was that he whiffed more often than he made contact, barely being able to hit his weight. While he weighed in at between 200 and 215 pounds, he regularly hit in the .220s or .230s. There was enough huskiness to the lad that the sportswriters of the time quizzed him about his eating habits, though nothing intriguing was revealed.

"I like to eat when I'm hungry," Seerey said. "But I don't do much eating between meals. An average breakfast, a fair lunch, and a hell of a big dinner manage to keep me going."[15]

Later in the '48 season, Seerey would produce the most stunning hitting feat of the campaign; a day for which he is still recognized as a Major League record-holder.

What began as a mish-mash for Boudreau to sort out proved to be a blessing, as all of the outfield candidates flashed a variety of strengths. No one, however, performed better than Larry Doby. Doby got off to a swift start, hitting well and fielding sharply. Boudreau watched all of the outfielders with an eagle eye, but the reporters more frequently asked about Doby. As

March began to fade into April, it was clear to them that Doby was claiming a spot, even if Boudreau wouldn't admit it yet.

"I'll keep Doby only if I feel quite sure he can play regularly," Boudreau said. "Right now I don't think he can. He's a good ball player, but he needs experience. If Doby continues the way he has been going I don't see how I can let him go. But he must play regularly. I won't have him sitting on the bench all year like he did last."[16]

A week into March, before Cleveland played even one of its scheduled 40 exhibition games, Mitchell, the most reliable pre-spring training outfielder, went down with a pulled muscle, which gave the other hopefuls playing time. Clark was the immediate beneficiary, and would start the season in left field. There was skepticism about the strength of Clark's arm throwing to the plate from distant precincts, but Veeck pooh-poohed that.

"He can throw well enough, and he will hit well enough to make up the difference."[17]

Doby never faltered during spring training and earned an everyday spot in the lineup. Somewhat remarkably, all seven of the other outfield candidates played for the Indians at some point of the 1948 season.

While there were still questions about Boudreau's outfield, there was a much shorter line at third base. Veteran Ken Keltner wasn't going anywhere; his spikes were rooted to the base. But his backup was still undetermined, and two intriguing candidates presented themselves. Al Rosen was a youngster on the way up. The question was whether or not he was ready. Rosen, like Hank Greenberg, was Jewish, and he was forced to deal with discrimination and abuse as he worked his way through the minors and in his days as a big-leaguer. By 1953 Rosen was the American League's Most Valuable Player, and a two-time home-run and RBI champ. But in 1948 he wasn't quite ready. Rosen appeared in seven games for Cleveland during the regular season and competing for a roster spot with Ray Boone . . . or so Boone might have thought. In the end, Boone played in just six games for the Tribe during their championship season. Although he also became a fine player, Boone in later years was better known for being the patriarch of one of the game's most distinguished families. His son Bob became an All Star catcher for the Philadelphia Phillies and his grandsons Aaron and Bret also played Major League ball.[18]

Rosen and Boone provided material for the writers in March, but they did not provide much ammunition for the fans during their cameos. It just wasn't their time. Clark ended up spelling Keltner.

* * *

Who was going to make the team? That's always the question when a big-league team embarks for spring training. While the club basked in the sunshine of a warm-weather paradise, the home fans dealt with the drudgery of winter, trudging through snow, and putting up with the mundane daily tasks of going to work or attending school. The fans looked to their local correspondents from the big-city dailies to clue them in on what was happening with their favorites and inform them what kind of team they would have come opening day.

Spring training baseball is the harbinger of spring in the north, and this was one time when Cleveland needed some cheering up. On March 11, one of those blizzards that form and blast the city from Lake Erie alighted on downtown, wreaking havoc.

"The worst snowstorm of the winter stopped Greater Cleveland in its tracks today," the front page of the *Cleveland Press* reported. "It made almost everyone late for work . . . and [put] thousands of autos out of service. It continued without relief to put more snow on the ground to a depth of six inches by noon and a predicted seven inches by nightfall."[19]

It definitely was more pleasant to be hanging out in Tucson then Cleveland. Veeck chose Tucson because he owned a ranch outside the city that he used occasionally to recuperate from a chronic asthmatic condition. Although Veeck sold the club in 1949, the Indians continued to train in Tucson until 1992.[20] While Clevelanders were digging out their houses and cars, the Indians were playing ball in the warmth and in their spare time sipping drinks served with little umbrellas in them. The mayor, the state, and the highway department all issued warnings telling everyone in Cleveland to stay home. Hopefully, the snowbound fans would still get home delivery of their *Cleveland Plain Dealer*, where they learned that "Two Tribe Hurling Jobs Seen Open."[21]

Boudreau depended on the judgment of a couple of crusty old coaches, Muddy Ruel and Bill McKechnie, (who later joined him in the Hall of Fame) in sorting out the pitching staff. It was judged that Bob Feller, Bob Lemon, Al Gettel, Steve Gromek, Bob Muncrief, Ed Klieman, and Bob Kuzava were keepers, and that the main remaining challengers were Gene Bearden, Mike Garcia, Bill Kennedy, Lyman Linde, and Edgar Jones. The assessment was partially correct.

At that point in his career, Garcia was too green to keep. He later became a mainstay of the staff and twice won 20 or more games twice for the Indians (1951: 20; 1952: 22), but appeared in just one game during the 1948 season, in which he pitched two innings. Nicknamed "Big Bear," Garcia won 142 games in the big leagues and he was a key man on the Indians' 1954 pennant winner when he was an All-Star for the third straight time.

Gettel, who had three years in the majors on his resume at the time, had won 11 games for Cleveland the year before. Gettel wanted to hold his spot as a regular in the rotation in '48, if only to keep financing his farm livestock—primarily horses.

"I'm just wild about horses," Gettel said. "I've invested considerable money in good riding horses and I aim to invest some more. That's why I've got to be a starting pitcher."[22]

Unfortunately for Gettel, it was not to be with Cleveland, and his future financing came from the Chicago White Sox. He appeared in just five games for the Indians in 1948 and took a 0–1 record to the Windy City after he was replaced in the rotation. Gettel was a by-product casualty of the sensation of spring training. The pitcher that got him moved to Chicago and basically rearranged the staff was Gene Bearden.

Bearden was a 6-foot-3, 200-pound left-hander who had kicked around the minors since 1940, and whose sole prior appearance in a big-league game in '47 put a 0–1 record and an 81.00 earned run average on his resume. He had served in the military in 1943 and 1944, and was a twenty-seven-year-old rookie grasping at career straws when he showed up in Tucson.

The southpaw was fortunate to be alive. While working as a machinist's mate in the engine room on the U.S.S. cruiser *Helena* near the Solomon Islands during World War II, Bearden was seriously wounded when two Japanese torpedoes struck the ship. Of the crew of 600-plus, more than 200 died. Bearden was clobbered by flying metal fragments that crushed his right knee and split his skull open. He was first rescued by an unknown ship's officer as he lay unconscious and then spent two days adrift on a life raft with compatriots while reaching only a semi-conscious state before being rescued a second time and taken ashore for treatment.

Bearden spent months in a Navy hospital in Jacksonville, Florida, undergoing a series of surgeries. He was told over and over that he would never pitch again, and might not be able to walk at full strength.

"I don't know how many doctors told me that," Bearden said. "I didn't know what to do. Finally, I ran across a doctor who told me he might be able to patch me up well enough. He worked with me for months."[23]

Bearden fought back. He brought strength and determination to a vigorous rehab program and returned to the New York Yankees' minor-league chain in 1945, although he kept silent about being wounded and the severity of the injuries, fearing he would be cut immediately.

When he resumed throwing, Bearden had an aluminum plate in his head and knee. He would set off metal detectors for the rest of his life, but he managed to regain his athletic skills. The trade that Veeck swung to bring Bearden to Cleveland also gave the Indians Al Gettel and Hal Peck. In exchange he sent Ray Mack and catcher Sherm Lollar to New York, who did not blossom until later employment with the Chicago White Sox.

Compared to his previous pitching motion, Bearden made some concessions. He cut back on the height of his leg kick and no longer employed a full wind-up. When he was traded to Cleveland, he didn't tell either Veeck or Boudreau about the extent of his war wounds either, only going public after he made the team and began having success.

Bearden was a miracle man for overcoming his war wounds, the sensation of spring training, and was about to become the story of the year in baseball as the unexpected star of the Cleveland Indians' refurbished roster.

Chapter Two notes on pages 278–280.

# 3

# PLAY BALL

**P**LAYING 40 EXHIBITION games in addition to a 154-game regular-season schedule can be an ordeal. Once the manager knows who he wants to keep and who he wants to cut, there's not much purpose to playing so many faux games.

The only defense for such a lengthy schedule was that in the 1940s, players did not come to spring training in shape and used spring training to get in condition. This was one time period when a player-manager had to concentrate a bit more on managing than on playing, as he formed the team that was going to represent the franchise for the next six months.

Lou Boudreau had not served during World War II. He was 4-F—the result of weak ankles. During his hardcore days as a basketball player, Boudreau had put so much stress on his ankles that he suffered from early onset arthritis. He could cover ground at shortstop, but was not deemed strong enough to cover ground on long-distance marches. He also played ball with his ankles protected and didn't overdo his playing time during spring training, rather he chose to ease into playing shape.

It wasn't until two weeks into March that Boudreau plugged himself into the starting lineup for an Indians exhibition game in San Francisco against the minor league Seals. As it was, he only played a few innings. A sportswriter watched as Boudreau unwrapped his ankles. "Got to start sometime and this is as good a place as any," Boudreau said.[1]

Boudreau was the most indispensable man on the team—in part because he was the boss in the dugout—but more importantly because he was the team leader on the field. By 1947, Boudreau was a five-time American League All Star and while owner Bill Veeck certainly laid it on thick when he gushed about Boudreau as he was shut out of one All Star game, he had earned the right to be called the best shortstop in the league.

Just like the other players who kept busy in the offseason with matters other than running, lifting weights, or working out— habits that had not been developed yet by professional athletes during their family time—Boudreau reported to Tucson out of condition. He weighed in at 186 pounds and figured that he was going to have to sweat off about nine pounds in the scorching sun, but wasn't exactly sure how he was going to lose the poundage without doing marathon-like training.

"This air gives me an appetite," Boudreau said.[2]

While no one expected Gene Bearden to force his way into the starting rotation, many expected Al Rosen to be the rookie that pushed Ken Keltner out of the way and took over at third base. Rosen got off to a slow start, even playing on Indians B teams in exhibitions and never really challenging for the spot. Rosen knew he might be in trouble when Boudreau, the man who would pass judgment on his immediate future, told him that his batting stance needed work. That's as fundamental as it gets, and Major League teams do not brings rookies to the Show so that they can tinker with their stances upon arrival.

While Boudreau was nursing his ankles, he occasionally played Ray Boone at shortstop. Boone was the quiet man of camp. The only thing he did to draw attention to himself was play well. Boudreau liked Boone's versatility and even for a brief fleeting instant thought of him as a back-up catcher.[3] At the moment, Jim Hegan was the starting catcher—despite rumors that Veeck was going to trade him. Boudreau must have read the papers because he started using the Joe Tipton as his catcher as the exhibition schedule dragged on.

Tipton was a rookie and Boudreau wanted to watch him do his stuff first-hand, not merely go on scouting reports. For a time he used Tipton so often that Hegan complained of boredom, or rather he hinted at it.

"I've had a long vacation," Hegan said. "A fellow develops a lot of power while he is resting."[4]

Eventually, Tipton made the club as a back-up, Hegan was retained, and the idea of using Boone as a fill-in behind the plate was scotched.

In one pre-season game, Boudreau employed five outfielders with the varsity—Allie Clark, Walt Judnich, Hank Edwards, Dale Mitchell, and Pat Seerey. Then he used Larry Doby, Thurman Tucker, and Hal Peck with the junior varsity. After a few weeks in Arizona, Boudreau was still confused about which trio constituted his best option, but it was a bit surprising that he hadn't clued into the fact that this represented a strength rather than a weakness. He spoke with a heavy sigh when analyzing the circumstances. "It looks as though it will have to be the same old story," Boudreau said. "We'll keep on switching and hope for the best."[5]

Before the end of spring training, Boudreau was cornered for a prediction about the season and picked his Indians for a second-place finish in the eight-team American League. Was he serious? Was he playing possum? Much later he said he was; that he believed the Indians could be winners.

For Boudreau, the spring training roster decisions leading into the season opener in April was a jigsaw puzzle to be worked out one step at a time. But no one in Cleveland would argue that the most important player to get into top shape before getting down to real business was pitcher Bob Feller.

Feller was the face of the franchise (and the right arm of it too). Except for time off during World War II, Feller had been the Indians' most important asset since 1936 when he signed with Cleveland while still a seventeen-year-old high school student in Iowa. By the spring of 1948, Feller was not only the team's ace, but the ace of the American League. He had been a five-time 20-game-winner and was coming off a 20–11 season in 1947. To some extent Feller had spoiled his public. It was taken for granted that he would repeat his success year after year; that his fastball was still motoring at a more rapid rate of speed than any automobile on the highway.

Testimony to Feller's nationwide popularity, especially in an era before any kind of regularly televised games, was seen in an Indians' exhibition swing to San Francisco for a series against the Pacific Coast League Seals. It rained on the day that Feller was scheduled to pitch and Boudreau, for one, said he didn't think there was any way the teams could get the ball game in and that even if they did, no one would come.

Hah, was Seals manager Lefty O'Doul's retort. He watched with a satisfied grin as 4,000 fans streamed into the soaked ballpark.

"Most of these people have never had a chance to see Bob Feller," said O'Doul, the former Major League hitter with a .349 career batting average. "You couldn't have kept them away from here with a tidal wave."[6]

The only problem was that Feller was not his usual overpowering self as spring training dragged on. Even as it passed into the third week of March, Feller did not feel right and said his arm was not ready for the rigors of the season. He started a game against the New York Giants in Los Angeles and got lit up as if he was some Class-D busher. Afterwards he soaked for a long time in whirlpool bath, totally immersing his body.

As it turned out, Feller had not even wanted to pitch that day, as he was still suffering from after-effects of a previous exhibition a few days earlier.

"I was still stiff and sore today," he said.[7]

It's difficult to believe that such a valuable commodity would be overused in spring training during the modern era of baseball, but it had been advertised that Feller was going to throw against the Giants and he was viewed as a workhorse. The Giants scored six runs off Feller in two innings, and New York won the game, 14–5.

"Generally speaking, I still feel better than I have in years," Feller said. "But it takes me a lot more time to get my arm ready. I'll get even with the Giants before the season opens."[8]

No one pointed out that it was irrelevant if Feller got even with the Giants or not since these were exhibition games and the only way they would face one another again would be if both teams made it to the World Series.[9] The important thing was for a healthy Bob Feller to be ready to fire those fastballs past American League teams when the games counted in the standings.

If Feller or the Indians had any worries about his readiness for the regular season, they dispelled them quickly. The interminable exhibition season finally concluded and Cleveland broke camp for the season opener at home. For the time being, despite initially being christened Municipal Stadium, the huge structure overlooking Lake Erie that was now the Indians' full-time home was called Cleveland Stadium. On April 20, 1948, the Indians drew the St. Louis Browns for the opener, and Feller drew the opening-day assignment.

After all of the challenges and contenders for jobs sorted through in Arizona, Boudreau declared a starting lineup that from the hindsight of many years later made perfect sense. There was one surprise at the time that in retrospect was not—Larry Doby had made the club and was starting in right field. A second surprise was that Boudreau skipped over the seemingly more reliable hitting credentials of some of the other outfielders to instead start Thurman Tucker in center, with Allie Clark being slotted in left.

The infield layout had Eddie Robinson at first, Joe Gordon at second, Boudreau at short, and Ken Keltner at third, with Jim Hegan as the catcher.

Cleveland scored one run in the first inning, one in the second, and two in the fourth to beat the Browns 4–0, as Feller twirled a two-hitter with three strikeouts. That was an anemic "K" total for Feller—especially in a complete game—but that was no big deal considering the result. It didn't even rate as Feller's finest opening-day victory. On April 16, 1940, pitching the opener for the Indians against the Chicago White Sox at home, Feller tossed a no-hitter, walking five and striking out eight in the 1–0 victory. It was a cold and blustery day with the wind blowing off Lake Michigan, and the crowd was announced as being only 14,000.

In a hint of things to come, the Indians drew 73,163 fans for Opening Day in 1948. Cleveland had the largest ballpark in the majors, and it was Bill Veeck's goal to fill it on every possible occasion no matter what it took to bring paying customers through the gates. The players thought it was impressive to look up at the massive stands jammed with loud rooters cheering their names and rooting for them. Showtime, Veeck's specialty, was part of it, but putting together a good team was just as important.

As someone who was on the team for more than a decade and always the victim of close calls, Feller watched with intense interest as Veeck worked wonders in performing trades to improve the franchise. Feller approved of Veeck's work.

"Bill Veeck deserves much of the credit," Feller said. "The moves he began making when he bought the club in '46 were producing surprisingly quick results. Our leaders, Veeck in the front office, and Lou Boudreau on the field, had us headed in the right direction."[10]

Jim Hegan, the man who was allegedly on the trading block, apparently had stored up all of his excess power and unleashed it against the Browns. He went 3-for-3 and drove in three runs.

While Doby was a long shot to make the team, he worked his butt off in spring training and gained Boudreau's approval. He batted .358 during the spring to claim a starting outfield slot. Even though he went 0–4 in the opener, the reason for Doby's sub-par performance was most likely do the fact that his wife Helen had just suffered a miscarriage.

In a rather peculiar start to the schedule, after the season opener in Cleveland, the Indians embarked for Detroit to face the Tigers in their home-opener on April 23. With Bob Lemon throttling the Tigers on six hits, Cleveland won again, 8–2, at Briggs Stadium. The Indians pounded out 15 hits, and eight of the nine starters (including Lemon) got into the hit column.[11] (Leadoff man Thurman Tucker was the only Indian to not get a hit, going 0–3.) Boudreau collected three of them, Keltner drove in four runs with two hits, and Robinson and Clark each contributed two hits again. Doby, though, made the big splash. He gathered three hits and scored two runs.

Doby was admittedly nervous for the Cleveland opener (as well as having his wife on his mind), but looked like a different player against the Tigers. He was about to become a major contributor to the Indians' offense, and this was his coming-out party.

"I was more relaxed," Doby said, "and I hope I can keep it that way."[12]

A few days into the season, the *Cleveland Press* revealed the results of a fan survey. Perhaps because they were used to disappointment, the Indians' supporters suggested they would be no better than a third-place club. As long as it was conducting such a survey, the *Press* sports department asked how the fans felt about having Hank Greenberg around in the front office. Some three-quarters of them wanted to see Greenberg in uniform and in the batting order as opposed to sitting behind a wooden desk out of sight. Unfortunately for the fans, that ship had already sailed. Although the fans couldn't know it at the time, there was a better chance that Veeck would send a midget to the plate before Greenberg took anymore swings.

It should be noted that the man-in-the-street interviews of those voting did turn up some extremely optimistic believers. One fan from Erie, Pennsylvania, said, "I still believe this is the year for the Indians." Another Cleveland fan said, "With the kind of support the Tribe gets, it's about time we get into a World Series."[13]

The Indians moved to 3–0 by beating the Tigers again on April 24, 4–1. Because of the long layoff between the St. Louis game and the series in Detroit, Feller was able to pitch again and was marvelous as usual, giving up one run on five hits while striking out six. Doby had two more hits and scored two more runs. Cleveland then swept Detroit the next day, with a 7–4 victory. This time Keltner was the main weapon on offense with three hits, three runs scored and four runs knocked in.

However, for the first time all season, the mound work was less than stellar. Al Gettel started and was run out of the game after surrendering four runs in two innings. That was his Cleveland swan song. For the first time in the 1948 season, the bullpen would be tested. Terms such as "closer," "set-up man," and "middle reliever" had not been coined and there was no such clear division of responsibility in bullpens. Generally speaking, a reliever was a pitcher who was not considered good enough to make the rotation. After Gettel got out of the second inning, Boudreau waved in a pitcher by the name of Bob Muncrief to start the third.

Robert Muncrief III, thirty-two, was a veteran right-hander who made the team partially based on experience; some might say serendipity was involved as well. Muncrief's middle name was Cleveland. His family was fond of former President Grover

Cleveland. (Not knowing they were going to raise a pitcher, there is no evidence they were thinking of Grover Cleveland Alexander.)

"It's fine with me, both as a name and as a club to work for," Muncrief said.[14]

During the 1940s, Muncrief experienced four different seasons where he won 13 games for the St. Louis Browns. The Browns were considered Les Misérables of the AL and anyone who could accomplish that with that team's lackluster run support was a budding superstar. He also achieved that while missing substantial time due to injury.

For a scary moment at the beginning of spring training it seemed entirely possible that Muncrief was doomed to again be heading to the disabled list, and maybe somewhere even worse. A batting practice line drive came with an inch of braining him. The ball nearly parted his hair. For once, Muncrief was lucky.

"Maybe that was the ball that had my name on it," Muncrief said. "You know how they say that there's one bullet that has your name on it. Well, maybe that was the bullet that was meant for me and it missed. Let's hope I can get through a whole season for once without getting hurt."[15] If that bullet-ball had Muncrief's name on it, it was misspelled.

This was Muncrief's regular-season debut for Cleveland and off-and-on during the summer he was able to contribute some useful innings when the starters had an off-day. He did exactly that on April 25, when the Indians encouragingly batted around against Tigers future Hall of Famer Hal Newhouser for six runs through six innings. Muncrief pitched 4.1 innings in relief, giving up three hits and no runs.

After Muncrief performed yeoman service, Boudreau turned to Russ Christopher to finish the game. Christopher filled the task of closer for Cleveland in 1948 and this was his first save, going 2.2 innings without permitting the Tigers a run.

Russ Christopher was an amazing tale. If he was pitching in the majors in the 2000s, he would have been an All-Star on Oprah. As a youngster, he suffered from rheumatic fever and nursed a heart condition forever after. Rather than baby him, his mother urged him to stay active and play baseball. Christopher turned out to be very good at the game and in 1942, at age twenty-four, made his debut in 1942 for the Philadelphia Athletics under venerable manager Connie Mack.

The righty toiled for the A's for six seasons, putting up some respectable numbers on occasion. He had a 51–62 record (including his first season, in which he went 4–13) with a 3.40 ERA before showing up on Bill Veeck's shopping list. Mack, who unlike some baseball magnates, suffered from an affliction called truth-telling, informed Veeck that Christopher was in poor health and he could not in good conscience sell him to the Indians for the $25,000 Veeck offered.

Christopher stood 6-foot-3 and weighed around 165 pounds. Veeck was not dissuaded by Mack's honesty and asked to speak to the player directly. Christopher was ill at that moment, and even as Veeck reached out to Christopher, he was lying in a hotel room bed freezing cold under the covers despite the warm weather. Veeck asked him if he could still pitch at the age of thirty. Christopher said, "I don't know. Look at me, I'm sick." Veeck replied, "I'm going to take a gamble on you." Christopher said, "I think you're crazy, but I'll do the best I can for you."[16] The pitcher also suggested that Veeck talk Mack down from the $25,000 on the table, but Veeck chose not to do so.

Not a thing about the transaction made any sense for the Indians, except that Veeck must have been relying on a secret intuitive power.

"He was a medical freak," Veeck said. "He was a blue baby grown up. His heart leaked blood instead of sending it to his lungs for oxygen."[17]

Yet there was Christopher on the mound picking up his first save of the season against the Detroit Tigers. Saves were not invented as a statistic until decades later, but were rewarded retroactively due to diligent research. Christopher amassed 17 of them for the Indians that season, and finished with a 3–2 record and 2.90 earned run average.

After sweeping the Tigers, the Indians added wins over the Chicago White Sox and St. Louis Browns to complete a 6–0 start to their season. But Cleveland didn't get out of the month before the first newspaper call to add starting pitching was sounded. That was because the fifth win in the streak was a 12–11 muscle show of hitting and a horror show of throwing. Actually, after a trio of Cleveland pitchers were treated rudely (including the starter, Don Black, who was knocked out in the third after giving up six runs), the bullpen again took command. Ed Klieman hurled three innings of no-run relief, followed by Christopher, who pitched five terrific innings, allowing three hits and no runs. He also catalogued the win.

Maybe things wouldn't be so bad after all.

Chapter Three notes on pages 280–281.

# 4

# THE BOY WONDER

**R**OBERT **WILLIAM ANDREW** Feller's baseball career started as fiction and ended in legend. Rarely has there been told a real-life, believable story to match his origins in the game. The high school boy turned major leaguer overnight with the fastest fastball of them all unleashed as if the horsehide was shot from a cannon.

His was a tale that leapt from the page of boys' literature, one belonging to the exploits of Frank Merriwell or Chip Hilton. It was fantasy come true. At his most fanciful, every boy who stands on a pitcher's mound surely takes a moment to imagine his surroundings miraculously transformed from the high school playground to a Major League stadium, the rowdy crowd of dozens calling his name transformed to one of 40,000.

Far-fetched. Impossible. Yet it was real. Bob Feller was seventeen years old, genuinely fresh off the farm with manure still sticking to his shoes—heck, still with a year of high school to complete—when the Cleveland Indians summoned him to the Show in 1936. The team recognized the skills of a prodigy in his right arm, bursting to be freed with the purest speed that almost any of them had ever seen.

The technological challenge of measuring the speed of a pitched ball in the thirties and forties had not yet been mastered with assurance, but the fascination was so great with Feller's arm strength that tests were devised to try and quantify the speed of his throws. Man has always been fascinated by speed, whether it is how fast a human can run, how fast a car can be driven, or how fast an airplane can fly. Feller, the sages of the game nodded, was as fast as any of them had ever seen, comparable to Walter Johnson, for sure. "Seen" being the operative word because those who stood in the batter's box sometimes complained that all they could do is hear Feller's heater as it passed, perhaps with a hiss. The conclusion drawn from what measurements could be mustered by Rube Goldberg–like contraptions were that "Rapid Robert" topped out at between 101 and 104 mph.

That's how fast he was in the minds of baseball aficionados. Feller did not mess with numbers—except in math class—but he could tell by the results that his fast was pretty fast. The lanky boy from Van Meter, Iowa, population 300, who grew up on a 360-acre farm some 25 miles from Des Moines, fanned just about anyone in the scholastic conferences and amateur leagues who waved a stick at him. Because his fastball had buzz on it, it was termed the "Van Meter heater."

Feller was raised by his dad, Bill, to be a ball player. Even Bob recognized later in life how peculiar it seemed for his father to shift from growing corn to wheat as he dug up some of his farmland to build a slick little ballpark on his own property. Yes, the comparison to W. P. Kinsella's novel *Shoeless Joe* was inevitable when the book was made into the popular movie *Field of*

*Dreams* in 1989. The Fellers beat Kinsella to the construction of a baseball field carved out of the crops. Probably the most famous Little League dad was Mickey Mantle's father, Mutt, who not only groomed his son for the big leagues, but named him after his favorite player, Mickey Cochrane. Feller pere was Mutt's equal, except for the naming rights. He played catch with Bob, taught Bob everything about the game, steered him into pitching, and represented him when the scouts arrived.

Although his dad was truly committed to making Bob into a ball player, that didn't mean that he got to shirk work on the farm. The chores were included in his son's daily schedule, along with pitch and catch.

"My father kept me busy from dawn to dusk when I was a kid," Feller said. "When I wasn't pitching hay, hauling corn, or running a tractor, I was heaving a baseball into his mitt behind the barn. If all the parents in the country followed his rule, juvenile delinquency would be cut in half."[1]

Even without sophisticated national tournaments, Internet publicity, and scouting newsletters, the siren song of a fastball such as Bob Feller's brought scouts to his doorstep in the communication-backwards 1930s. One thing the Fellers did was play it straight with the suitors in the sense that they found one they liked representing a team they believed was honest, and stuck with it even when the process became sticky.

The Fellers hitched their wagon to scout Cy Slapnicka of the Indians and didn't waver when bigger offers came over the transom, or even when Commissioner Kenesaw Mountain Landis got involved with the situation and could have made Feller a free agent. No thanks, they said. They weren't interested in anyone except the Indians, even if the contract offer was for just one dollar.

Once the tricky stuff was sorted out the Indians upped the ante a little bit, but Feller collected in the low thousands, not Robber Baron money. A player cannot be classified as a bonus baby when his bonus is only enough to cover some chewing gum and a few soft drinks, but the Indians did baby Feller. They understood instinctively that he was going to be a franchise player and made sure he wasn't overworked—at least at first.

Yet not even his protectors, Slapnicka and manager Steve O'Neill, could resist the temptation to test the 'Boy Wonder' against big-league hitters once he showed up under their wings in the summer of '36 between his junior and senior years in high school. Feller would become known as a strikeout artist and his first Major League strikeout came in an exhibition game on July 6, 1936, recorded against Leo Durocher, still a shortstop for the St. Louis Cardinals before he began his more renowned managing career.[2] Feller pitched three innings that day and struck out eight of the nine men he faced.

The thing was that Feller did not look out of place or over-matched against big-league hitters. On August 23, 1936, in his starting debut, Feller struck out 15 members of the St. Louis Browns, a record for a first start.[3] The shame of it was that there were only 9,000 witnesses in the park. In the first game of a doubleheader against the Philadelphia Athletics on September 13, Feller struck out 17 batters, an American League record at the time. That was 17 Ks at 17 years of age. Golfers take pride in shooting their age as they pass into their sixties, seventies, and eighties, but Feller is almost the only baseball player to ever strike out his age. That shortened rookie year, Feller went 5–3 in 14 games and struck out 76 batters in 62 innings. There was no reason whatsoever to send Feller to the minors for seasoning when he could do that, especially at such a young age.

For those who felt that Feller being right off a farm where his expertise on alfalfa, cows, horses, pigs, and chickens equaled his knowledge of where to place his fastball was bound to be all cornpone, he was actually preternaturally calm. The kid never got ruffled, not even when facing the biggest names in the game at the plate.

"Not in my entire pitching career was I ever scared of any hitter or any situation," Feller said.[4]

It would have seemed more likely for his knees to be knocking so violently in fright that it could be heard in the press box, but no, Feller had it all, including poise. When the season ended, Feller returned to Iowa and while given props for his achievements he sought to blend in as a regular student. Once he earned his diploma, the 6-foot, 185-pound Feller returned to the Indians for the 1937 season.

By 1948, the Indians' magic summer, Feller was viewed as the greatest pitcher in the history of the team. He won 24 games in 1939, 27 in 1940, and 25 in 1941. Around that time, his father Bill was stricken with brain cancer and was gradually fading. When the Japanese bombed Pearl Harbor, dragging the United States into World War II, Feller could have remained home to manage the family farm as the sole supporter of his parents and younger sister, but decided to immediately enlist for military service and spent the next three years (1942–44) serving his country.

There has been much speculation over what type of final statistics Feller might have compiled if he had played baseball those years instead of serving in the navy, but Feller never dwelled on that out loud. When he returned to the Indians he pitched some in 1945 and returned to his "normal" self in 1946 by winning 26 games. In 1948 he was coming off another 20-win season.

After his overpowering start in April, Feller was shelled in his next two outings, losing to the Detroit Tigers and Philadelphia A's. He then promptly picked up two more wins in early May, the second one a complete-game six-hitter over the White Sox. He was sitting on 4–2 by the middle of the month.

One thing owner Bill Veeck understood was the concept of putting fannies in the seats and everyone in baseball knew that on days Feller was scheduled to pitch, attendance grew. Feller's contract with Veeck had an attendance bonus clause written into it. His base salary was $50,000, but he made thousands of dollars extra when the Indians attracted bigger crowds. Feller's deal earned him five cents a person for every attendee over 500,000. Plus, he had another bonus in his contract calling for payouts for each win he accumulated over 15.

Before the 1948 season began, Veeck jokingly informed the press that his high-paid pitcher, had more or less become a partner in the franchise because of the bonus payoffs.

"Feller now owns everything to the left of first base," Veeck said.[5]

During that immediate post–World War II era Feller was indeed one of the biggest names in the game, alongside Ted Williams and Joe DiMaggio, and Stan Musial in the National League. Feller made additional money from endorsements and when the regular season ended he pulled together teams of major leaguers and went barnstorming across the country playing exhibition games. When the big leagues had just eight teams in each league and before television took hold, millions of Americans lived outside of immediate access to seeing the top caliber of baseball available in the United States. Feller capitalized with his traveling All-Stars. Sometimes his teams traveled in tandem with Dizzy Dean's All-Stars and sometimes they played a series of games against Satchel Paige's All-Stars. There was a growing fascination with the talent in the Negro Leagues just before the color barrier was broken in the majors, and Feller and Paige worked together to schedule games between whites and blacks. The two became friends, and Feller sung Paige's praises long before there was ever a glimmer of thought that they might become teammates on the Indians.

By 1948 Feller had earned his place as the king of the Cleveland franchise; he was the rock on the mound that the rest of the staff rotated around as if he was the sun and they were planets. But there was some criticism coming his way. It was suggested that some speed had been lost from his fastball and that he may have overdone the workload on his golden right arm with all of the barnstorming.

While Feller was one of the highest paid players in the game, the reality was that he needed the money, every dollar he could raise. It was not revealed until many years later that Feller was sometimes teetering on the edge financially because of mental health and substance abuse issues his first wife, Virginia, faced. That was not something that anyone talked about publicly in the 1940s, and Feller, a proud man, would not have been likely to tell anyone outside of his household about it. He tried to remain the head of a functioning family while bringing home the bread, but his financial circumstances were much more significantly dire than anyone ever knew. Far from being motivated by greed,

Feller was propelled by necessity. He had to make more money, or else be in danger of losing his home.

Feller put on a good face and persevered and it was decades before anyone knew the strain he had been under when he was at the top of his game. As evidence about how little Feller's strained relations with his wife were known in 1952, a lengthy as-told-to story appeared in the magazine under the name of Virginia Feller. The headline pricelessly read, "He's My Feller!" It was also revealed that when Virginia met Bob in 1940 she didn't know who he was or anything about baseball. In fact, she despised the sport. "A ball player!" she learned when being fixed up on the blind date. "I detest ball players and I hate the game."[6]

Mrs. Feller did drop some insight to Feller's thinking while he was away at war as a chief petty officer for the Navy on the U.S.S. *Alabama*.

"Bob was certain his name would never again appear in a Major League box score," Virginia Feller said. "Knowing how much baseball meant to him I prayed, not only for his health, but also for the day when he would be wearing a Cleveland uniform again."[7]

Virginia Feller said, and Bob Feller echoed, that in some ways the biggest thrill of his career was the first game he pitched after returning to the Indians from the service. Feller made nine starts in 1945 and finished 5–3 after his discharge from the service. Not only was that the same record he posted as a rookie nine years earlier, he felt like a rookie a second time, too, after so much time off.

Many baseball players served their country during World War II and many like Feller lost some of their prime years while wearing another kind of uniform. Although he saw combat and was decorated with eight battle stars and six campaign ribbons for the missions he served aboard ship in the Pacific and in the North Atlantic, Feller did not like being referred to as a hero.

"I'm no hero," he said. "Get this straight. The heroes didn't come back. Only the survivors did."[8]

Still, Feller was feted by the people of Cleveland when he returned to the Indians. He was the star attraction at a luncheon on August 24, 1945, and the city threw a parade in his name. That night Feller pitched for the first time since 1941 and the Indians beat the Detroit Tigers, 4–2. Feller went head-to-head with Hal Newhouser, who was 20–7 entering the game. Feller threw a complete game, allowed just four hits and two runs, had 12 strikeouts, and gained an emotional win.

"I had been away four years and people were saying I was washed up," Feller said. "They had a right to say it, too, since few come back after being away so long. But this game proved to me that I was still able to pitch."[9]

The great ones are great because they bring something extra to the table beyond sheer talent. Feller had that grit and dig-deep stuff inside him. He won that big game upon his return, but there were still skeptics when he reported to spring training in 1946 for the same reason. He had been away too long, some wrote. He had lost a few mph off his famous fastball. Sportswriters backtracked fast when he hurled a no-hitter in game two of a doubleheader against the New York Yankees on April 30. It was his first in six years, and second of three that he tossed in his career. Feller also threw 12 one-hitters.

"I never was any better," Feller said of the no-hit sizzler versus the Yankees. "I had everything that day."[10]

That night Feller took manager Lou Boudreau, trainer Lefty Weisman, and his coaches out to dinner at Toots Shor's, the famous New York watering hole and restaurant that was a favorite among big-time athletes. Feller tossed 133 pitches that day, not a common occurrence in the baseball world of the 2000s. Feller also let loose some of his pent-up frustration to sportswriters, firing off a few sarcastic lines.

"Why do you want my picture?" he asked photographers. "I'm all washed up in this town." Clearly the reports of his premature pitching demise had stung. He told the sportswriters he would talk to them as long as they wanted until it threatened his impending appointment at a local hospital. "I want to find out what's wrong with my arm. I've been reading that I can't pitch anymore."[11]

Touché. Feller did walk five in that contest, however. That was a weak point, the chink in his armor. He could be blindingly fast and strike out men who had no idea where the ball was going, but he could also be wild. When first starting out in the bigs, nobody on the Indians wanted to tamper with his form. They sat back in awe of his blazing fastball. Feller led the American League in strikeouts seven times, with a high of 348 in 1946, but he also led the AL in walks four times, including issuing an incredible 208 free passes in 1938.[12] The man threw a lot of pitches.

"I didn't know much," Feller said of being a polished pitcher instead of a thrower when he was a teenager. "I just reared back and let them go. Where the ball went was up to heaven."[13]

While he may not have been known for his pinpoint control, Feller's reputation as the man who brought the heat was one he milked with batters, and with them knowing that he was someone who might accidentally throw high and tight helped keep those hitters from digging in too deep in the batter's box.

"It's a help to have a reputation as a strikeout pitcher," Feller said. "It makes the batters feel they've got to prove themselves against you, rather than vice-versa. But for a real help there's nothing like a reputation for having a hot fastball that's a little bit wild. Then they really worry up at that plate."[14]

When Feller was first the rage, with the hype suggesting his fastball could beat Walter Johnson's fastball to the plate by a measured mile, not everyone wanted to believe it. Some hitters scoffed at the early reports, and one player in particular would just never admit that Feller was as fast as a speeding locomotive. Dick Bartell, a two-time National League All-Star, was a member of the New York Giants when they engaged in a lengthy spring training exhibition series against the Indians when Feller was being introduced to the masses.

Nope, Bartell insisted, Feller was not as fast as Van Lingle Mungo. He kept repeating that opinion. Feller got a little bit irritated, which may have been Bartell's purpose, but the teenager never said a word. When Bartell finally batted against Feller, the infielder struck out. But he still wouldn't admit that Mungo's speedball did not take precedence. Day after day Bartell came to the plate against Feller during the exhibition games and Feller would strike him out, doing so 16 times in 19 at-bats. Bartell created more breezes with his bat than any hurricane ever did, but he would never concede the point that he believed Mungo threw faster. Not that it mattered much since Feller got him out just about every at-bat.

"Oh, Bartell," Feller said later, "yeah, he sure was stubborn."[15]

Feller became an instant civic institution in Cleveland pretty much from the time he fanned Durocher. They went gaga for him in his hometown, too.

By 1937 Feller was pitching well enough that the Cleveland Press signed him up to write the story of his life in a series. He was still eighteen at the time. Since Feller had done virtually nothing in his life up to that point besides graduate from high school, lift a milk pail and tote that hay bale, and throw fastballs, it was not riveting stuff that was in danger of being highlighted in the cover headlines in *True Magazine*. However, the *Associated Press* did report when Feller received his high school diploma in Iowa, and the *New York Times* ran the story. It was also reported that the Indians insured Feller for $100,000 when he flew home for the event.

The road to the top in any professional sport is lined with the wannabes, the almosts, and the failed prospects who never lived up to the promise shown as young players, but Feller was the genuine article and he was one of the can't-miss players who did not miss and became a Hall of Famer.

And he wasn't merely a Hall of Famer, either, but was designated as someone symbolic of an era in the game. Ted Williams, who may have been the best hitter that ever lived, called Feller, "the fastest and best pitcher I ever saw during my career."[16] Stan Musial, who was the National League's Williams at the same time, said Feller was "probably the greatest pitcher of our era."[17]

Most of those credentials were established by the start of the 1948 season. But after more than a decade in the game, Feller had not played for a pennant-winner, nor appeared in a World Series. That was what he craved at the start of the Indian summer.

Chapter Four notes on pages 281–282.

# 5

## WHO'S ON FIRST?

**T**HE CRUSH OF outfielders vying for playing time did not end with the conclusion of spring training. While the comedy team of Abbott and Costello had made famous their baseball routine of "Who's on First?" the Indians seemed to determined to befuddle their fans with the question, "Who's in Left?"

To the surprise of many, probably even him, Dale Mitchell did not see that much action during the first days of the regular season despite being the team's best returning hitter with a .316 average in 1947. Manager Lou Boudreau instead started Allie Clark in left field.

The Indians got off to a hot 6–0 start, and then lost four games in a row before winning five in a row to stand at 11–4. By the end of May, concluding that month with two straight doubleheaders, the Indians had a 23–11 record and definitely looked like a pennant contender.

Boudreau, who was an acknowledged standout at short, had to earn the other part of his salary as manager by going on gut instinct when he wrote out his lineup card each day. With the glut of outfielders on the roster, he had to guess who might be on each day. Some days Allie Clark, who was a better hitter than fielder, came through with two hits. Then Boudreau began swapping him out for Dale Mitchell, and Mitchell would come through with two hits.

Rarely did the two men appear in the same game unless one of them pinch-hit. After several weeks of contemplating whether Clark or Mitchell should be the regular starter in left, Boudreau hit on a new scheme. On some days he inserted Clark at third and played Mitchell in left. The only problem with that was it left regular third baseman, Kenny Keltner, a superior fielder and also a dangerous hitter, on the bench.

As the Indians moved through April and May while winning two-thirds of their games, Boudreau had a few days that in particular had to plaster a wide smile on his face. On May 7, the Indians shut out the Washington Senators, 4–0, with Clark and Mitchell each having two hits in the game. That may have been the moment Boudreau realized Cleveland was stronger the more he used both men rather than alternating them. Add to the fact that the winning pitcher, Bob Lemon, threw a four-hit shutout while going the distance and improving his record to 3–1.

The next day at Griffith Stadium, the Indians topped the Senators, 6–1. The winning pitcher was rookie Gene Bearden, recording his first career victory.[1] Bearden went 8.2 innings, surrendering just three hits and only one run, which was unearned.

But probably no game gave Boudreau the chills quite the way Cleveland's 13–8 thumping of the Chicago White Sox did during the second game of a doubleheader on May 30. In that game Clark and Mitchell each produced two hits—as did

Keltner. Even better, although poor Bill Kennedy, destined not to play much of a role in Cleveland after scrambling to make the squad out of spring training, was clobbered in the first inning, replacements out of the bullpen were the difference makers. Lemon gained the win, lifting his record to 7–2. Russ Christopher, fine-tuning the role of closer, collected his seventh save by finishing the final two innings.

It may well have dawned on Boudreau as the calendar page turned to June that Lemon, not Feller, might be the staff ace in 1948, and that the unheralded Bearden might be their sorely needed extra starter.

At the end of May, the New York Yankees were 21–16, the Boston Red Sox were 14–23, and the Detroit Tigers were 19–20. All three of those teams finished ahead of Cleveland in 1947. The Indians' superior start was an indicator that something special might be brewing in Cleveland that summer.

In these days of reality TV shows it would be an interesting competition to see which Indians pitcher had the more unusual back-story that mitigated against his success. Feller missed all of that time during World War II, Bearden had serious war injuries and had never pitched in the majors before, and Russ Christopher was coping with a heart ailment. But for all of that, it was hard to top Lemon.

Members of Lemon's high school class in Long Beach, California, would not be the least bit surprised to hear of his baseball success. As a senior Lemon was the California high school player of the year. The Indians signed him and thought for certain he would be their shortstop of the future. That's right; Lemon was an infielder, not a pitcher. As it turned out, when it came to facing big-league hurling, he was no hitter, either.

To his credit, Lemon scrapped and hustled and reached the majors as a late-season call-up in September of 1941. He was twenty years old, made it into five games, came to bat four times, and stroked one hit. He was now a career .250 hitter. The next year he was back in the minors and again took the welcome call promoting him to the majors. For the second year in a row he made it into five box scores, coming to bat five times—striking out three of them—and never reaching base.

Lemon spent the next three years in the military and by the time he reappeared in Cleveland after World War II, he was twenty-five years old. Lemon got into 55 games that season and batted .180. His average was almost identical with his weight and unlike Bob Feller's 17 strikeouts at 17; Lemon's numerical oddity did not excite Indians management.

Not quite sure what to do with him, even as he still played some in the field Lemon obtained baptism as a big-league pitcher and wasn't half bad. He finished 4–5 in 1946, but his earned run average of 2.49 sparkled in 94 innings. Hmm, went the big thinkers in the front office. Agreement was reached between Indians officialdom and Lemon that his future would be on the mound rather than in the six hole. This was particularly obvious because while Lemon was at war, Boudreau became a fixture at short.

There was another reason why Lemon did not make it big at shortstop. He had a problem in the field that bugged him—his arm was sometimes too strong. While playing in Wilkes-Barre, Pennsylvania, in 1940, Lemon's throws after fielding ground balls were so erratic that fans inhabiting the seats behind first base learned to pay attention at all times lest they be beaned by errant tosses. At one point it became such a local joke that fans shouted warnings when the ball was bounding Lemon's way.

Lemon underwent a short trial as an outfielder in the Indians chain, too, but neither his bat, nor his negotiations with fly balls, seemed to be of Major League caliber. Lemon kept trying to tough it out, trying to live his dream as an accomplished pro, but even he grew discouraged in 1947 and informed Boudreau, "I'm no good to you. Send me out."[2] Such pleas are only made out of despair.

Basically, Lemon hit rock bottom; but that made him ripe to try something completely different. He harnessed the strength in his arm and learned how to find the plate better than he ever found first base. It turned out that being a pitcher was the right position for Lemon; all of his time spent dabbling at short and in the outfield was a distraction. That 1946 ERA was eye-catching and in 1947, Lemon became a full-time hurler.

That season he went 11–5, mixing his work as a starter and a reliever. He was twenty-six years old and still studying his new-found trade, but all signs were pointing in the right direction. Lemon pitched in 37 games and started 15 of them, finishing with an earned run average of 3.44. Lemon was ten years older on the learning curve than the typical recruit, but he picked up things fast and 1948 would be his breakthrough year.

The more Lemon pitched, the better he got. Opposing managers didn't know what to make of him. National League managers who only saw him in spring training were impressed.

"The bottom just drops off of that ball," Giants field boss Leo Durocher said of Lemon's sinker. "He's all of what I've heard. We might have a guy or two in the National with as much stuff and brains, but I doubt it."[3]

Who knew? Who saw this coming? Absolutely nobody.

Like Feller, Lemon was signed out of high school by Cleveland. His signing bonus was $300 and some walking around money at a rate of $50 monthly until he finished high school. His first minor-league outpost was in Oswego, New York, where he did not leave a strong first impression. After starting 0-for-18 he broke down in tears. After that he started to hit, well enough to get promoted up the ladder in the Indians chain.

One of the eyewitnesses to Lemon's throwing debacle in Wilkes-Barre was future Indians teammate Jim Hegan, who later had the honor of catching Lemon's good stuff from the mound.

"Hell, he was likely to bean some guy in the fifteenth row," Hegan said of Lemon's wild and crazy throws off grounders.[4]

After Lemon was released from the service it was hinted that he might be the club's replacement for Ken Keltner at third base. At the time, Keltner was aging and holding out for more money. The opportunity drove Lemon, but he couldn't make himself indispensable enough to oust Keltner. What was little-known to the Indians was that Lemon had done some pitching during the war while he was stationed in far-off bases and fared quite well. He thought of it merely as a diversion, a relaxation while he was away from the front. Even after Lemon struck out at third Boudreau believed his only option was to try Lemon in center field. But then Lemon flopped with that .180 batting average.

Of all things, when his future with the Indians looked dire, Lemon began playing around in his spare time, tossing knuckleballs to back-up catchers. The knuckler is often the pitch of last resort for hurlers, but it helped some players on the Indians begin to look upon Lemon as a pitcher. Yet the defining moment in his transformation came from outside the organization. One day before a game in New York against the Yankees, Boudreau was shooting the breeze with New York's All-Star catcher Bill Dickey. Dickey shared military duty with Lemon in the South Pacific and he caught some of his games.

"How about pitching that kid?" Dickey said to the Cleveland manager. "He showed me the best curve of anybody in Hawaii during the war. Give him a real test. You'll see."[5] Boudreau was ready to jettison Lemon to the minors, but he looked at him in a new way. That's when Lemon got his bullpen trial and recorded that attention-getting ERA in his limited work.

Lemon was not at all surprised that he could not beat out Keltner. When he saw Keltner play up close every day he knew he wasn't as good as the veteran. His service pitching saved him, though, and once he got the chance to throw for the Indians Lemon became dependent on Mel Harder for advice.

\* \* \*

In a twenty-year career—all spent with the Indians—Mel Harder won 223 games and was a four-time All-Star. In 13 All-Star innings, Harder never allowed a run. He retired in 1947, but almost immediately became the team's pitching coach and held that job for years. When he stepped back from the mound, though, he willed Lemon his little black book on hitters.

"I threw practically the same pitches he did," Lemon said. "So when he quit I inherited his book. I was very fortunate. He spent a lot of time with me."[6]

In addition to his pitching tenure, Harder was an Indians coach for sixteen years and came to be regarded as one of the great teachers in the game. Lemon was essentially his first pupil, but others soon followed. In later years, Herb Score, the Indians'

1955 rookie of the year, said, "If Mel Harder couldn't teach you a curveball, then no one could." Score was not Harder's only prominent fan. Hall of Famer Early Wynn said of Harder, "He taught me to throw the curve." Lemon was always grateful to Harder for his assistance. "Mel did it all for me," he said. "He changed my mechanics. His word was gospel."[7]

While Lemon gave thanks to Harder for his help, Boudreau heaped credit on one of his favorite baseball men, coach Bill McKechnie. Boudreau called McKechnie "Pops" because he was like a father to him. Boudreau said after the Dickey tip that he asked McKechnie to devote attention to Lemon.

"'Pops,' I told him in spring training," Boudreau said, "'I want you to take Lemon to the bullpen, look at him, work with him, and when he's ready to be a starting pitcher, let me know.' Not long after that McKechnie came to me and said, 'Louie, you've got yourself a pretty good pitcher . . . Lemon is ready.' He was right. I was blessed to have both Lemon and Bob Feller on my team—and blessed that I never had to bat against either of them in his prime."[8]

Leading up to the 1948 season, owner Bill Veeck signed Lemon to a new contract and predicted that he would become a 20-game winner. Everyone laughed and figured Good Old Bill was just doing what he did best, hyping things up.

Lemon began winning games so fast in the early months of the season that he made a believer out of those doubters.

Although Boudreau publicly said before the season's start that he thought the Indians would finish second, privately he liked the way the team came out of spring training at a sprint and started winning right away. Privately, he thought more optimistically.

"I thought we could win because we were beginning to jell as a team," Boudreau said.[9]

He also understood that if the Indians did not win the pennant after Veeck's earlier attempt to trade him, his expressed concerns about his managerial capability, and all of the deals that Veeck swung to beef up the club, that he was likely to be fired. Throughout 1948, Boudreau felt it was win-or-else for him.

Much like McKechnie was for a time Lemon's personal coach, Boudreau had the smarts to keep Harder around when he retired and also made sure he worked with Lemon. There was also a coach who served for a few months during that long exhibition season who was brought aboard for a distinct purpose.

One of the greatest Indians players of all time was Tris Speaker. Beyond his Hall of Fame ability in the outfield, Speaker was also the manager of the 1920 Cleveland championship team—the only title team in franchise history going into 1948. As terrific as "The Grey Eagle" was as a hitter—and he was that with a .345 lifetime average—many believed that he was the best fielding center fielder of all time. Speaker's assignment was to work specifically with Larry Doby. Doby had been an infielder most of his life, but it was apparent that the best use of his talents in the majors was in the outfield. During his short trial in 1947, Doby had looked skittish circling under fly balls. If he was going to be an everyday player for Cleveland, he had to be more sure of himself in the field. Speaker was his teacher.

"No man ever knew more," Veeck said of Speaker as he drilled Doby day after day in the hot Arizona sun until he picked up the nuances of fielding the outfield. Speaker supervised as Doby chased flies and positioned himself in front of line shots that bounced.[10]

A few years later when he spoke at a Cleveland baseball dinner, Doby listed several people he was indebted to, and Speaker was one of those he singled out. Doby did improve steadily as a fielder and much of what he gleaned from Speaker stayed with him for the rest of his career.

Chapter Five notes on pages 282–283.

# 6

## THE PIECES FIT TOGETHER

---

**MAYBE IT WAS** because he didn't hit for power, but Dale Mitchell might be one of the least-remembered first-rate hitters in baseball history. The man could wield a stick the way a symphony conductor could wave a wand. From the moment that Mitchell burst onto the Cleveland scene in 1946, he showed management that wherever he played in the field he was at home in the batter's box.

Mitchell threw left and batted left. He was from Colony, Oklahoma, and spent some time at the University of Oklahoma. Few recall what he did in the classroom, but during his baseball career for the Sooners, Mitchell batted .467. As a senior he hit .507. In fact, the Sooners baseball team plays its home games at L. Dale Mitchell Park. Mitchell was already twenty-five when he got his chance in 11 games during that September call-up for the Indians in '46—hitting .432 in the trial. Not only had he attended college, but he spent twenty-seven months in the air force during World War II, so he was definitely a rookie who had experience shaving.

Mitchell said at Oklahoma that he followed the instructions of his coach to just meet the ball, and set up so many meetings between bat and ball that he never saw a reason to change his style. He also said he picked up important pointers from Roy Deal, the coach of the semi-pro Oklahoma Natural Gas team.

In 1947 Mitchell was a Cleveland regular and batted .316 as a rookie. He had a 22-game hitting streak that season and manager Lou Boudreau said he liked the way Mitchell moved in the field. "This boy could be the center fielder we have been looking for," Boudreau said.[1] He wasn't, but in reality, despite the glut of outfielders in camp in 1948, Boudreau was going to find a place to use Mitchell.

It also wasn't certain where Mitchell belonged in the order. He had a tremendous eye at the plate. In 4,358 career at-bats, Mitchell struck out just 119 times. Mitchell always maintained a good on-base percentage, though he wasn't a speed demon and had only sporadic success stealing bases.[2] Yet Boudreau concluded he was the team's best lead-off man and when installed in that slot in the batting order, Mitchell performed.

In a June 6 game against the Philadelphia Athletics—a game Cleveland won 11–1—Mitchell stroked four hits and drove in five runs from the lead-off position. June was good to the Indians, going 16–11 for the month and raising their record to 39-23. The Yankees made up some ground and were at 38–26 and the Red Sox woke up after their abysmal May. Boston went 18–6 during the month to improve to 32–29, winning nine out of eleven at one point.

One asset that Mitchell brought to the plate was patience. At 6-foot-1 and 200 pounds, scouts thought he should bang the ball farther more often. Instead, he mostly made good contact.

"I'll pull the ball if it's pitched inside," Mitchell said. "Otherwise I'll try to hit into left field."[3]

Mitchell was another one of Tris Speaker's spring training pupils, as the organization thought as Boudreau had: Maybe he would make a good center fielder. Speaker blinked hard the first time that Mitchell trotted over to him and called him "Teach" because he was carrying an infielder's glove instead of an outfielder's glove. That was the first fielding lesson. Part of the Speaker curriculum was to teach young prospects how to get a good jump on the ball, how to back-pedal on a struck ball, and how to adopt the proper form for long throws. It didn't take with Mitchell and he was shifted to left field, which was a better fit. Few could match Speaker, and the Indians weren't asking Mitchell to be that fine in the field. But Mitchell could bat with anyone and Speaker, about as good at the plate as he was in center, gave Mitchell glowing marks for the way he handled himself facing pitching.

"The man has one of the best batting eyes in baseball," Speaker said.[4]

The A's game was hardly Mitchell's only notable contributing at-bat during the month of June. In a 10–8 victory over the New York Yankees on June 11, Mitchell slammed three hits and drove in two runs. He had a nice two-hit game against the Washington Senators during the second game of a doubleheader on June 27, as well. Once installed in the order, Boudreau didn't ever have to worry about Mitchell steering the train off the tracks. He was soft-spoken, rarely drew attention to himself, didn't make outrageous statements, and came to play every day and he usually hit every day.

Mitchell said he developed his hitting strategy early upon entering the pros. He did not picture himself as the next coming of Babe Ruth or Jimmie Foxx, but upon analysis decided his best chance to stick was to spray hits.

"I figured when I first came up that I'd have to hit the ball somewhere most of the time, or not play," Mitchell said. "So I just tried to meet the ball and hit it safe. If I had taken the big cut, who knows? I'd probably have missed so many pitches I'd have been out of there in a hurry." Indeed, Speaker sided with Mitchell's approach. "Dale is always going to be a good percentage hitter. That's because he always hits the ball some-where. I'd say that of all the hitters around our league today he has the best chance to go as high as .400."[5]

That was really quite the endorsement. Speaker was of one of the few generations that produced .400 hitters. Ted Williams hit .406 for the Red Sox in 1941, and that is the last time anyone in the game has accomplished the feat. But from Speaker's vantage point, Williams' achievement was not so old. They were still in the same decade; now the world isn't even in the same century.

Most hitters of Speaker's time—notably his good friend Ty Cobb—disparaged the more modern hitters of the 1940s for investing so much energy in going for the long ball instead of batting for average. That was one thing that made Speaker's comment extraordinary.

Yet that is the way Mitchell stood out as a hitter. He was a throwback to the Bill Terrys and Rogers Hornsbys. Speaker more than once floated the notion that Mitchell had the goods to be a .400 hitter. He was on his way to a .336 finish in 1948, a far cry from .400, but Speaker was certain that Mitchell was going to improve all of his talents and hadn't yet reached his potential.

"Young Dale Mitchell may become one of those rare birds—a .400 hitter," Speaker said. "If .400 is still humanly possible,

Dale's the boy that can do it. He hasn't learned how to run bases yet. We'll teach him how to slide in spring training [of 1949]. Then watch him go."[6]

That overall rawness in Mitchell's game was one reason Boudreau held him back from the starting lineup in April as the manager sorted through his outfield options. Gradually, Boudreau became a believer in Speaker's touting and also said aloud that Mitchell could be a .400 hitter. Boudreau said that if "any Indian ever again hits .400" it would be Mitchell.[7]

There is no question that good baseball was being played in Cleveland from opening day and there was no question that the Indians were the Greatest Show on Earth. Bill Veeck followed through by televising home games, but despite the other owners who acted as naysayers, the free games on the tube did not harm attendance. As Veeck predicted, it just made more people into Indians fans. Seeing some games on TV whetted the appetites of residents who wanted to take in games in person. They wanted to see for themselves what all of the hullabaloo was about.

Veeck was always full of surprises. Long before ball clubs crammed their schedules full of giveaway days for free caps, bats, bobble-heads, and the like, Veeck was handing out free stuff . . . only Veeck's gifts came with a twist. They were not necessarily baseball oriented. Some days it looked as if Veeck had raided a local state fair. It wasn't always clear whether or not it was a good thing to be declared a winner at Cleveland Stadium. The so-called lucky winner might be handed a 50-pound block of ice. What was he supposed to do with that? Or maybe the prize was a live turkey, a guinea pig, or a white rabbit. Veeck was into animal giveaways, mostly, but not always, little ones that a family's little ones would enjoy as pets.

However, he was also into giving away other off-beat prizes—sometimes by the bushel. Those bushels might contain apples, peaches, or tomatoes. Usually the presents were good for laughs, but not everyone who was proclaimed the winner wanted to take his bounty home with him.

A May 23 doubleheader against the Yankees pulled in 78,431 fans. Another Yankees game on June 23 brought in 65,797. But a game played on a weekday against a weaker opponent like the Washington Senators or the St. Louis Browns could leave the stadium feeling like a mausoleum with merely 7,000 or 8,000 people in the house. Veeck had to keep hustling.

That's one thing that Veeck was good at. He slept short hours and spent his waking hours focused on improving his ball club, as well as dreaming up fresh ways to lure fans to the park and entertaining them. He never lost sight of the goal of winning a pennant. At one point, although it had been stated that Veeck began working for the Cubs as a thirteen-year-old, he contradicted that notion and said he was eleven when he started doing odd jobs, the point was the same. He always wanted to work in baseball and own a team.

"I still can't think of anything I'd rather do for a living," Veeck said when he was into his tenure with the Indians. "The pay is adequate and in the off-season there are occasional periods when you seldom have to work more than thirty hours a day. If you like to get to bed at a reasonable hour you'd better think twice before you buy that ball club. The only way I know how to run a ball club is the hard way . . . the hard way requires you sign your life away to the customers. For running a ball club successfully, as I see it, is a job of salesmanship—personal salesmanship."[8]

Anyone who worked in close proximity with Veeck in his front office, and anyone who owned a telephone and worked in a key position of administration with another team in baseball, knew that Veeck did not get much sleep. He smoked at a crazed rate and was convivial with friends and the sporting press, downing much liquid refreshment. But his brain never rested, even when his body was forced to—he had to soak his sore leg in tubs, but always read books as he reclined. Sleep was not on the day planner, except for the rare occasion when it was convenient as opposed to necessary.

Veeck would try anything to fill his ballpark. Sometimes he was criticized for taking too large of a risk and trying something in poor taste. Sometimes things just worked out for the best. On June 13, 1948, one of the most poignant moments in baseball history played out.

Babe Ruth revolutionized the game with his slugging in the 1920s, and was pretty much conceded as the man who saved baseball after the disastrous "Black Sox" scandal of 1919 infuriated and disappointed fans. He wanted to manage the Yankees after he retired, but owner Jacob Ruppert countered with an offer only to manage AAA Newark. Ruth spurned the prospect and never again held a prominent place in the sport. In 1946 Ruth was stricken with throat cancer and by 1948 was a physical shadow of his once-bulky self as he was losing the battle for his life.

The Yankees celebrated the 25th anniversary of Yankee Stadium and announced that Ruth's No. 3 uniform was going to be retired. Weak and failing, Ruth appeared for the ceremony. Indians first baseman Eddie Robinson recounted Ruth's appearance at Yankee Stadium that day. He said that over the years between Ruth's retirement and that game, the Yankees had switched the home team and visiting team locker rooms. So the Indians' clubhouse was where the Yankees' used to be and Ruth's locker, with his name still on it, remained in place.

"Babe wanted to dress one last time in his own locker, so he used our clubhouse on that day," Robinson said. "He appeared to be a little shaky and as he started up the dugout steps to go onto the field [and] I grabbed a bat out of the bat rack and handed it to him for support. He used the bat as a cane while he walked out to home plate and leaned on it during the ceremony."[9]

The photograph of Ruth leaning on the bat addressing the packed stadium in "The House that Ruth Built" became an iconic image of the sport and won a Pulitzer Prize.

After Ruth struggled through his farewell speech with a voice that wobbled, Robinson took the bat, asked Ruth to autograph it, and then took it home. Robinson said for several years he displayed the bat alongside a photo of Ruth walking back to the Indians' dugout in a restaurant he owned in Baltimore.

Eventually, Robinson sold the bat to famed sports memorabilia collector Barry Halper, a friend of his, for what he said was $10,000. However, it was a Bob Feller bat. Feller, who pitched against the Yankees that day, did not know until a day later that he was missing a bat and didn't know where it had gone. He figured out that it was his bat Ruth had used, though. In 2001, the bat made its way back to Feller, and it is now on display in the Bob Feller Museum in Van Meter, Iowa. The Feller Museum paid $95,000 to obtain the bat.

"It's the most important bat in the United States," Feller said. "It's the last bat he [Ruth] ever had in his hand."[10] At least it's the last bat that Ruth held in a public appearance. The Yankee

Stadium one was his last and he died two months later at the age of fifty-three.

Feller not only lost his bat that day, but he lost the game as well, although he only gave up two runs in a 5–3 defeat. While Feller was instantly aware of the bat's historical significance, neither he nor anyone else would have imagined in 1948 that a sports memorabilia market that didn't exist in that decade would bring such huge prices for game-used baseball equipment a half century later. The bat actually went from Robinson to Halper, to the Upper Deck Company, a baseball card manufacturer, which gave it to a Seattle-area near-retirement-aged couple as a contest prize. Then the Feller Museum bought it.

By the 1948 season, Veeck had owned the Indians for less than two full years. But he had replenished, restocked, reshaped, and reloaded the roster. He obtained Gene Bearden and Russ Christopher for the mound and that was just the start. He had added Joe Gordon in trade and Larry Doby from the Negro Leagues. But even after the season began and the Indians started well, Veeck was still on the lookout for that one player that could help, the one that might be the difference maker between winning the pennant and finishing second in the American League.

Something told Veeck that St. Louis Browns pitcher Sam Zoldak could help his Indians. Zoldak was on the verge of thirty and the southpaw had won nine games in each of the previous two seasons. His earned run average was in the 3.40s, so it seemed as though he had pretty good stuff. Veeck's prior acquisition of Bill Kennedy had not paid off, as he only appeared in six games with a 1–0 record and an ERA of 11.12. Veeck shipped Kennedy to St. Louis along with $100,000 for Zoldak.

It was a long-shot deal, but there was a general belief that Cleveland could use another pitcher. There was not another soul in baseball who believed that Zoldak was worth $100,000, and there were loud chuckles when Veeck announced the trade on June 15. It was said that Kennedy was a throw-in and that the Browns bit because of the cash. That was such a large number for a transaction of that type at the time that when Zoldak died from cancer in 1966, the six-digit figure was in the lead of his obituary and in the headline in some newspapers.

Zoldak's nickname was "Sad Sam" because of the look in his eyes, but he was a happy man to join the Indians. In 1948, $100,000 was big bucks. Zoldak said he teased his Indians teammates about his price tag. "I used to kid the other Cleveland players about it," Zoldak said. "I'd tell them, 'This club paid $100,000 to get me from St. Louis. What did they pay to get you?' You know something, though? I wasn't worth it."[11]

Despite that self-deprecating remark made years later, Zoldak actually was worth the payout. Zoldak had arm problems in 1947 (Veeck took a pass at acquiring him that season), and reported to St. Louis' spring training by telling his trainer that his "flipper" was feeling fine. Zoldak was not a hard thrower by any means. He did not blow the ball past hitters, but thrived on location. Zoldak was 2–4 with St. Louis when Veeck beckoned, but once he showed up in Cleveland, he was nearly as effective as Bob Feller. Zoldak went 9–6 with the Indians, and his 2.81 earned run average gave his team a good chance to win every time out.

The pitching staff was looking better every day as 1948 wore on, but few hurlers in the league could compare to the failed infielder, failed outfielder-turned-pitcher Bob Lemon. Lemon on the mound was most assuredly no lemon, and his best work capped the month of June for the Indians.

The Indians visited the Detroit Tigers for a game at Briggs Stadium on June 30, and it was a very good crowd for a Wednesday game, with 49,761 on hand. Lemon took a 10–6 record into the game against right-hander Art Houtteman, who was 2–9. Houtteman was about to pitch one of his best games of the season, but Lemon was about to pitch one of the best games in the history of the Cleveland franchise.

Cleveland scored two unearned runs in the first inning—and no one crossed the plate after that. Houtteman gave up just five hits, but Lemon gave up none. That day he hurled the 12th no-hitter in Indians history in a 2–0 victory in which he faced just 30 batters. The three hitters over the limit came from walks.

Doing his best to capture the drama of the moment, *Cleveland Plain Dealer* scribe Harry Jones wrote in his lead: "Make way you immortal pitchers of baseball. Move over and allow room in your hallowed Hall of Fame for a newcomer by the name of Bob Lemon, a young upstart hurling for the Cleveland Indians, for tonight he, too, achieved greatness."[12]

Lemon was twenty-seven, but had only been pitching regularly for two years. His eleventh win of the season was his fifth shutout. Suddenly, he was the staff ace. It took just one hour and thirty-three minutes to complete the game, and the last out was recorded on an infield play. Future Hall of Famer George Kell was at the plate with two outs in the bottom of the ninth and Lemon handcuffed him on a sinker. Kell took his cut, but only got a slice of the ball. It bounded high back to the mound. Johnny Berardino covered first for Cleveland and Lemon tossed the ball to him with a gentle underhand motion.

That was the last time the swirl of activity around Lemon was peaceful for the next couple of hours. First, he was mobbed on the field by delirious teammates. Then he was mobbed in the clubhouse.

"Gee, what a thrill it was when that last out was made," Lemon said. In keeping with the usual baseball superstition, once it became apparent that a potential no-hitter was in the offing, Lemon was shunned by his teammates in the dugout between innings. "The fellows on the bench didn't talk to me from the sixth inning on. I thought at the time it was funny, but wasn't quite sure what was happening."[13]

That was proof positive that sometimes during a no-hitter the pitcher is the last to realize it. If the hurler doesn't stare at the scoreboard and read the line score with the running tally, sometimes it slips his mind as to what may or may not have been allowed. Mostly he has spent his time staring in the other direction, at the catcher's finger signs, or the enemy batsmen evaluating him sixty feet, six inches away.

For Cleveland, Dale Mitchell collected two hits, and Johnny Berardino, Lou Boudreau, and Walt Judnich contributed one each. The runs were scored by Mitchell and Boudreau and the Tigers made two errors, one by Kell and another by Johnny Lipon. Boudreau's double was the big blow and Hank Edwards got an RBI without getting a hit.

Kell was heavily involved in the action all night. In the fourth inning he whipped a shot to left that had trouble written between the stitches of the ball, but ended up nestled in Mitchell's glove for a big out. It wasn't as big a play, but it was important when third baseman Ken Keltner speared a slow bouncing ball in the fifth and threw out Hoot Evers.

"I had as good stuff as I've ever had," Lemon said, "and I got wonderful support. You don't see many catches like that one that Mitchell made in the fourth."[14]

Once Lemon finally realized that he was pitching a no-hitter, he said he was nervous about it for the duration of the game. Lemon said the clue, even if his brain was not computing the numbers, was his teammates ignoring him. That was like hitting a gong in terms of alerting him to the situation. It was Lemon who chose to joke with catcher Jim Hegan in the ninth inning when the tension was at its thickest. He threw a good imitation of a wild pitch to Kell and when Hegan walked towards the mound he didn't even smile when Lemon said, "That one was just a little wide, wasn't it?" Lemon figured that would be worth a grin or something, but Hegan said, "Yeah, it just missed the corner."[15]

The game was close enough that Lemon had to worry about winning and not just throwing the no-hitter. A couple of mistakes could have changed the result very quickly. He also said he may have pitched even better his previous outing against the Philadelphia Athletics—in some ways. In that game his fastball was faster, but in this one his control was better.

"I was afraid all the way," Lemon said. "Afraid I might walk somebody and have one of those left-handers hit one into the stands and tie us."[16]

Deep down, at least until Kell was tossed out at first, Lemon may still have preferred to be playing the infield. Continued success on the mound, highlighted by a no-hitter, though, was scrambling his thoughts sufficiently that he admitted that as long as it went like this he could get used to this pitching stuff.

"Yes, I guess this pitching racket is all right," Lemon said. "I feel pretty good right now."[17]

Many years later, long after Lemon retired, he was asked to recount the one game of his career that would never forget. Although he had been a 20-game winner and part of a pennant-winner and World Series champion, Lemon chose the no-hitter, calling it the "game that was most exciting to me."[18]

A no-hitter is forever.

Chapter Six notes on pages 283–284.

# 7

# THE GOOD KID

THE JOB OF player-manager—two workers for the price of one—appealed mightily to the skinflint tendencies inherent in the souls of Major League Baseball owners. Still, the tradition of having a man in uniform as both an active player as well as the team's field leader stemmed from the belief that the best man in the lineup could be the best leader.

This was not always true, but employing one person for both jobs was a longstanding proposition when Lou Boudreau became manager of the Cleveland Indians in 1942 at age twenty-four, two months before his twenty-fifth birthday.

The very first player-manager in baseball history was Bob Addy, an outfielder for the Philadelphia White Stockings in 1875. Prior to Boudreau's ascension, such luminaries as Cap Anson, Jim Bottomley, Dave Bancroft, Frank Chance, Ty Cobb, Frankie Frisch, Rogers Hornsby, Nap Lajoie, John McGraw, Mel Ott, George Sisler, and Tris Speaker among others (and all eventual Hall of Famers) acted as player-manager for their clubs. One critical attribute to becoming a player-manager was that he had to be a star, lest the risk be that no one would pay attention to his orders. Ironically, in later years, baseball people decided that back-up catchers and utility infielders were as a rule better managers than superstars who expected too much of their players.

The practice has faded out and the Cincinnati Reds' Pete Rose was the last Major League player-manager. He retired as a player in 1986.

More unusual in Boudreau's case than his appointment was his age. Already an All-Star shortstop, Boudreau was exceptionally young to take over a ball club as its skipper.

Cleveland owner Alva Bradley was looking for fresh blood to count on after he dismissed manager Ossie Vitt and his initial moves didn't pan out. Vitt alienated much of the team with his harsh demeanor and a player revolt sent him packing before the 1941 season. Bradley wanted a better working environment. He took steps to ensure that when he installed a new management duo with Cy Slapnicka as general manager and Roger Peckinpaugh as manager. Slapnicka quit the GM job in September of 1941, though, because of illness. Peckinpaugh, who had previously managed the team some years earlier, was now managing the New Orleans minor-league club.

Slapnicka's departure at the end of the '41 campaign was a surprise. Bradley promoted Peckinpaugh to GM and then they and the team's board of directors met with Boudreau. The announcement that young Boudreau was going to run the team off the field as well as lead it on was a bombshell. Boudreau was not on Bradley's radar screen at first. Boudreau sold himself to the boss and the other decision-makers.

Boudreau knew he was a long-shot to get such a position of authority at his age. In fact, Bradley had nearly decided on hiring veteran skipper Burt Shotton. Boudreau wrote Bradley a letter outlining his case.

"I was only twenty-four years old at the time, with just four seasons of professional ball behind me," Boudreau said. "I figured I had nothing to lose because I didn't tell anybody about it—not even my wife. I told him I was qualified to handle the job. I thought he might ignore it [the letter]."[1]

Instead, the Indians hired Boudreau as the youngest manager in baseball history, giving him a two-year contract. There was definitely outside skepticism.

One Cleveland newspaper reporter referred to the choice of Boudreau as "Baby Snooks" and suggested that the job would "ruin" the All-Star infielder.[2] Others referred to Boudreau as the "Boy Manager."[3]

Initially, Boudreau had to contend with a perception that he was merely going to be Peckinpaugh's puppet since the older man had so much baseball experience. Boudreau admitted he relied on Peckinpaugh as a sounding board, but insisted he was his own man.

"I called the shots from the beginning," Boudreau said. "Some of my decisions were not so good, I'll admit. But I made them. I was in charge. Not Peckinpaugh."[4]

Boudreau was named manager of the Indians only two weeks before the Japanese bombed Pearl Harbor on December 7, 1941, and thrust the United States into World War II. At the time he was two years younger than Joe Cronin when he took over the Washington Senators and three years younger than Bucky

Harris when he took over the Senators. The "Boy Manager" tag had also been applied to them.

Bradley undertook an extensive search in his quest for a managerial replacement, but he found all other candidates wanting. He too wondered about Boudreau's youth, but eventually looked past that flaw.

"The more I inspected the qualifications of various other candidates the more convinced I became that we couldn't afford not to take advantage of Lou Boudreau's natural gift for leadership," Bradley said. "I don't know of another man of whom I could be so certain that he would be thoroughly respected by players, press, and public. Lou is smart, he's a great ball player, a fine young man, a fighter and a leader."[5]

Until President Franklin D. Roosevelt issued his so-called "green light" letter to Baseball Commissioner Kenesaw Mountain Landis, it was unclear if the sport would even be played in 1942. But FDR suggested baseball would provide good entertainment and a distraction for the hard-working laborers on the home front.

Cleveland finished 75–79 and in fourth place in the American League's eight-team circuit in 1942. The Indians went 82–71 the next year, then finished 72–82 in '44 and 73–72 in '45. In 1946, Cleveland finished 68–86. That record was one reason why new owner Bill Veeck was not convinced the team had the right manager running the Indians, even if he greatly admired Boudreau's playing abilities.

However, Boudreau escaped his near-exile when Veeck was prepared to trade him and the city rose up in support, essentially vetoing the trade. Although he was from Illinois and Boudreau might have been more likely to have a preference for playing for the White Sox or Cubs, he fell in love with the city of Cleveland, the city's fans, and the entire Indians' organization. He did not want to depart, but was very concerned that he would not last as manager much longer under Veeck.

Veeck vastly underestimated Boudreau's ties to the city and the reciprocal feelings among the team's backers. Boudreau earned his goodwill on the field even if the team overall had troubles in the standings. Hal Lebovtiz, a long-time Cleveland sports columnist, wrote that Boudreau "in the 1940s . . . was a household name. Every kid in town mimicked his strange stance, resembling a question mark. He was the exceptional athlete who, despite bad ankles and lack of speed, always seemed to position himself perfectly, the flawless, graceful shortstop and the clutch hitter. A leader by example, his performance was an inspiration to his teammates. He was clean cut, personable, and more handsome than most movie stars. The whole town took to Lou. Women went gaga over him."[6]

While many of his players went off to war, including, and perhaps especially, ace pitcher Bob Feller, Boudreau stayed in his baseball uniform. He had ankle problems that prohibited him from running any distance. In 1945, doctors examining his ankles with X-rays couldn't be sure if he had broken his right ankle for the third time or not. Also that year, Boudreau went to work at a war materials manufacturing plant in his hometown of Harvey, Illinois. But he played for Cleveland again in 1946 and stayed on as manager. By then Boudreau was a six-time All-Star and he led the American League in batting in 1944 with a .327 average.

One thing Veeck did was supply Boudreau with an older, seasoned coach who had been around the dugout before in Bill McKechnie. McKechnie, later installed in the Hall of Fame as a manager, was Boudreau's eyes and ears when he was on the field. He served as mentor and savvy advice man, and Boudreau later said he "was a big, big help to me."[7] McKechnie was a loyal supporter who played a somewhat unheralded role during the memorable 1948 season, keeping his pulse on the mood of the team and backing Boudreau in his decisions.

"I have never known another year like the one we had in Cleveland in '48." McKechnie said. "Every day was like the final game of the World Series. And that year Lou Boudreau was the greatest shortstop and leader I have ever seen."[8]

Cleveland has never known another baseball season like '48, before or since, but it was one that unfolded gradually. At first there was some optimism. At the end, there was the culmination of a magnificent pennant chase.

"It was quite a year," Boudreau said. "The pressure kept building and building until I thought we'd all burst."[9]

Popularity saved Boudreau when Veeck was ready to trade him, but he knew entering the 1948 season that even if he was as popular as Santa Claus, that if the Indians didn't win big that year he was going to be ousted as manager. Many likeable managers have been admired, but their tenure ends when they no longer put up more W's than L's and they don't lead their team to the playoffs, pennants, or the World Series. Results count. Boudreau may have wanted to stay in Cleveland forever, but managers rarely leave on their own terms.

In February of 1948, Boudreau was honored and spoke at Cleveland's Man of the Year Dinner sponsored by the Cleveland Chapter of the Baseball Writers' Association of America. He took the occasion to make some news. He was so committed to Cleveland, he said, that even if he could no longer remain as manager, he wanted to remain as a player. However, he intended to win as a manager and prove to Veeck that he could handle both tasks.

"That put the fat squarely in the fire," Boudreau said. "Either I won in '48 or I started taking orders from somebody else. It was as simple as that."[10]

Out to save the job of Boudreau the manager, Boudreau the player was never better. It was added fuel to his fire. Veeck later said of Boudreau's '48 brilliance, "He was out to prove I was a jerk. He was right."[11] Boudreau was the sparkle on the diamond, the clutch hitter when the bases were loaded, and the ubiquitous player who made the key play of the game over and over. Always regarded as a superior fielder, Boudreau was also on his way to compiling a .355 batting average, the highest of his fifteen-year career. His enthusiasm was infectious in the clubhouse. He struck out only nine times all season and blamed umpires for three of them, claiming they screwed up the calls. His on-base percentage was .453 that season, which was also a career high.

Boudreau said he wrote that fate-altering letter to Bradley because he believed, even at his young age, that he could master being an everyday player and the team's manager.

"It appealed to my competitiveness," Boudreau said. "I knew it would be a great feat if I could do it successfully."[12]

Several years into coping with the dual role, the jury was still out on a verdict of just how successful Boudreau was. The 1948 season changed the perception of his reign. No player-manager in baseball ever combined the two jobs so remarkably. As a manager, Boudreau led his team to the pennant and its first World Series in twenty-eight years. As a player, he won his league's Most Valuable Player award, the first shortstop to ever win the award. That combination achievement cannot be improved upon during a single season.

Although several Indians players were recording their finest seasons, Boudreau played in a spectacular zone nearly all year. As evidence that 1948 was a magical year, Boudreau tried things he never even considered doing before. He stole home plate to help the Indians to a doubleheader sweep over the Boston Red Sox as more than 70,000 fans roared at Cleveland Stadium.

"It was the only time I ever stole home or tried to steal home," Boudreau said.[13] He stole the plate on the pitcher who wasn't paying much attention to the runner at third not known for his theft ability.

Once, as he put it, Boudreau admittedly managed himself into a corner by exhausting his bench. He realized he had no one left to catch. So Boudreau strapped on the shin-guards, grabbed the round mitt, and pulled the mask over his face. Unsurprisingly, the opponent, the White Sox, tried to steal on him. Once he was beaten, but the next time he threw out a runner going into second. That was a sign that Boudreau had goofed up his managing strategy more than anything else, but it also showed his willingness to take one for the team. Veeck later forbade him from doing anything so risky to his health again. The Indians needed him at short.

Boudreau's fingerprints were all over the Indians. He made the cuts from the roster; he made the batting order; he listened to advice, but determined the starting pitching rotation; he hit the heck out of the ball and played shortstop like a demon, almost as if he had a magnet in his glove that attracted batted balls. This was his team and this was the role he felt he was born to handle. If his job depended on the outcome of the season, Boudreau was making sure he would never look back with any kind of regret that he hadn't poured his heart and soul into the operation.

"It was the pressure that also created the greatest challenge of my career," Boudreau said. "Nobody wanted to win the pennant more than I, not even Veeck."[14]

One thing Boudreau benefited from was having a player like Boudreau on his team. Not only because of his skills, but because of the fire he brought to the field, the hunger for victory. Managers love ball players who go hard all of the time, who uplift their teammates, showing that hard work by example makes a difference. That was Boudreau all over, although it was especially obvious in 1948.

Boudreau had always been that type of athlete. He was a spark-plug in high school football and basketball at the University of Illinois. Boudreau only knew how to play a sport one way, and that was giving it his all. However, unlike some players known for that style of participation, his personality off the field was not hard-edged.

"He was the greatest shortstop I ever saw," said Indians pitcher Bob Feller. "He was afraid of nobody. He was a great manager, teammate and friend. Just a great man. There is not a more gracious man than Lou Boudreau."[15]

One thing that Boudreau always admitted about Veeck is that once the owner signed him to a two-year contract to run the club, he did everything in his power to acquire players that would help Cleveland win the pennant. There was no hint of undermining Boudreau. They were in it together, and Veeck never stopped tinkering, never stopped attempting to add talent throughout the season. If Boudreau felt he could use more pitching, Veeck tried to provide. It was almost as if money was no object, although that was not the case. Veeck was not a flush owner who also possessed his own key to a personal vault.

Revered in Cleveland because of his baseball accomplishments, Boudreau was well-remembered in Illinois for his collegiate days. But when he returned to Chicago as a Cubs broadcaster, he created an entirely new group of friends.

"He always called the players 'Good Kid,'" said Hall of Fame outfielder Billy Williams. "I guess he was a whiz-kid. He knew the game really well and he used to talk a lot about the game."[16]

Boudreau even began calling some of his own relatives "Good Kid." Grandson Peter Golaszewski recalled an occasion when he was a junior college player and his famous grandfather was in attendance for a playoff game—the only game he saw the boy play. Wouldn't you know it that Golaszewski messed up a ninth-inning fielding play that led to an opposition inside-the-park home run and defeat.

"Keep your head up, Good Kid," Boudreau said to Golaszewski. "Your team would never have been in this position without you."[17]

The same might have been said of Boudreau in 1948 with regard to the Indians' achievements.

Cleveland held first place in the American League from the end of May into July, but the Philadelphia Athletics were closing fast. On July 8, Cleveland blasted the White Sox 14–1 on 15 hits. Boudreau notched two of them with three runs scored and three RBI. Dale Mitchell, Joe Gordon, and Hank Edwards each collected three hits.

Seventy games into the season the Indians' record was 44–26. More than half of the season remained and while Cleveland had played well, the AL pennant race was no runaway. The Indians kept watch on the Red Sox and the ever-dangerous New York Yankees, but neither was of more immediate concern after the Independence Day holiday than the Philadelphia A's.

The A's, still managed by the revered Connie Mack, hit the 70-game mark a bit earlier, the day before the holiday, with a 43–27 record. Mack managed more games (7,755) over more years (53) than anyone in baseball history and, like Boudreau, began as a player-manager. Later, ironically since the Hall of Fame leader had once held down the double role, Mack became identified as the manager who never wore a uniform, only a street-clothes suit, in the dugout.

Mack had assembled the talent for two distinct dynasties with the A's, but no one felt that his '48 bunch would be a contender. It lacked the star power of his earlier champions. Yet Philadelphia's success made Cleveland wary. Yes, it was appropriate to worry about the Red Sox and their slugging lineup, and the Yankees and their normal threat, but things were getting altogether too crowded at the top if the A's were going to nudge their way into the picture.

Never content to sit back and see how things played out with the roster he amassed unless it was in complete command of the AL terrain, Veeck went shopping once more to buttress the Indians. He made one of the most daring, unexpected, and startling acquisitions in baseball history.

Believing that he could remedy any concerns that Boudreau had about weakness in the bullpen, Veeck signed Negro Leagues legend Satchel Paige. Short of obtaining Cleveland veteran Cy Young's autograph on a contract—at age eighty—there was nothing Veeck could have done to astonish and shake up the baseball establishment more.

Chapter Seven notes on pages 284–285.

# 8

# LARRY DOBY—UNDERRATED STAR

**T**HE MAN CLEVELAND Indians owner Bill Veeck chose to integrate the American League was vastly different in temperament and background than Jackie Robinson, the man Branch Rickey chose to integrate Major League Baseball and the National League.

Rickey, a far more meticulous operator than Veeck, laid the groundwork for Robinson's appearance in a Major League game as a barrier breaker with deliberate and careful research, massive scouting, and in-depth character analysis. As has famously been explored, Rickey well understood that Robinson, as the first African American in the majors in the twentieth century, was going to be subjected to hateful and disgusting abuse. But he also knew that if Robinson, fiery by nature, got into fistfights defending his honor, the criticism would be heaped on him, not those guilty of verbal attacks. So he informed Robinson he wanted to hire someone tough enough not to fight back.

Robinson had experienced plenty in his life, including wide-spread discrimination in the army, and he had been in his share of scrapes. He knew what he was in for as well as Rickey did.

Although he was originally from South Carolina, Lawrence Eugene Doby was raised in New Jersey, a product of the comparatively liberal north. He played ball in Newark and had not suffered as much discrimination because of the color of his skin as had Robinson and many other black players of the time that had toured the South.

Veeck's heart was in the right place. He recognized it was wrong that baseball had shut out African Americans and he had explored various avenues of how to break the color line over the years. At the least, now that he had finally become the owner of a big-league club, he was on the prowl for any talented black players that could help his team. Once rebuffed when he made his intent known to stock a team he hoped to purchase with the best players in the Negro Leagues, Veeck moved more cautiously.

In 1947, Larry Doby was twenty-three years old, but he was a seasoned twenty-three. He joined the Newark Eagles as a seventeen-year-old second baseman and then spent time in the navy during World War II. During his first season back in New Jersey, Doby and another future Hall of Famer, Monte Irvin, led the Eagles to the Negro Leagues championship. Compared to Robinson, Doby was shy and sensitive, but he was no push-over; not with his playing background and his military service.

Robinson opened the 1947 season in the Dodgers' lineup on April 15. Doby was signed by Veeck and the Indians in early July, approximately eleven weeks later. While Rickey shepherded Robinson carefully through a two-year process of spring training and a year in Montreal in the high minors, Veeck brought Doby right to Cleveland and deposited him on the Major League roster. Veeck and Doby became great friends and Veeck always referred to him as Lawrence, Doby's given first name. But neither Veeck nor Rickey could be full-time protectors of Doby and Robinson. There was no way to insulate them from the cruelties of bigots, whether that meant harsh language shouted by fans in the stands or from letters penned by insulting idiots. The owners also could not make their teammates love them.

Not everyone on the Indians was enamored with the arrival on the roster of an African American player. There was a tepid welcome in the clubhouse. Doby's Cleveland signing did not equal the fanfare attached to Robinson's, nor has he always been mentioned as prominently as a pioneer. Being second always is a consideration, just as it is in the standings.

"People said that Jackie Robinson made it easier for me," Doby said years later. "Heck, we're still having problems in 1994. It was eleven weeks between the time Jackie Robinson and I came into the majors. I can't see how things were any different for me than they were for him."[1]

Even some of the seemingly most astute members of the baseball press did not quite pick up on that. Dan Parker, a long-time New York sportswriter, took note of Doby's signing with the Indians and issued a view quite contrary to Doby's thoughts. He praised Doby's skills and said that Newark owner Effa Manley had been talking him up as a supremely talented player for a couple of years.

However, Parker wrote, "Announcement of the deal Thursday created only a minor sensation compared with the news a year ago last winter that Jackie Robinson had been signed by the Montreal Royals. Jackie having done the pioneering, things will be much easier for Doby. The racial issue in baseball seems to have lots its virulence."[2] In Doby's mind, Parker was living in a different world than he was, and perhaps that was true.

Later on, Veeck, who paid $10,000 to the Eagles for Doby and added $5,000 more when he made the Indians, admitted that Manley, the only woman in the National Baseball Hall of Fame, offered to let him have Irvin for $1,000 and an additional payment later if he made good. Far from demonstrating the type of initiative he had planned when he attempted to take control of the Phillies, Veeck declined. "Effa," Veeck said, "I think I'm going to have enough trouble bringing in one black. I'm afraid two may not be twice as complicated, but would instead [be] arithmetical, geometric. This shows how bright I am."[3] Indeed it was a terrible decision. Irvin ended up sharing the New York Giants' outfield with Willie Mays and becoming a Major League star.

Doby said that he hadn't known anything of the Indians' interest in him until about two weeks before the deal between Cleveland and Newark became official. Veeck did not meet Doby until July 5 when they were preparing for a press conference. They became so close Doby characterized their relationship as like father and son. Hoping not to let any emotions fester, Veeck rushed Doby to the Indians while they were on a road trip against the White Sox in Chicago. Inevitably, though, some members of the team vocalized their harsh feelings about playing with an African American as a teammate. Veeck reacted strongly by responding to his team, saying, "I understand that some of you players said that 'if a nigger joins the club' you're leaving. Well, you can leave right now because this guy is going to be a bigger star than any guy in this room."[4] That proved essentially to be true, since Doby ended up in the Hall of Fame.

Veeck introduced Doby to the Chicago press in the Bard's Room at Comiskey Park, the after-hours bar and club where newsmen were always welcome after they filed their stories. Then, whether it was a poor miscalculation or not, since he had thrown the weight of the owner's authority in support of the signing, he asked player-manager Lou Boudreau to speak to the team and then introduce Doby to the other players.

Boudreau gave the club a pep talk while Veeck was handling the public introduction, telling the Indians to embrace Doby since he was "part of our team. He'll be wearing the same uniform as we are, so we'll fight for him as well as you'd fight for me or anybody else. Just as you fellas have to earn your job, he's going to be treated the same way. He's going to have to earn his spurs. He realizes that."[5]

Boudreau had not been in on the signing of Doby. In Brooklyn, manager Leo Durocher had been more involved in the acclimation of Robinson to the Dodgers. But when called upon on short notice (about a day's worth of knowledge about what was transpiring) Boudreau rose to the occasion in standing up for his new player. Boudreau was a veteran college athlete before he turned professional in baseball, and had been around black athletes his entire life.

Doby and Boudreau had a private, sit-down session in the manager's office where Boudreau welcomed him to the team and provided such salient information as the bunt sign. Rickey made it clear to Robinson that he would likely not face calm seas and was fully realistic about the type of vicious names his player would be called. Boudreau had not made nearly the study of the issue as Rickey had, but was no dummy and realized Doby might be walking into a tinder box. "Shrug it off," is what Boudreau said by way of advice in case Doby was verbally assaulted.[6] That may have been simplistic, but it was better than saying nothing at all.

One of the worst parts of becoming a racial pioneer for both Robinson and Doby was not the hatred expressed by bigots outside the clubhouse, but the inability to know who to trust in the inner circles. A team is a private club where the prevailing sentiment is supposed to be much like the Knights of the Round-table. Robinson and Doby lacked that luxury at first, uncertain who was really on their side on their own team. It could make for a lonely existence.

Boudreau's take on what happened next as he and Doby made the rounds of the clubhouse, the manager making introductions between Doby and the other players, was a more polite viewpoint than Doby described later. Boudreau said no Indian refused to shake the African American player's hand, but that some made their discomfort obvious by giving him "what we call a 'cold fish,' a limp hand. There were a few who didn't look up."[7]

Later, Doby said that not every player was willing to shake hands with him. Eddie Robinson refused, he said, as did Les Fleming. Fleming played 103 games at first for Cleveland in 1947, batting .242. He was nearing the end of his seven-year Major League career and was not a member of the Indians during their 1948 championship season.

When the players ran onto the field for warm-ups, various accounts have Doby playing catch with Boudreau and others with Joe Gordon. Doby was not in the starting lineup for his first game in an Indians uniform against the White Sox. The game was won by Chicago, 6–5. But Doby did make it into the game, pinch-hitting for relief pitcher Bryan Stephens. Doby was a left-handed hitter. He swung and missed at the first pitch he ever saw in the majors, one thrown by Chicago's Earl Harrist. He struck out swinging. It was an inauspicious debut.

Although later a Bill Veeck–generated myth grew up around that initial at-bat—that second baseman Joe Gordon had comforted Doby after striking out—apparently that was not the case. Boudreau, the boss, did speak to Doby, saying, "Well, now you know some of what it is all about. You are now a big leaguer."[8] Veeck may have told his tale to show how well-received Doby was by his teammates and that right from the beginning when he made a mistake someone was around to console him.

Doby never did view his debut season as a love fest. He struggled all year long, took to heart many insults he heard, and didn't play with the same verve and flash he had exhibited with Newark. The summer of 1947 was a difficult time for him. Because he was not playing well, Boudreau didn't use him much. Doby got into just 29 games and batted an awful .156. He was a lost rookie. Under other circumstances—if he hadn't been the pioneer African American player in the American League—Doby almost certainly would have been sent to AAA to sort out his swing. But after the high-profile announcement of his signing, that was not an option for Veeck and Boudreau. They just hoped Doby would come around. He never did in '47.

Veeck was not going to demote Doby. One very important reason was the naysayers, the bigots, the enemies of progress and change who had written to him and assaulted him for hiring a black player.

"When I signed Larry Doby, the first Negro player in the American League, we received 20,000 letters, most of them in violent and sometimes obscene protest," Veeck said. "Over a period of time I answered them all. In each answer, I included a paragraph congratulating them on being wise enough to have chosen parents so obvious to their liking."[9]

He was not going to back down, nor give those pen pals any satisfaction. Veeck also noted that when he worked fundraising for the Combined Jewish Appeal in Cleveland, he received 5,000 hate letters. When he converted to Catholicism, he said, he received 2,000. Somewhere along the way he realized that many of the names taking the trouble to spew venom at him were the same, making the writers equal-opportunity bigots.

Although it was not publicized at the time, when Doby was overly stressed and felt he could not go to Veeck for reassurance, he called Jackie Robinson on the telephone to talk about their shared fate.

"I'd call Jackie late at night to get things off my chest," Doby said. "Jackie and I agreed that we shouldn't challenge anybody who called us names or caused any trouble. We figured if we spoke out we'd ruin things for other black players. Whatever bitterness I felt at the time I took out on the baseball field. I tried to concentrate on baseball on the field and to get away from it off the field. For me, playing was the joy. My happiest moments were on the baseball field."[10]

That may have been true in general, but Doby did not exhibit much joy over the remainder of the 1947 season. His usual facial expression was a mask, as he tried not to reveal too much feeling.

"When I first got there I didn't have any preparation to help me deal with it," Doby said. "I had to deal with it as I saw fit. I didn't have anyone to hold my hand."[11]

Veeck, as he had a tendency to do anyway, oversold Doby at the introductory press conference, telling the world that Doby was better than Robinson. He may even have thought so since Doby was hitting .415 for Newark at the moment. By the time Robinson burst on the scene in Brooklyn, he was fully prepared and made a splash immediately. He distinguished himself on the field, and especially with his hitting and base running.

Doby couldn't even get on base. He kept to himself, rarely said anything in the clubhouse, and played like an overmatched minor leaguer while used sparingly.

"During that whole first year," Veeck said, "he was a complete bust."[12]

Veeck did his best to act as a sympathetic ear to Doby and earned his everlasting admiration. Veeck was also sensitive to the fact that some players treated Doby shabbily. He was building what he believed could be a championship team and he didn't want any poison in the clubhouse atmosphere in 1948. Doby became a lifetime fan of the man who gave him his chance in the big leagues and stood by him when things were tough.

"He didn't see color," Doby said of Veeck. "To me, in every sense, [he was] color blind. And I always knew he was there for me. He always seemed to know when things were bad, if things were getting to me. He'd call up and say, 'Let's go out. Let's get something to eat.' The next year Bill Veeck eliminated about five of the guys who were discourteous to me."[13]

Yet Doby grew up on the premises in 1947, watching, learning, soaking information in. When the Indians gathered for spring training the next year, the most painful part of Doby's apprenticeship was over. Even before he left Cleveland for the winter the team had presented him with homework. Coach Bill McKechnie gave him the book *How to Play the Outfield* by major leaguer Tommy Henrich. Interestingly, Doby played some professional basketball in the offseason, at least partially because he was insecure about his future in baseball.

In the spring, though, Doby drilled with Tris Speaker, grasping how to play the outfield, and earned a spot as a starter. Boudreau was pleased because in spring training he had a surfeit of outfielders and was waiting on some to emerge from the pack. Doby worried him in 1947, but excited him in 1948. Boudreau called him "a catalyst" on the team's offense. Not only did Doby begin to live up to his advance billing, he was a transformed player who became a team leader on the field with his performance.[14]

In 1948, a much more important season for the Indians than 1947, Doby loomed as a much more important figure on the team. He was still a pioneer, but he was going to have to be a contributor to stick. First, even before the Speaker tutorial, there was the matter of spring training accommodations.

The Santa Rita Hotel, spring home of the Indians, refused to allow an African American player to stay within its walls with his white teammates. Doby was farmed out, not to the minors to play ball, but to the home of a private black family, to stay with. The arrangement did not facilitate Doby's closeness with his teammates.

By the middle of the 1948 season Doby had not only distinguished himself by playing better than his outfield competitors, he was showing he had the power as a home run threat to disturb American League pitching. Then, on July 7, 1948, the Indians signed Negro Leagues legend Satchel Paige. That gave Cleveland two African American players and, naturally enough, in accordance with the thinking of the times that made them automatic candidates to room together on the road.

However, Doby and Paige were completely different types of people. Besides skin color, they had little in common. Paige was forty-two and Doby didn't turn twenty-five until after the season. Paige not only loved to fish, but brought the catfish he'd caught back to the room and cooked it on a hot plate. The smell basically made Doby gag. Paige had developed the habit over the years of carrying a pistol with him and Doby was afraid Paige might accidentally shoot him. It was like a bad college dorm marriage.

The entire situation would have been comical if it was part of a television sitcom, but it was ironic in the lesson for Indians management in showing that, gee whiz, not all black players are alike. The big picture—roommate life aside—was that Doby was a transformed player from 1947, heading towards a .300 season, nearly doubling his average from the previous year.

Chapter Eight notes on pages 285–286.

# 9

# THE METHUSELAH OF THE MOUND

**THE MAN WHO** may have been the greatest pitcher in baseball history watched in dismay as the world passed him by. Then, in an instant, Satchel Paige went from being overlooked to grandly exposed in the baseball fraternity.

For years Paige had blown away hitters with his mix of blurring fastballs and complicated off-speed stuff featuring a "hesitation" pitch. He engaged in stunts such as waving his fielders in and striking out the side and bragged about his throwing prowess in a way that would not otherwise become part of the athletic landscape until such broad personalities as Muhammad Ali and Joe Namath ascended in the 1960s.

He was baseball's best-kept secret, a pitcher on par with Dizzy Dean and Bob Feller—and those finest Major League mound stars said so too—yet he operated in the shadows where there was little media attention.

A showman deluxe, the gangly Paige befuddled hitters wherever he traveled—and boy did he travel—in the Negro Leagues, in foreign countries, and for barnstorming exhibitions. No one could hit his stuff with any consistency. He jumped teams and contracts at will because he was bigger than the boundaries set by his leagues and his clubs, chasing the dollar wherever it was offered. Sometimes he had large wads of cash in his pockets, and that's why he took to carrying a handgun.

Paige knew how good he was and he wasn't shy about telling anyone willing to listen. Mostly those were black Americans who turned out in droves when his name appeared on a marquee. They were also sportswriters representing newspapers like the *Chicago Defender* and *Pittsburgh Courier* whose audiences were black readers.

More than once Paige was told that if he were only white he would be signed by a Major League club in a second. But he knew that without being told. He knew that the work he did for the Pittsburgh Crawfords, the Kansas City Monarchs, and other black teams, or the throwing he did in Mexico, the Dominican Republic, or in other Latin American nations where he was welcome, was more than just good enough. Paige was endowed with a rubbery right arm of extraordinary endurance, a fastball of super speed, and a confidence level that enabled him to master every situation on the ball field he faced, even if he was facing a Josh Gibson or Buck Leonard, two of the most feared Negro Leagues hitters of the day.

It was the rest of American society that occasionally kept Paige off balance, though few prominent African Americans coped with the hatred and discrimination that pervaded the country in the 1930s, 1940s, and beyond as well as he did. No one ever invented a machine that could measure motivation, but if there was a graph chart to accompany such results, Paige's hunger and desire to prove himself would have been over the top.

It was not skill alone that lifted Paige to the top of his game. He was a star in personality as well. Some people are born with charisma as well as talent, and Paige was a man who innately understood how to please an audience. Pitching skill is one thing. A player must possess enough talent to overwhelm big-league hitters. But putting on a show at the same time, ah, that was something special—something that only a few could master. Paige was the king of the hill when it came to combining outstanding performance, crowd-pleasing chatter, and colorful antics.

There was part of Paige that was definitely a guy who enjoyed hamming it up, but he never lost sight of his primary goal—to set the batter down and chalk up an out. Paige could be playful and purposeful simultaneously, but whether it was couched in such a way that the flavor of the moment was remembered by onlookers or not, Paige never was anything but serious about his pitching.

Paige was immensely proud and quite aware that his gift on the mound was what set him apart from others. He deeply resented being stuck on the outside looking in at the National Pastime, but he rarely showed his frustration in either deed or words except when tested on the field. He said a lot, but when it came time to get the important message across, he always let his arm do the real talking.

"Satchel's the greatest pitcher ever lived," said Ted "Double Duty" Radcliffe, both a teammate and opponent of Paige's.[1]

No one—not even Paige—knew how many games he won as he crisscrossed the country, switched leagues, and swapped teams. He sometimes made cameo appearances lasting three innings. The show was the thing in exhibitions. Fans wanted to go away saying they had seen the great Satchel Paige work his wizardry.

Paige grew up in Mobile, Alabama, not one of the forward-thinking American communities on race during the first two decades of the twentieth century. However, Mobile was a cradle of great baseball stars, including future Hall of Famers Hank Aaron and Billy Williams.

Paige's given name was Leroy and he was one of John and Lula Page's (the spelling of the last name changed later) eleven children. Growing up, Paige's favorite hobby besides baseball was fishing, a passion he indulged the rest of his life. During his youth he earned his nickname of "Satchel" through work carrying suitcases for arriving passengers at the local train station. He developed a gizmo that enabled him to tote more than one at a time, earning the lifetime sobriquet. However, Paige also got into trouble as a teen and was sent to the Alabama Reform School for Juvenile Negro Lawbreakers for five years and it was there he truly learned the art of pitching. His motion was perfected partially by repetitive rock throwing. Eventually, he made his professional debut, being paid $50 a month, for the Chattanooga Lookouts in 1926.

Paige was brilliant at getting what he wanted: a larger paycheck, the right to drive his own Cadillac to games rather than riding the bus, or being the headliner when the most important games were played. Paige was always stung that he was not wanted in the majors because he was black. Much like basketball player Darryl Dawkins, who later named his spectacular slam dunk, Paige had a variety of names for the repertoire of his pitches, changing them on a whim. Some were crisper than others, but among the titles applied were "bat dodger," "hurry up ball," "wobbly ball," "nothin' ball," and "midnight creeper." Cool Papa Bell, another of the brilliant Negro Leagues players of Paige's vintage, said, "Bob Gibson was fast, but Satchel was faster than all of them."[2]

If Paige was ever the least bit timid on the mound, he had outgrown any hint of trepidation by the time he was pitching for pay. He learned early that his best pitches were too much to handle for even the best hitters. When you strike out 17 opponents in a game, as Paige was doing in his teens, it becomes apparent early that you can fool most of the hitters most of the time. Usually, a leveling out process follows when even the best pitchers can't dominate. But things never evened out for Paige. He never found a league he couldn't dominate.

"All I know for sure," Paige said in his folksy way, "is that there's a fellow at that plate with a big stick in his hand. It's him and me and maybe he'll hurt me. But if he does, he's got to hit that fastball."[3] Those fellas carrying big sticks rarely did.

Paige was a mythmaker. In an era when little was documented and often only second-hand by newspapermen who were not present at the event, he could spin his skills any way he wanted. There was no Internet, no TV, and no radio of Paige's games. The eyewitnesses shrunk back into their homes when a game ended. Paige was free to embellish and he was a marvelous story-teller. The basic facts of the matter might be authentic in terms of wins and losses or number of strikeouts, but Paige had a talent for telling a tale breathlessly, building drama. Satch's version might be a life-and-death account, such as pitching for Presidente Rafael Trujillo, supposedly at gunpoint after spending a night in jail in the Dominican Republic. Paige could charm any listener and his feats were impressive enough to support any back story.

The American South was often seen as divided from and separate from the North during the early years of the twentieth century as it had been during the Civil War. It remained backward on race relations with full-scale discrimination and Jim Crow laws in effect to restrict African Americans. There were "colored" and "white" drinking fountains in public places, segregated seating at movie theaters and ballparks. There were lynchings of blacks across the region for no better reason than a young African American male looking the wrong way at a white woman.

Daily doings and achievements by blacks were ignored—beyond the boundaries of the South. It was as if newspapers and magazines considered the minority population of the country to be invisible. That is one reason why descriptions of Negro Leagues baseball stars often referred to them as playing "in the shadows." It was as if whites and blacks lived in parallel universes.

The first true crossover American sports superstar was heavyweight champion Joe Louis. He was followed by Olympic sprinter Jesse Owens, whose multiple gold medals earned in the 1936 Summer Games in Berlin seemed a personal insult to German dictator Adolf Hitler. Jackie Robinson was next in line as the third athlete whose accomplishments earned fans of all colors and ethnic backgrounds.

Paige was an athletic god in the black community, but for much of his career was known as a superior baseball player only by a sliver of the sport's constituency. Mainstream Americans did not follow Negro Leagues baseball. However, those who did not reside in Major League cities were the beneficiaries of traveling All-Star teams playing exhibitions in the offseason, usually in the early fall after the World Series.

Dizzy Dean, the St. Louis Cardinals' brash and brassy hurler who won 30 games in 1934 for the World Series champs, was a pioneer at pulling together postseason, pieced-together barnstorming clubs that often toured with and played against Satchel Paige–led all-black ensembles. Across the great divide of segregation these types of encounters showed Paige and his teammates that they were just as good as the white players. It provided empirical evidence otherwise unattainable.

Dean and Paige were quite the pair. They both threw fast; they both had disputes over their dates of birth; and they both liked to do nothing more in the world except talk a good game. They teased one another, entertained the public with one-liners, and became great friends. Dean was as much cornpone as Webster's in his speech, especially when the Arkansas boy tried to please his constituency. But he was never condescending to Paige, and he was always laudatory on the radio when he broadcast games and in the newspapers where he penned a column. Whether Dean could spell well or not was unknown, but his editors apparently felt attention to detail was not necessary when he wrote.

"I know whose the best pitcher I ever see and it's old Satchel Page (sic), the big, lanky colored boy," Dean wrote. "Say, old Diz is pretty fast back in 1933 and 1934, and you know my fastball looks like a change of pace alongside that little pistol bullet old Satchel shoots up to the plate. It's too bad those colored boys don't play in the big leagues because they sure got some great players." Dean added, "If old Satchel and I played together we'd clinch the pennant mathematically by the Fourth of July and go fishin' until the World Series. Between us we'd win 60 games."[4]

In later years, after Dean's Hall of Fame career was shortened by injuries, Paige and Cleveland Indians star Bob Feller engaged in similar touring showdowns and also gained mutual respect for one another. Paige was older and in theory on the downside of his career. It was the 1940s, not the 1930s prime of Dean. Yet Paige and Feller had their own road show. These barnstorming adventures were all about money and nothing spoke louder to Paige than the color green. However, it was also important to him that he show well. It wouldn't do at all to come off as inferior to his white counterparts, even if Paige was believed to already be in his forties. Feller and Paige were also well aware that many of the baseball fans who would attend their events were curious about the black versus white aspects of the contests. Were blacks just as good at baseball at whites?

"The whole trip was because of racial rivalry," Feller said of a 1946 tour.[5]

With each star pitcher serving as captain of a racially divided team, the two groups of All-Stars toured the hinterlands where only minor league ball was regularly played. Stops included visits to Pennsylvania, Ohio, Missouri, Colorado, and California, and there were more than 250,000 paying customers. They did it again in 1947. Feller was not generous in his assessment of the African American talent, which his team bested regularly in 1946. "Maybe Paige when he was young," Feller said, indicating he was the only one among the opposition that was Major League–ready.[6] Much later Feller added to his impressions of Paige, saying he had "perfect control" and "could spot a hitter's weaknesses very quickly, quicker than anyone I ever knew."[7]

Although he rarely admitted his deepest true feelings, Paige did believe that if and when the white man opened to black players, his would be the first name called. Many times over the years he had heard the patronizing and infuriating phrase, "If only you were white" about the likelihood of a big-league contract being offered. It was a shock to Paige when Branch Rickey and the Brooklyn Dodgers announced the signing of Jackie Robinson as the first twentieth-century African American player.

Paige believed he was going to be the chosen one, if there ever was a chosen one. To many, Paige was too old. One of the great mysteries of his life was the pitcher's actual age. Many theories abounded and Paige played along with them when outsiders sought to trace his Mobile, Alabama, birth to a specific date. Paige had also attained a certain stature in the sport. To some baseball fans his was the only name known in Negro Leagues ball. He was not going to be a man to kowtow to any elements of discrimination if he integrated the sport, and perhaps white owners feared that he was too much his own man.

Famously, when Rickey signed the much younger Robinson he asked him to turn the other cheek to the firestorm of discrimination coming. Paige did not have the makeup to cope with an order not to fight back as Robinson adjusted to in his first years. Paige disarmed some discrimination with cleverness and humor, but he was a very different kind of person than Robinson. Robinson was more disciplined and was married. Paige was a free-wheeling guy and a playboy at various times of his life.

Robinson made his Major League debut for Brooklyn in 1947. The Dodgers were in the forefront of integration. They were signing other African American ball players, too, like Roy Campanella, Don Newcombe, and Dan Bankhead. Bankhead became the first African American to pitch in a Major League game on August 26, 1947, when he hurled 3.1 innings for the Dodgers against the Pittsburgh Pirates.

Once Robinson jump-started the integration of the majors and others had started to follow, Paige believed his ship had sailed; the last opportunity for him to appear in the white majors was gone. *How about that*, he probably thought. The majors were looking for black talent and they didn't even know his phone number. They were dismissing him because he was too old. A certain amount of intimidation might also have played a part in teams ignoring Paige. He was set in his ways and the reputation that preceded him was of a player who didn't work hard, who had a general disdain for the clock and keeping appointments (such as clubhouse arrival times).

However, Americans at-large had caught a glimpse of this enigmatic figure some years earlier. In an unprecedented divergence from its usual journalistic practices, *Life* magazine ran a spread on Satchel Paige, a "negro" baseball player locked out of the majors because of his skin color in June of 1941. In twenty-first century America, it is difficult to get across how significant *Life* magazine coverage was at that time. It was the official barometer of American life. It was the most important magazine in the nation. If *Life* magazine wrote about you and displayed photographs of you, that meant you really were somebody.

Paige was a sportswriter's dream. All he had to do was act his usual self and the writer would go away smitten by this genius of the mound who could tell tales like Mark Twain. And Paige knew exactly what he was doing. "The sportswriters loved me acting the big shot and living it up like that," Paige wrote later in life. "They started talking about me like I wasn't even a real guy. I was something out of a book."[8]

Early in his pitching career Paige realized there was no percentage in hurrying to the mound. He might strut off of it, but when he entered a game Paige was in no rush. He recognized that until he threw the first pitch no action would transpire, so he maintained control of the pace. Paige also had a very noisy stomach that often gave him indigestion and was known to sip Pepto-Bismol or equivalents while on the mound. That was all back-drop to his legendary list of rules for smart living that became part of the Paige legend.

Entitled "Time Ain't Gonna Mess With Me," by *Collier's* magazine, and later referred to generally as "Satchel Paige's Rules For Staying Young" by a variety of publications and in books, Paige listed:

1.  Avoid fried meats which angry up the blood;"
2.  "If your stomach disputes you, lie down and think cool thoughts;"
3.  "Keep the juices flowing by jangling around gently as you move;"
4.  "Go very light on the vices, such as carrying on in society. The social ramble ain't restful;"
5.  "Avoid running at all times;"
6.  "Don't look back. Something might be gaining on you."[9]

Some people probably remember portions of Paige's advice better than the man who had offered it. It was typical Paige. His comments were part sincere, yet offered with a wink given that he rambled as much socially as anyone in the sport. The "Don't look back" comment was the most enduring.

In 1948, it was getting more difficult for Paige to look forward. He saw a new world opening in baseball and he wasn't part of it. Suddenly, Major League teams (at least some of them) were looking for talented African American players, and they weren't looking at him. In 1946, Paige had sent new Cleveland Indians owner Bill Veeck a telegram asking when he was going to be summoned to Cleveland. He was not hired at the time, but Veeck wrote him back a note that was hopeful in content, implying that patience was going to be needed.

The Dodgers were the most progressive team, almost seeming to be cornering the market on black talent. But the Boston Braves were showing signs of aggressiveness, as were the New York Giants. The American League was slower to integrate, but Veeck had made Larry Doby the first African American player in the AL only months after Jackie Robinson joined the Dodgers.

Veeck may well have once at least mentally committed to stocking a Major League club with black talent, but the 1948 Indians were not the early 1940s Philadelphia Phillies. This was a club on the verge of capturing a pennant, perhaps capable of reaching its first World Series in nearly three decades. Yet by July Veeck was not completely convinced the Indians could go all of the way. He felt the squad needed some bullpen help.

The energetic owner was quite aware of Paige's skills, but he wondered if he had enough left in his arsenal to play big-league ball in 1948. Like almost everyone else, Veeck was not sure how old Paige really was. It eventually came to light (after some light-hearted shenanigans by both Veeck and Paige) that Paige was born on July 7, 1906. That made him forty-two years old, not an age that appealed to any team looking for young prospects. But that wasn't what Veeck was looking for anyway. He was in the market for immediate help to give manager Lou Boudreau more options in the bullpen.

Veeck was friendly with Abe Saperstein, the creator and long-time owner of the Harlem Globetrotters. Saperstein and Veeck had both been based in Chicago for years. No one knew the African American sports scene better than Saperstein, and Veeck asked him to scout for potential fresh young black talent. A couple of African American players had been signed by the Indians organization, but they were only minor leaguers.

In 1948, Veeck approached Saperstein again and asked if he could arrange a tryout for Paige with the Indians. Veeck ran his brainstorm past Hank Greenberg, who had settled into the front office after his aborted fling in the field during spring training. Veeck was also aware that his own pitcher Bob Feller and Paige had developed a good rapport from their barnstorming experiences. Manager Lou Boudreau was not consulted in advance, but asked by Veeck to come to the ballpark to watch a pitching prospect throw.

"What could I do?" Boudreau said. "Veeck was the boss. I said I'd be there in an hour. It was then I met Satchel Paige for the first time. I told Satch to loosen up, to run or whatever, and let me know when he was ready. He struck out his hand, jiggled it, then said, 'Mr. Lou,' which is what he always called me, 'I'm ready. I pitch with my arm, not my legs.'"[10]

Initially Boudreau did not respond warmly to the idea of the ancient (in his mind) pitcher becoming an Indian. Boudreau said he played catch with Paige for perhaps ten minutes while other witnesses on the scene, Veeck, Greenberg, Saperstein, and *Cleveland Plain Dealer* sportswriter Gordon Cobbledick watched in silence. Paige may have been old by baseball standards, but he also had a point to prove. To demonstrate that he was throwing as efficiently as ever he gave Boudreau a handkerchief that was folded up into small squares and asked him to put it on the plate in any position at all.

"First I put it on the inside corner," Boudreau said. "He wound up and threw ten pitches—fastballs and sliders, all with something on them—and nine of them were right over the handkerchief. He told me to move the handkerchief to the other side of the plate and he threw ten more pitches the same as before. His fastball had a hop to it and his slider was tremendous. Seven or eight of his pitches were right over the handkerchief and those that missed didn't miss by much."[11]

The point was made that Paige had remarkable control. Of course, no one was in the batter's box and pitching against live hitters was much different. It was Veeck who insisted that Boudreau take a turn in the box. After all, he was one of the best hitters in the American League. Boudreau said he struck a few line drives, but saw enough to know that Paige still had the goods. Joking about Paige's true age began immediately upon his signing, Veeck told the reporters Paige was forty-two. Paige said he was "only about thirty-nine." Boudreau said he thought Paige might be closer to forty-nine or fifty. Boudreau saw value in Paige as a reliever and spot starter to mix into the pitching rotation.[12]

Although there was no such thing as a media storm to match the hurricanes of the 2000s, within the context of the times, the Indians signing Paige was big news.

The *Sporting News* offended both Veeck and Paige with its high-and-mighty reaction that bordered on the hysterical. The weekly *Sporting News* was the Bible of baseball and it was more conservative than extreme right politicians. Owner J. G. Taylor

Spink authored an editorial, accusing Veeck of making a travesty of the game by inking Paige. "If Paige were white he would not have drawn a second thought from Veeck," Taylor wrote. "To bring in a pitching 'rookie' of Paige's age casts a reflection of the entire scheme of operations in the major leagues. To sign a hurler of Paige's age is to demean the standards of baseball in the big circuits."[13]

It was not unusual for someone to accuse Veeck of trying out a gag for publicity value. He was more proud than chastised most of the time when such a thing occurred. However, Veeck had too much respect for the black ball players who had been marginalized to trifle with their feelings. He knew Paige could still play. Veeck, who always called Paige Leroy, his real first name, and Paige became close friends and as it became apparent that Paige was a valuable addition to the Indians, the owner sent messages to Taylor tweaking him about the newcomer's success and even suggesting Paige should be considered for rookie of the year honors.

The Paige accuracy and ball placement with the handkerchief was a neat trick and Boudreau said, "Now I can believe some of the tall stories they tell about his pitching."[14]

Indeed, for Paige the handkerchief ploy was somewhat routine.

"I don't pitch for home plate," he said later. "I stick a small match box or a tiny piece of cigarette paper in front of the catcher instead," Paige said. "I figure if I can throw over a small target like a match box I sure can get it over a great big plate."[15]

Paige lore and legend would only be magnified in the coming days and months. By coincidence, Paige signed with the Indians on July 7, 1948, which, given the prevailing belief surrounding his date of birth once the smokescreen was eliminated, would have been his forty-second birthday.

More than twenty-two years after Paige first pitched for cash for the Chattanooga Lookouts, he was a member of a Major League franchise. If some of the disquiet that followed the signing stemmed from American League owners still resistant to signing African American players, that was their problem as far as Veeck was concerned. Other AL teams might be stand-offish on that front, but the public was ready for the infusion of black talent. Paige was a big enough name to put bottoms in the seats and that was always a prime Veeck consideration, though more than anything he wanted to field a winner.

Boudreau scoffed at the idea that Paige's acquisition was all about attendance and nothing else. "Bill signed Paige because we needed another pitcher, preferably one with sharp control who could be of service as a relief man and a spot starter," Boudreau said. "Paige was signed for what he could do, not for what he could draw."[16]

Still, Veeck gave Paige a generous $40,000 deal covering the remainder of the season and paid Saperstein a $25,000 finder's fee, although Veeck certainly could have "found" Paige without his assistance.

When Paige was hustled before the somewhat astonished Cleveland press, he was calm and collected not only in demeanor, but in speech.

"I'm starting my Major League career with one thing in my favor," Paige said of the best birthday present he ever received. "I won't be afraid of anybody I see in that batter's box. I've been around too long for that."[17] Paige was disingenuous on another front, that day informing his listeners that he had been born on

September 18, 1908. Not quite, although a birth certificate with any date on it was never produced for Paige.

Paige swiftly donned an Indians uniform and two days later, on July 9, made his Major League debut, which also happened to be the first appearance in an American League game by an African American pitcher. Paige came out of the bullpen after starter Bob Lemon struggled in the fourth inning as the Indians trailed the St. Louis Browns, 4–1. Paige, as was his way anyway, strolled slowly to the mound from the pen.

Never in his life did, or would, Paige admit to being nervous, but he did say that on this occasion he came about as close to that sensation as was possible.

"I knew all those folks in the stands were studying me," Paige said of the 37,840 in attendance. "Folks been eyeing me all my life. But these folks were different. I could feel it. They were like people at a circus. They were asking themselves, 'Can that old man really pitch?'"[18]

That day Paige pitched two innings, gave up two hits, struck out one batter, and surrendered no runs. He was a Major League pitcher with a 0.00 earned run average, although the Indians lost to the Browns, 5–3. It was a game that was much larger in the scheme of baseball history than the final score. For Paige it marked the culmination of a remarkable journey, not that there weren't still thrills to be had now that he was a member of Major League baseball's exclusive club.

It was not long after that when Boudreau employed Paige in another role—starter. On July 9, no one knew whether or not Paige would get into the game. But on August 3, 1948, it was well-publicized that Satchel Paige was going to be the Cleveland Indians' starter against the Washington Senators that night at

Cleveland Stadium. Fans began pouring into the ballpark hours before the game and when Paige wound up for his first pitch, the turnstiles had registered the arrival of 72,434 of them. By then Paige's record was 1–1 in relief.

On this day the ball was handed to Paige first, not with him coming out of the pen. There was no rush to the mound, no reason to glance at runners on base. He was starting fresh. Paige pitched seven innings, allowed three runs, and the Indians won, 5–3, moving their record to 56–38.

During this time period, when Paige put on Cleveland's uniform for the first time, when he appeared in his first game as a reliever, and when he made his first start that one question was repeated. Everyone kept asking him if he was nervous. Years later, even his son, Robert Leroy Paige, asked the same question. In a way Paige dodged a direct answer, but he always gave the same one. "I knew I could pitch," he said.[19]

Obviously he meant that since he knew he could pitch there was no reason on God's green earth for him to be nervous.

And there wasn't, really, for Paige was an instant success. He may have been thrust into a stressful situation as the first African American pitcher in the American League, trying to help a team win a pennant, and yet being looked at askance for his age, but Satchel Paige never shied from a challenge and probably the last time he had been truly nervous was being sent to reform school by his thirteenth birthday.

Pitching make him nervous? Heck no, he'd been doing that almost his entire life. The guys toting the bats into the batter's box were the ones that should be nervous.

Chapter Nine notes on pages 286–287.

# 10

# HELP FROM EVERYWHERE

**B**RINGING IN RETIRED star Tris Speaker to work doggedly to make Larry Doby into a smoother fielding outfielder was the type of thing the Indians had tried before. In 1947, also in spring training, the Indians hired Rogers Hornsby to work with outfielder Pat Seerey on his hitting. The intensive course lasted eight weeks.

For Seerey, making contact with the ball was often as elusive as scientists seeking to determine if there was life elsewhere in the solar system. Both swung and missed frequently, Seerey striking out about 100 times a season in limited action and routinely hitting in the .230s.

Hornsby is regarded as one of the greatest hitters of all time. His lifetime batting average of .356 is second best in history to Ty Cobb's .367. Hornsby hit over .400 three times and won seven batting titles. However, he was not a patient man and despite being given numerous coaching and managerial jobs he never attained renown as a tutor.

By 1948, it was produce or else for Seerey and it became "or else." Seerey appeared in just 10 games for the Indians in

1948 before the club gave up on him, trading the outfielder and pitcher Al Gettel to the White Sox for third base–outfielder Bob Kennedy. Ironically, soon after the deal, Seerey recorded the highlight moment of his career. On July 18 against the Philadelphia Athletics, Seerey smashed four home runs in a single game. That tied the all-time record of four round-trippers in a game, a mark that has been equaled several times since, but never broken.

While that show of destructive power might have indicated the Indians made a mistake in shipping out Seerey, that was not the case. While he did crack 18 home runs and drive in 64 runs, Seerey still batted just .231 in 105 games for Chicago that year.

There was a glut of outfielders vying for starting roles when the season began, but the Indians thinned the herd. Doby advanced ahead of the others. Dale Mitchell was a regular. Seerey played himself into a job in Chicago. Allie Clark was hindered by a broken wrist suffered in April. It was still crowded, but manager Lou Boudreau took advantage of his choices to use the others as he saw fit.

One of those outfield hopefuls was Hal Peck. Peck was a left-handed hitter who, like several of his teammates, had overcome physical obstacles to become a Major League player. Peck was from Genesee, Wisconsin, and was a fine prospect in 1942. But just when he reached the cusp of big-league attention, a shooting accident nearly cost him his foot and career.

How Peck came to sidetrack his career was through a hunting accident of sorts, but one far from typical. While home on the outskirts of Milwaukee, Peck and his mother heard a noise coming from the bushes outside their home. As his mother was convinced that the troublemakers were rats that had been sneaking into the house stealing food, Peck grabbed a shotgun and set out after the culprits.

On his way to the bushes, Peck stumbled and as he fell, the gun went off and buckshot sprayed his left foot, not only putting a hole in the foot, but blowing off two toes. Known for his speed as a runner, Peck fretted that his baseball career was finished. It took more than a year to recover and he had to wear a special shoe made just for him.

Peck made his Major League debut with the Brooklyn Dodgers in 1943, getting into one game. He played in just two contests the next year, but was a regular for the Philadelphia A's in 1945, batting .276. When he came to Cleveland in 1947, Peck recorded his best season, batting .293 with eight homers and 44 RBI. He had earned the chance to play regularly, but couldn't fend off the challenges the next year. Instead, during the pennant scramble he became an element off the bench for Boudreau. Peck batted .286 in 45 games and rarely went to the plate more than once in a game.

Peck collected 35 at-bats as a pinch hitter during the summer of 1948, notching eight hits and gathering five walks, even breaking up a no-hitter against the Athletics.

"I'm happy I got timely hits in key situations," Peck said.[1]

Probably the biggest long shot in the spring training outfield sweepstakes was Thurman Tucker. One thing that made Tucker stand out was wearing glasses at a time when few players did. Sometimes players with glasses were teased and some doubted their ability to see as sharply as those who didn't wear them. Indeed, Tucker did not hit like his competitors, but had shown that he was a better glove man over several seasons with the Chicago White Sox. Boudreau was a very good fielding shortstop and understood the value of a good glove. Surveying his choices to patrol the outfield, Boudreau saw the still-learning Doby and the limited-range Mitchell manning the corners. While many were surprised, he anointed Tucker to be his centerfielder.

Tucker was already thirty when Veeck obtained him over the winter in a deal for catcher Ralph Weigel. Tucker had posted two seasons where he hit .287 and .286, but mostly was a pedestrian contributor with the bat. It was his speed in the outfield and ability to cover ground that had made his acquisition appealing to Veeck. The Indians envisioned Tucker more as a versatile outfield back-up, yet came to rely on his smoothness afield.

Throughout the sport Tucker was known for his resemblance to comedian Joe E. Brown, but the ironic fact was that Tucker was taciturn while Brown was famed for his big mouth. In contrast to the others playing outfield for Cleveland, Tucker had virtually no pop in his bat. He hit exactly one home run in 1948 and just nine for his career.

In 1944, Tucker surprised the baseball universe by getting off to a wicked hot start at the plate and woke up one day leading the American League in batting average. The fast start even earned him a place in the All-Star game. It was a transitory moment, however.

"I led the league in hitting for about half the season," Tucker said. "Then I got tired and went twenty-eight times without a hit."[2]

Boudreau didn't care too much about how well Tucker hit, as long as he kept his average respectable. Tucker batted .260 in 1948 while appearing in 83 games. He had his big moments, but his glove wasn't so great that he could monopolize a place in the lineup.

Another player in the outfield mix was Hank Edwards. Before World War II, Edwards was a top outfield prospect in the Indians' system. In 1946, reintegrating into the Cleveland lineup, Edwards batted .301 with 10 home runs and 54 runs batted in while playing in 124 games. He also hit a league-leading 16 triples.

However, Edwards did not keep up his high level of play, batting just .260 in 1947. That drop in average raised uncertainty about Edwards' ability to contribute and that made him just another outfielder with high hopes coming out of Arizona in 1948. Edwards saw spot duty and batted .269 as the pennant race unfolded and never again had as solid an all-around year as he experienced in 1946.

Injuries played significant roles in limiting Edwards after 1946. He hurt his right shoulder in spring training of 1947, although he did play in 108 games. Edwards barely made it out of July in one piece in '48. Starting in right field in the opening game of a doubleheader against the Boston Red Sox on August 1, Edwards was tracking a fly ball close to the wall at Cleveland Stadium, and then leapt at the last minute for a stunning catch. However, he bashed the wall and suffered a dislocated right shoulder, re-injuring the same wing he'd hurt the year before. Basically, one by one the Indians' outfielders either played themselves into regular jobs or played themselves out of the lineup.

Not to be overlooked in the ever-changing pattern of the outfield was Wally Judnich. Judnich was one of Veeck's pickups from the St. Louis Browns and posted a .257 batting average in 79 games for the Tribe in '48.[3] It was Judnich's only season in Cleveland, but he had a knack of getting on base and had a .411 on-base percentage.

Overall, it was a strange situation. Pennant contenders usually had more settled lineups. Few managers over the first half of the twentieth century platooned players. George Stallings had remarkable success doing so with the miracle Boston Braves of 1914. Casey Stengel was soon to be hailed as a genius for the way he juggled his players with the Yankees, but Stengel had not yet established that as a notable trademark during his losing years running the Brooklyn Dodgers and Boston Braves.

By nature, Boudreau was not inclined to platoon, but to gain maximum advantage from the talent he had on hand in 1948 he could not stick with a set outfield. He was forced into making more judgment calls as the season went on. Of all the accomplishments Boudreau could be proud of during the '48 season, the way he smartly handled the manning of the Indians' positions based on the individuals available at the time was probably the most overlooked.

This was not a team that was fully formed in spring training, not a team where Boudreau could just roll out the balls and let his guys play. It took some care and nurturing, some fine-tuning for the Indians to be at their best. Boudreau was like a chiropractor providing adjustments.

One of the biggest surprises by mid-season—as big a surprise as the signing of Satchel Paige, although in a different way— was the slump of Bob Feller. Here were the Indians, poised to capture their first pennant in nearly thirty years and their ace, their star, their most reliable thrower, was sitting on a 9–11 record. That didn't figure and no one really understood what was wrong. Strangely enough, Feller, based on his reputation, was still selected for the All-Star team.

"I had misgivings," Feller said. "A guy who isn't pitching at the .500 level doesn't belong on anybody's All-Star team. My election that year was just for old times' sake. Although it was a nice gesture, it was something I didn't deserve."[4]

While baseball people may have raised their eyebrows and questioned the choice of having Feller participate in the All-Star Game, Boudreau was concerned about the decision for a different reason. He was counting on Feller getting some time off to regroup and come back to the rotation refreshed for the final couple of months of the regular season. Boudreau went to Veeck and made his case that Feller should skip the game. Feller agreed, but then Indians management blundered. Rather than having the team announcing that Feller needed time off for rest, Veeck told Feller he should fake an injury. When Feller refused to lie, Veeck then issued a statement indicating Feller was pulling out of the game for unspecified reasons. That didn't go over well with anyone and created a media storm.

Even after Veeck publicly back-tracked, no one believed that Feller wasn't behind the entire mess and that he just wanted to blow off the game. It was an overblown non-event that we're used to seeing today, but not in the 1940s, and it was one of the unhappier episodes in Feller's career. Cleveland and Feller got past that contretemps and Feller did heat up as the summer weather did, putting together a much better second half of the season.

By the end of July the Indians' record was 53–38, which was very good, but not good enough for a runaway in the pennant race.[5] There were other teams feeling just as good about themselves. After their slow start, the Red Sox rebounded and by the end of that month had a record of 57–38, which gave them a two-game lead over Cleveland in the AL. The Philadelphia A's were 58–40, good enough for second place, and the Yankees record was 54–39, which left them tied with Cleveland for third place.

It was crowded near the top of the standings and as optimistic as the Indians were, there was no reason for any of those other clubs to feel discouraged. As the season turned to August, the Indians and the Red Sox met in a series that loomed large.

After falling to the Red Sox on July 30 (losing 8–7) to start a four-game series, the Indians won the next three games (a victory on July 31 and in a doubleheader on August 1) at Cleveland Stadium, taking games by scores of 10–9, 12–2, and 6–1. It was an important three-game winning streak, both psychologically and in the standings.

Feller started the game on the last day in July and pitched five and two-thirds innings, giving up four runs with five walks and only one strikeout, and Steve Gromek got the win in relief. In the first game of the doubleheader, Bob Lemon, an Indians true All-Star that season, went the distance and improved his record to 14–9. Boston collected just six hits while being bombarded by the Indians' bats. Doby had three hits, scored two runs, and drove in four. Lemon contributed with his bat as well, knocking in three runs on three hits while scoring twice. He hadn't forgotten how to hit despite moving to the mound to make his living.

Sam Zoldak, the man everyone said Veeck overpaid for, won in the nightcap. Eddie Robinson's three hits and Kenny Keltner's two safeties provided the Cleveland offense.

It was too soon to tell how it was all going to play out with four teams hanging tough as August began, but Feller, none too pleased with his own performance, raved about how Boudreau was playing—and running things.

"He was showing us how to win," Feller said, "by doing everything at a level of excellence that other players seldom reach. And he was going an outstanding job as our manager, too, making the right moves in games and handling his pitching schedule—the hardest part of managing—so well that all of us were effective, especially in the second half of the season."[5]

Partially because Boudreau was fulfilling the double role as player-manager and because he was so young when he took over the team, he always seemed to have to defend his judgment to outsiders. He simply felt he was born to lead and that he was able enough and smart enough to make the big decisions without waiting for his beard to turn gray and without spending years accumulating wisdom.

It takes a certain arrogance to rule from such a position and viewpoint and Boudreau had that inner conceit that enabled him to think that way, though he would merely tell you he was channeling his confidence and positive thinking. Sometimes when questioned about how he could lead a group of grown and grizzled men, Boudreau expressed surprise that anyone would question his credentials.

"The job never scared me," Boudreau said. "Why should it? I was elected captain of my high school and college basketball teams in my sophomore year. When I was fifteen, coaches were talking things over with me. Say, I even was elected president of Phi Sigma Kappa, my fraternity, when I was a sophomore. I expected some of the older guys on the team would be jealous of me, but I knew I could handle them."[6]

So there it was. To Boudreau the Indians were just one big brotherly fraternity.

Chapter Ten notes on pages 287–288.

# 11

## THE KNUCKLEBALL MAGICIAN

---

**G**ENE BEARDEN'S NAME does not ring out among modern baseball fans anywhere except Cleveland, a place where it never should be forgotten. Bearden was the X factor of 1948, an unknown player in spring training who was a hero by October.

Whenever a team makes a run to a championship, it is likely that someone on the roster will inject themselves into the mix unexpectedly and succeed to a wild degree when they weren't even expected to make the team.

More than sixty-five years after Bearden emerged from nowhere to become one of the best pitchers in the American League in 1948, he remains one of the most astounding one-season wonders in sport. It was almost as if Bearden made a deal with the devil, trading a season of his life for baseball immortality. Rarely has any athlete in any sport burst upon the national scene so dramatically, played such a pivotal role for his team over the course of one season, and then virtually disappeared as a consequential player so quickly.

Southpaw Henry Eugene Bearden was born in Lexa, Arkansas, in 1920, and in 1948 he had a better year than Harry Truman, who was only elected as the next president of the United States. Bearden pleased the baseball voters of the entire country with the possible exception of Massachusetts.

It didn't make much sense and nobody saw it coming, but Bearden was the Indians' miracle man, with a better political platform than any other candidate in the pitching rotation—even Bob Lemon and Bob Feller. All Bearden did all summer long was win and baffle batters with the little-used knuckleball.

After high school Bearden became property of the Philadelphia Phillies, and in 1939 was invited to the team's spring training camp in New Braunfels, Texas. At eighteen, he was almost immediately homesick for the small-town life of Arkansas and his family and friends.

"I had never left my parents for any great distance for any real span of time," Bearden said. "My mother says I cried at the railroad depot."[1]

Spring training amounted to a cameo for the teenager and he made his professional debut with Moultrie in the Georgia-Florida League in 1939, where he went 5–11. It was not a particularly impressive start. In 1940, Bearden pitched in Florida, for Miami Beach, and showed a newfound maturity, finishing 18–10 with a 1.63 earned run average. He returned to Miami in 1941 and played well again, going 17–7 with a 2.41 ERA.

"Everything is fine when I win," Bearden said. "I'm a great winner. When I lose, I'm tough to live with. Ask my wife. Miami Beach was paradise. I was winning."[2] During Bearden's first season in Miami, his pitching made him so popular that the fans held a "Gene Bearden Night" and gave him such gifts as two suits, a suitcase, shirts, underwear, and a fishing rod.

The Phillies planned to promote Bearden to a higher classification in Ottawa, but he did not want to leave the South and preferred staying in Miami. He got a raise and had another good year. Bearden went fishing with his new rod afternoons before reporting to the ballpark. One day he hooked and landed a monstrous sailfish that measured six-foot-five and was longer by two inches than he was tall. Life was good. The multi-talented Bearden played the outfield when he wasn't pitching and drove in 65 runs in 1941.

Life stopped being very good for most people in the United States later that year when the Japanese bombed Pearl Harbor and drove the country into global conflict that lasted until 1945. By 1943, Bearden was also at war, serving in the navy, was wounded and taken to Jacksonville Naval Hospital for treatment. He had suffered a concussion and leg injuries.

Bearden spent months hospitalized before he could think of resuming his baseball career, although it was on his mind during the long hours of recuperation. He walked with a limp when he was discharged from the hospital, so he had some ways to go. The one-time machinist mate torpedoed on the Helena and rescued on a raft at sea was not content simply to get well, but wanted to rebuild his body into that of a successful professional athlete.

After two years away from baseball and sidetracked by his serious physical ailments, Bearden regrouped and began pitching for Binghamton. He again had instant success, finishing the 1945 season with a 15–5 record. The performance was really more than he could have asked for and his showing was impressive for the grit demonstrated. No longer affiliated with the Phillies, Bearden ended up in the New York Yankees organization. When Indians owner Bill Veeck was looking for pitching he tried to pry loose Frank Shea from New York. The Yankees refused. Instead, Veeck ended up with Bearden.[3]

When Bearden caught fire in 1948 there was considerable moaning and groaning in New York with interrogators wondering who was responsible for giving up on Bearden. Veeck made the trade with the New York higher ups, but he knew about Bearden because of a tip from Casey Stengel, who had worked for him in Milwaukee. Stengel was now managing for Oakland in the Pacific Coast League when he passed along the word that Bearden was a worthy player.

Bearden briefly played for Baltimore in the International League but refused to stay there, and then improved his stock value with a 15–4 season for Oakland, where Stengel enjoyed his talent. He was coming off of that solid showing at Indians spring training in 1948, ready, he was sure, to make his mark in the majors after a one-game trial in '47. (Bearden allowed three runs in one-third of an inning pitched.) Cleveland was on the fence about Bearden, as he had trouble with wildness. While the Indians had an opening in the rotation, manager Lou Boudreau was open-minded and Veeck kept running in candidates.

Bearden had raised questions about his stability when he blew off his assignment to Baltimore the year before and later said he felt sportswriters and some people in the Indians organization thought he was crazy.

"I wanted to be taken seriously," Bearden said. "I figured the only way to do it was by hard work. In my mind I had decided that this was the do or die year. If I wasn't ready for the big leagues now I never would be. I wasn't getting any younger. I knew the Indians were looking for at least one left-handed pitcher. Four of us were seeking that spot, Bill Kennedy, Bob Kuzava, Dick Rozek, and myself. Kennedy seemed a sure bet to make it. I was determined to be looked at, too."[4]

Bearden had some very good moments in spring training and at other times he was hit fairly hard. He was just good enough to hang on and make the team leaving Tucson, but Bearden was pretty much at the bottom of Boudreau's to-use list. Once the season began, he sat around the bullpen or the dugout being ignored. During that time period, in April and early May, Bearden was aware that his old Oakland team was trying to get him back and he thought it would be okay to be a star in the high minors rather than ride the bench in the majors. A couple of times rain rearranged the rotation and washed out Bearden's chances to start.

In advance of the Indians May 8 contest against the Washington Senators, Boudreau gave Bearden the message he wanted to hear: He was going to start that day. It was the pivotal game of Bearden's career. He dominated Washington that day, pitching eight and two-thirds innings, allowing just three hits and one unearned run in a 6–1 victory.

"I'll never forget that game," Bearden said. "In the ninth I got two outs. I was so close to my first Major League victory, and so anxious to finish, that I almost lost it. I walked four men. Russ Christopher came in for the final out."[5]

After the game Boudreau stopped by Bearden's locker to compliment him on throwing a good game. Boudreau liked what he saw from Bearden, though he wasn't sure whether it was a one-shot win or not. Making the staff had been a long road for Bearden and Boudreau thought of him strictly as bullpen material at first.

"Our initial plans were to have rookie Gene Bearden work in relief," Boudreau said. "Our thinking was that if Bearden could control his knuckleball it didn't matter that his other pitches were only so-so, which was the reason the Yankees had been willing to trade him."[6]

After the May 8 triumph, it was "Nice going, Gene." But one game did not change everyone's perception of Bearden's capabilities. He was no one's idea of a pennant-winning staff anchor. Boudreau started Bearden against the Yankees a few days later.

"In the first inning I faced Joe DiMaggio," Bearden said. "It was the first time I ever pitched against the man I had been reading about all these years. There were two men on when Joe came to bat. I put them on base by walks. I was wild. Joe sent them all the way around. He hit a home run. Luckily for me the game was called in the fourth inning on account of rain."[7]

Ten days after his first win, May 18, Bearden took the mound again for a start against the Philadelphia A's. He was sharp and dominating as the Indians won, 6–1. Bearden pitched a complete game, allowing six hits and one earned run. *Hmm*, Boudreau began thinking, *maybe this guy can start for us regularly after all.*

Years later, Hank Greenberg, who watched the season unfold from his vantage point in the front office, said that Boudreau showed a lot of moxie turning to Bearden as a starter. The pennant race was heated and close and Boudreau knew he had to win to hang on to his managerial job. Bearden was unheralded, with almost zero Major League experience. "It was a daring move," Greenberg said. "It took a lot of guts." Boudreau didn't deny it. "I never disputed that it took a lot of guts. But I did what I thought was best."[8]

There have hardly ever been more than a few knuckleball pitchers who prospered in the majors at the same time. For one thing, the pitch is difficult to master and usually becomes the

Regarded as the best friend fans ever had, Bill Veeck, who later owned the St. Louis Browns and Chicago White Sox (twice), was the Indians owner who swiftly built the pennant-winner after taking command in 1946. *Photo courtesy of the National Baseball Hall of Fame Museum, Cooperstown, NY*

Lou Boudreau fulfilled the dual roles of starting shortstop and team manager brilliantly, winning the American League's Most Valuable Player award and leading his team to World Series victory. *Photo courtesy of the National Baseball Hall of Fame Museum, Cooperstown, NY*

Cleveland Stadium, also known as Municipal Stadium, was a huge ballpark and enabled the Indians to not only set a Major League Baseball record for attendance of 2.6 million in 1948, but to attract more than 80,000 fans to individual World Series games. *Photo courtesy of the National Baseball Hall of Fame Museum, Cooperstown, NY*

Bob Feller is regarded as the greatest player in Indians history. He struggled some in 1948, but was still able to win 19 games. *Photo courtesy of the National Baseball Hall of Fame Museum, Cooperstown, NY*

By 1948, converted position player Bob Lemon was a star pitcher. Just when his career looked doomed he found himself on the mound and in his career won 207 games. *Photo courtesy of the National Baseball Hall of Fame Museum, Cooperstown, NY*

The miracle man of the Indians' 1948 season was previously unheralded southpaw rookie Gene Bearden, who parlayed a virtually unhittable knuckleball into a 20-victory campaign and crucial playoff and World Series wins. *Photo courtesy of the National Baseball Hall of Fame Museum, Cooperstown, NY*

Third baseman Ken Keltner was a seven-time All-Star highly regarded for his fielding, but was also a major contributor with his bat. In 1941, Keltner almost single-handedly stopped Joe DiMaggio's hitting streak at 56 games. *Photo courtesy of the National Baseball Hall of Fame Museum, Cooperstown, NY*

Eddie Robinson manned first base for the Indians during the 1948 run to the AL pennant and World Series. *Photo courtesy of the National Baseball Hall of Fame Museum, Cooperstown, NY*

Dugout photo of Gene Bearden (left), Lou Boudreau (middle), and Bob Feller (right) before a game on October 6, 1948. *Photo courtesy of AP Images/John Lindsay*

Although less publicized than the other Indians starters, Steve Gromek won Game 4 of the 1948 Series—a crucial win for the Indians—and then spontaneously hugged Larry Doby in front of photographers. The iconic image of the white Gromek and black Doby received national attention. *Photo courtesy of the National Baseball Hall of Fame Museum, Cooperstown, NY*

When he joined the Indians in 1947, Larry Doby became the first African American player in American League history, and the future Hall of Famer blossomed into a star in 1948. *Photo courtesy of the National Baseball Hall of Fame Museum, Cooperstown, NY*

Initially a second baseman, Larry Doby's fielding was rough around the edges when the Indians made him an outfielder, but he received extensive tutoring from Hall of Famer Tris Speaker, for which he was forever grateful. *Photo courtesy of the National Baseball Hall of Fame Museum, Cooperstown, NY*

Satchel Paige was already a legend when the Indians signed him as a reliever and spot starter in July of 1948 as a 42-year-old rookie. Paige became the first African American to pitch in a World Series and the first whose career was primarily in the Negro Leagues to reach the Hall of Fame. *Photo courtesy of the National Baseball Hall of Fame Museum, Cooperstown, NY*

Pitcher Satchel Paige (left) sharing a laugh with player-manager Lou Boudreau. *Photo courtesy of the Boston Public Library*

After finishing in the first regular-season tie for the American League pennant in the sport's history, the Indians had to get past the Boston Red Sox and their slugging leader Ted Williams. This was something Indians manager Lou Boudreau was an expert at, having devised the "Williams Shift." *Photo courtesy of the National Baseball Hall of Fame Museum, Cooperstown, NY*

One obstacle for the Indians in getting past the Boston Braves to capture their first World Series since 1920 was besting Warren Spahn, whose 363 victories are the most ever by a left-handed pitcher. *Photo courtesy of the National Baseball Hall of Fame Museum, Cooperstown, NY*

A panoramic view of Municipal Stadium in Cleveland as the largest crowd in baseball history, 86,288 persons, watched Game 5 of the 1948 World Series on October 10, 1948. Joe Gordon is at bat in the last half of the first inning for the Indians with manager Lou Boudreau on first with a single on a line smash that caromed off the glove of Boston pitcher Nelson Potter. Waiting in the batter's circle is third baseman Ken Keltner. *Photo courtesy of AP Images*

More than 500 sports reporters were accredited to write about the 1948 World Series between the Cleveland Indians and the Boston Braves. *Photo courtesy of the National Baseball Hall of Fame Museum, Cooperstown, NY*

After falling behind 1–0 to start the World Series, the Indians won the next three games. Here, left fielder Dale Mitchell crosses home plate with a crucial run. *Photo courtesy of the National Baseball Hall of Fame Museum, Cooperstown, NY*

Team photo of the 1948 World Series Champion Cleveland Indians. Front Row (left to right): Eddie Robinson, Ken Keltner, Al Rosen, Mel Harder, manager Lou Boudreau, President Bill Veeck ,Coach Muddy Ruel, Joe Gordon, Johnny Berardino.
Second Row: Sam Zoldak, Ed Kleinman, Steve Gromek, Russ Christopher, Gene Bearden, Bob Lemon, Satchel Paige, Bob Feller, Bob Muncrief, Lefty Weisman.
Top Row: Allie Clark, Hal Peck, Larry Doby, Hank Edwards, Dale Mitchell, Bob Kennedy, Jim Hegan, Ray Boone, Joe Tipton, Thurman Tucker.
Seated: Bill Sheridan, batboy. *Photo courtesy of AP Images*

pitch of choice for throwers who have not otherwise been able to consistently deliver Major League stuff. Pitchers whose fastballs are a few mph too slow or who cannot conquer the intricacies of making other pitches work for them turn to the knuckler in desperation. What set Bearden apart was his interest in learning a knuckler when he was still in high school.

Of course, the reason why he sought to develop the pitch was because he couldn't make his curveball curve to his satisfaction. Bearden's high school coach discouraged the knuckleball's use, however, because he felt he still had to have a curve that worked. Bearden dropped the pitch from his repertoire for a while, but later made it work for him in the pros. The game against the Yankees went unfinished, so Bearden was 2–0 and began to get regular appearances. He was officially part of the starting rotation.

Bearden kept piling up the wins and he did so with ease. On June 8, he beat the Red Sox, 2–0, on a five-hit shutout to improve his record to 6–1. After a 2–1 win over the Senators and Early Wynn in a pitcher's duel on July 18, Bearden improved his record to 8–3.

"I pitched each game as it came up, never looking ahead," Bearden said. "I bore down all the time, figuring there were never any softies at the plate. When you let up, you get your brains knocked out. About the first of July Lou began to rest me. He explained to me that he foresaw a close race right down to the finish and wanted his pitching staff rested—and ready for it. As far as I'm concerned, I'm ready to pitch every day. My control seems better the more I pitch."[9]

The more Bearden pitched the better he got and the more Boudreau came to trust him. The fans loved him as well. Here was this relative unknown pitching at an All-Star pace. The other aspect that entertained fans about Bearden's success is that not many people at the time actually knew what a knuckleball was. It had received little publicity over the years and before Hoyt Wilhelm, Phil Niekro, and others gained fame with it the rarity of its use was even greater. As the end of the 1948 season grew near, the *Cleveland News* felt compelled to have a writer explain to the fan base just what a knuckleball was.

"It's just another pitch," Bearden said. "Some fellows throw it with their knuckles. That's how it got its name. I throw mine with my fingertips. You might call it a 'fingertip ball.' I file my fingernails way down."[10]

The knuckleball is not part of most pitchers' arsenal. The fastball is pre-eminent. The curveball is a close second in importance. A changeup is necessary regardless of what speed a hurler throws. Sliders, screwballs, and other pitches have been deployed. The knuckler goes against the grain. Usually the ball is thrown so slowly that it makes hitters believe they can easily bash it. But it moves so elusively, especially when thrown well, that it messes up a hitters' timing. They don't know what to make of its dips and twists. The pitch is unpredictable and not even the finest knuckleball throwers claim that they know exactly what the ball is going to do once it leaves their hand. That common theme does not inspire confidence in their managers and it takes a special breed of catcher to stay on top of knucklers as well. The receivers often risk embarrassment because the ball headed their way makes a sudden sharp turn and bounds away. The result can be a passed ball and a base runner advanced.

To some degree the knuckleball used well is almost a secret weapon. The pitch just doesn't behave like others and it has a great capacity to make hitters look silly. Although Bearden said he fooled around with the pitch when he was in high school, once admonished not to use it, he put it aside until 1946. By then, after his time in the minors and being wounded in the war, he was searching for something that would separate him from the masses of minor league pitchers who never make the big time. He became a self-taught practitioner of the dark art of knuckleball throwing.

"Nobody showed me," Bearden said. "I was just fooling around to see if I could add another pitch to my fastball and slider. I found the batters didn't like it, so I kept on using it. Now it's my main pitch. The fastball and slider are just mixed in, now and then, for variety. I use it so much my fingertips have developed calluses. It comes off the fingertips so it doesn't spin. It dips, wiggles, waves or jumps. When I throw it slow, it jumps. Of course, it's a fooler mostly because it dips as the batter is about to hit it. I throw the knuckler with the same motion I use for my fastball. The amount of speed depends on what it does. I put three fingertips on the smooth part of the ball and grip it with my thumb and little finger."[11]

Those who stand in the box waiting for a knuckler hate it. Teammates of Bearden's loved to watch him perform his tricks.

"You can almost count the seams," Boudreau said of watching the knuckler approach the plate in slow motion. "A curve is a spinning pitch. A knuckler doesn't spin, it simply appears to fall away more sharply than a natural pitch does."[12]

Many managers don't believe in anything they can't understand. But most managers are also happy to watch their pitchers whiff batters and get them out any way they know how, whatever method works for them.

Another of Bearden's teammates, Thurman Tucker, talked of facing knuckleball pitchers in the past who made all sorts of strange things happen to the ball. Dutch Leonard pitched for the

Dodgers, Phillies, Senators, and Cubs in a long career and won 191 games. Jackie Robinson once said that he was glad he didn't have to bat against him every game. Tucker felt the same way.

"I was batting against Dutch Leonard's knuckleball once and it rose up and hit me right on the chin," Tucker said.[13]

The inability to follow the ball's flight is what puts off many hitters. Every day they grew used to seeing fast stuff, breaking stuff, and the change of pace pitch, but the knuckler bothered them because it didn't follow any rules. The more chances Boudreau gave Bearden, the more he accomplished. Despite his late start as a starter as the season wore on, Bearden was on the cusp of winning 20 games. He threw shutouts frequently and complete games about every other time out and rarely gave up runs.

Indians first baseman Eddie Robinson said that watching Bearden throw that fluttery stuff was mesmerizing while standing in the field.

"When Gene is pitching I have to concentrate to remember I'm in the ball game," he said. "It's like watching a show, to see the way that ball acts when he throws it."[14]

When the season began, Bearden was making a salary of $7,500. The more he achieved for the Indians, the more he was rewarded. Although under no obligation, owner Veeck appreciated what Bearden was doing and how important it was for the team, so he gave him a bonus of $2,500 in June and then another $2,500 bonus in August.

Bearden pitched so well for so long over the summer of '48 that he became increasingly superstitious about his wardrobe. In the movie *Bull Durham,* Crash Davis (Kevin Costner) informs his team's young pitcher that he must respect a streak and that he should not change anything during it. In keeping with that policy, by the end of the season Bearden was fiercely protective of a particular sweatshirt that was torn and wearing very thin.

"I only won 10 straight with it," Bearden proclaimed. "Don't let anything happen now."[15] The sweatshirt was being held together by safety pins and Bearden had even grown extremely protective of those "lucky" pins.

Besides the sweatshirt which stood by him so steadfastly during the run to the pennant, Bearden swore allegiance to a floppy white, cloth hat given to him on a golf outing early in the year by his roommate, third baseman Ken Keltner. That evolved into his lucky hat and near the end of the year when it went missing after a game Bearden was nearly panicked in the locker room. He searched his locker space, a trunk, and nearby lockers, hot after the hat.

"Somebody must think it's funny," Bearden said, indicating by his tone that he definitely did not consider the situation humorous. Pitcher Bob Feller rode to the rescue. He had secreted the hat in a coat pocket. "I really ought to swipe this thing," Feller said. "I could use a little luck myself."[16]

Most of Bearden's good results stemmed from reliance on the knuckler, not his reliance on specific attire, although you might not have been able to tell him that. He was constantly getting asked how he did it, but after a while he just laughed when the question was put to him: What made the knuckler do what the knuckler did?

"I don't have to explain it," Bearden said. "I just have to pitch it."[17]

It was the perfect answer to an unanswerable question. Bearden himself was the answer to the Indians' pitching rotation needs in 1948.

Chapter Eleven notes on pages 288–289.

# 12

## TOP *THIS* INFIELD

**A**T TIMES KEN Keltner was the best third baseman in the American League. He broke into the majors at twenty in 1937 and was a seven-time All-Star. When player-manager Lou Boudreau glanced to his right during the 1948 season, he had to be comforted by the sight of the always-ready defender.

Keltner did many things well. He could hit for power, and when he was on he fielded third base like a protective wall, knocking down everything that was clubbed his way. That reputation was built slowly, though. At first Keltner was an erratic fielder, making 30 errors during the 1942 season. Yet he became a rock on the left side of the Indians' infield for more than a decade. He is also one of only a small number of players in Major League history more famous for specific glove work in a game than a hitting exploit.

Born in Milwaukee in 1916, Keltner attended high school in that city, grew to a husky 6-foot, 190 pounds, and returned to Wisconsin after retiring from baseball. Keltner appeared in just one game in 1937, but became a regular in 1938 when he smacked 23 home runs and drove in 113 runs. He only rarely hit for average, but was a middle-of-the-order slugger who could produce runs.

After that break-through year, Keltner hit a career-high .325 in 1939 and then his life took an unusual turn. At the end of the season, Keltner was out of work. In those days players typically did not make large salaries—a far cry from the kind of big money they began making later when their lifestyles became that of the rich and famous and diverged from the rank and file.

The baseball season was over by October, and Keltner had nothing to do until spring training beckoned. He had not obtained the kind of off-season work many players sought. Instead, he filed for unemployment compensation. Under the laws of the state of Ohio, Keltner felt he was entitled to $15 a week while out of work. He felt he was just like any other seasonal worker. The public did not agree. No one equated playing Major League Baseball with migrant fruit picking. Ohio turned down the request, but did not put a lid on the story.

Once his application became known a firestorm of criticism descended on Keltner. It was as if he had broken rules by taking performance-enhancing drugs. Not only did the booing hit Keltner locally in Cleveland, the story spread and he was virulently booed through the entire next season. Once word got around, Keltner basically clammed up. Likely realizing that anything he said would make his situation worse he did not explain much, offer his side of the story to any degree, and took his lumps.

"I got nothing more than I expected," Keltner said. "I made up my mind last winter to take what was coming and keep my mouth shut. I was determined not to let the stuff get me down and it didn't."[1] However, although he would not admit to being at all bothered by the continuous verbal abuse, Keltner's average did dip to .254 during the long season.

The verbal harassment of Keltner ran its course and in 1941, Keltner, looking to rebound at the plate and put the incident behind him, turned in a single spectacular game that provided him with the greatest fame of his career. It was a by-product of someone else's play, but made him a household name at the time and turned out to be the best-known performance of Keltner's 13-year Major League career.

The occasion was July 17, 1941, when the Indians met the New York Yankees. There were more than 67,000 fans in attendance at Cleveland Stadium. The Yankees won the game, 4–3, behind Lefty Gomez, but the biggest news of the day was that New York center fielder Joe DiMaggio went 0-for-3. By failing to hit safely in the contest, DiMaggio's record 56-game hitting streak came to an end. More than anyone else, Keltner was responsible for adding a period to that chapter in baseball history.

Al Smith was the Cleveland starter and facing DiMaggio in the first inning fell behind on a 1–0 count. On the next pitch, DiMaggio blasted a shot down the third-base line. Keltner stabbed at the ball back-hand, caught it, and threw DiMaggio out at first. Fully prepared for such a DiMaggio swat, Keltner was playing deep. He had a long throw, but completed it.

In DiMaggio's second at-bat of the day, he walked. In the seventh inning a similar play arose involving Keltner. Once again DiMaggio got good wood on the ball, ripping it down the third-base line, and again Keltner, playing the slugger deep, speared it and threw DiMaggio out. Both times the ball was hit well and seemed likely to land for a hit, and both times Keltner made the tough play. DiMaggio had one more at-bat and hit a grounder to Boudreau at short, which resulted in a double play. The two plays that were best-remembered, though, were the very hard-hit balls that took extra effort from Keltner to handle.

"I'm the guy that stopped the streak," Keltner said later. "I'm very proud of that. He hit them at me and I caught them after he hit them. That made me. If those balls got through me, where would I be? Nobody would even know about me."[2]

The attention from newsmen that followed DiMaggio's hitting streak at a time when baseball was the biggest game in the country was the type usually reserved for huge crimes or war battles. When the game was over DiMaggio praised Keltner's big plays. He later left the park with shortstop Phil Rizzuto and told him, "Do you know if I got a hit tonight I would have made $10,000?" Rizzuto didn't know what DiMaggio was talking about. "Heinz 57 people were following me," DiMaggio added. "They wanted to make some deal with me."[3] No one really knows if anything would have come out of such talk if DiMaggio had hit in 57-straight games instead of 56.

For the rest of his life, Keltner was best known as the player who stopped Joe DiMaggio's hitting streak.

However, in 1948, that was backburner stuff as the Indians sought their first title in nearly thirty years and Keltner was one of the most important contributors in making it happen. That season, Keltner hit a career high with 31 homers and 119 runs while batting .297. He was one of the best clutch hitters on the club that summer, which proved to be Keltner's last as a full-time starter.

"We were more closely knit than teams are now," Keltner said years later of the '48 club. "We made our trips on trains and had togetherness. There wasn't much money, but a lot of fun."[4]

If there had been some worry in spring training that Keltner might be fading and that the Indians might need a new third baseman, Keltner dispelled it quickly. He played in 153 games in the 154-game regular-season schedule, plus a one-game playoff. Keltner's home run and RBI totals ranked second on the team in both categories.[5] Keltner was one of three infield starters who knocked in more than 100 runs that season (the others being Joe Gordon (2B, 124) and Lou Boudreau (SS, 106).

The Indians were grooming Al Rosen to take over for Keltner at third and Rosen was knocking on the door in spring training. But Keltner handled the challenge and Rosen played just five games with the Indians in 1948, collecting one hit in five at-bats, and spent most of the season in the minors.

Rosen was nearly eight years younger than Keltner, but did not wrest the third-base job full-time until 1950. He immediately became a slugging force and won the Most Valuable Player award in 1953, then starred when the Indians won another American League pennant in 1954. Rosen was Jewish, and like star Hank Greenberg before him, was subject to anti-Semitic comments as Jackie Robinson was breaking the color barrier and had to fend off racist comments.

"I can only tell you this, there was anti-Semitism throughout my playing days," Rosen said of his 10-year career, "and it came from the stands, it came from the managers, the coaches and players. But as time went on, and particularly after the birth of Israel as a nation, I think that a new aura took over and people had more respect for Jewish athletes or Jews generally. I have broad shoulders. I took it upon myself. Cleveland was great for me. I loved every minute of it."[6]

Rosen did not complain that he was held back by the Indians due to religious intolerance—and that is something that owner Bill Veeck never would have countenanced. Instead, Keltner must be credited for holding off Rosen in order to maintain his own hold on the third-base position. In 1948, Keltner was still at the top of his game and Rosen wasn't quite ready for everyday Major League play, though periodically he gave hints that tempted the Indians to bring him up from the Kansas City Blues. In August, Rosen hit five home runs in five at-bats in AAA after being a unanimous American Association All-Star.

Rosen was an almost on that team, but not a big contributor in the pennant race. While Rosen wasn't yet able to contribute, Joe Gordon was. Gordon had a tenacious grip on second base and was in his prime, if the tail end of it, when Veeck pried him loose from the Yankees in 1947. Rarely did the Yankees make trades where they dispensed of anyone with major value, but it so happened that New York needed pitching when Veeck dangled Allie Reynolds in a deal.

A college graduate from the University of Oregon, Gordon played only briefly in the high minors before joining the Yankees. When he reported for duty at Yankee Stadium, a security guard at first refused him admittance, saying, "I never heard of a Joe Gordon." Gordon replied snappily, saying, "You will."[7] He was right.

Gordon was a six-time All-Star with New York and won the AL MVP in 1942. He was a rare middle infielder who could hit with power and has gone down as one of the greatest hitting second basemen ever. Three times Gordon drove in more than 100 runs in a season while with New York. Still, Gordon established career bests in homers (32) and RBI (124) during the 1948 pennant run, leading the Indians in both categories.

Perhaps it was inevitable playing in New York, the most high profile of markets, and with his last name, but Joe Gordon was appropriately nicknamed "Flash." Although still an All-Star and still capable of putting together outstanding numbers the way he did in 1948, Gordon missed a couple of seasons of play due to World War II service, and what was perceived as a minor slide in ability is what made him expendable. Just as likely, Gordon was correct in assuming that Yankees President Larry MacPhail held a grudge against him. For some reason Gordon believed MacPhail didn't like him and ordered manager Bill Dickey not to play him. Dickey used Gordon in the lineup anyway, and the friction increased between Gordon and MacPhail.

"MacPhail didn't like me from the start," Gordon said. "He accused me of quitting on him. That's a damn lie. I never quit on anybody in my life. He called me in his office and insulted me all over the place."[8]

If so, that was foolish, because Gordon was a star player only motivated more if made angry. The trade to Cleveland didn't bother him much and Gordon instantly stepped into the starting lineup and formed a solid double-play combination with Boudreau. He was a leader in the clubhouse and one of the first players to welcome Larry Doby to the team when he was signed as the first African American to play in the American League.

Not only did Boudreau call Gordon a "great" guy to have around, he also said his work around the second-base bag could be mesmerizing.

"So help me, sometimes I get so interested watching Joe make one of those patented plays of his," Boudreau said, "I forget I'm in the ball game, too. I act just like any other spectator. We have a great spirit on this club and one of the main reasons for it is Gordon. The guys all love him—and they respect him. Everybody who knows Gordon respects him. He's a real star."[9]

It was Ossie Vitt who handled Gordon's ascension with the AAA Newark Bears, and who predicted greatness for Gordon, early on calculating that he would be as good a second baseman as Charlie Gehringer, Rogers Hornsby, Frank Frisch, or Tony Lazzeri. Gordon could not match some of them for average, but exceeded the performance of others among that elite crowd in the field or by hitting for power.

"Don't laugh, because I'm not kidding," Vitt said. "He's going to be the greatest second baseman of all time. I know that's putting a kid up there a long ways that's never played in a Major League game, but when you see this kid you'll agree with me."[10] No one ever laughed at Vitt's analysis, and Gordon fit in with that Hall of Fame company when he was elected in 2009.

Although MacPhail was originally going to make the trade shipping out Gordon to the Indians for pitcher Red Embree, he was smart enough to ask Joe DiMaggio's opinion before consummating the deal. DiMaggio spoke up in favor of grabbing Reynolds, which turned out to be the right choice. The trade turned out more balanced for both sides when the Indians surrendered Reynolds, and if the trade would have gone through as planned (Embree for Gordon), it would have ranked among the greatest steals of all time. Gordon later said MacPhail was so angry at him he offered him his outright release, but then changed his mind. The mercurial MacPhail could lose his temper and lose control of his emotions, but something stopped him from simply letting Gordon walk away with no return. In the end MacPhail made an excellent trade with both sides benefiting. The Indians with both Gordon and Reynolds in 1948 would have been even more formidable.

In the short run, the Indians benefited more than the Yankees. On June 12, Cleveland visited New York and Yankee Stadium for a doubleheader. As part of a 25th anniversary celebration marking the opening of the palatial baseball field, Yankees management invited back many stars of the past and threw a dinner honoring them following the two day games.

Interestingly, Reynolds pitched the opener for New York, in which Cleveland won 7–5 when Gordon hit a two-run homer in the top of the seventh. The Indians won the second game as well, this time by a score of 9–4. Gordon was even better in game two, as he stroked three hits, including two more home runs, while scoring three runs and driving in four. While it may be a little bit of an overstatement, at least some observers of the Indians quartet suggested the group of Keltner, Boudreau, Eddie Robinson, and Gordon was among the finest infields in history.

In 1948, Gordon was off to a sizzling start that made it apparent before even mid-year that he was on pace to set career highs in homers and RBI. While the rest of the team slowly came together, Gordon was a leading figure from the start. There wasn't a moment all year when Boudreau had to worry about his second baseman.

The one-fourth of the infield that Boudreau wondered about was first base. Keltner, Boudreau, and Gordon were AL All-Stars at their position. Coming out of spring training Boudreau had settled on Eddie Robinson as his first baseman, but at that point in what would become a long career as a player and in team management, Robinson was more of a question mark.

Robinson was twenty-seven and had never played more than 95 games in a Major League season. His 1947 season ended in August because of a fractured ankle. Before that he had lost time to World War II service and while he was liked within the organization, his track record was more of a blank than a file folder brimming with credentials. Robinson won Boudreau's confidence during spring training and was named the first-base starter in 1948, appearing in 134 games. He beat out Allie Clark for full-time work and although his average settled at .254, Robinson hit with good power, amassing 16 home runs and 83 runs batted in. He was a good piece of the daily puzzle, someone who basically stayed healthy and was reliable over the long season. There really was no second-teamer. Clark played in 81 games, but his work was spread out over a handful of positions.[11]

Like so many others, Robinson had his baseball career interrupted while fighting in World War II, and while serving for his country in the navy, his right leg was paralyzed from a bone tumor. The body is an athlete's career vessel. It must be physically fine-tuned and speed, strength and/or flexibility are what provide him with his special skill. Doctors treating Robinson felt he would be lucky to walk normally again, never mind compete professionally. Robinson fooled them and regained his strength. After that he had to regain his baseball skill, but it was no easy road back to the majors. After much perseverance, Robinson was ready in 1948, which represented the culmination of his comeback and the big opportunity to play all of the time.

Robinson went from being flat on his back to the cleanup hitter in the order for the pennant-chasing Indians. He so thoroughly out-played Elbie Fletcher, the other contender for the first base job early in '48, that Fletcher was released by the Indians in May. Robinson also benefited from the resistance of Hank Greenberg to making a comeback. If Greenberg had wanted to play any more than he did in his fleeting appearance in the spring, he would have been given every chance at the job. Instead, Greenberg, who preferred beginning a front-office career, spent more time mentoring Robinson than competing with him, offering advice on how to play around the first-base bag.

"A lot of fellows have been nice to me since I joined this club and Hank is one of them," Robinson said. "Being a right-hander in the field like Hank, he was able to teach me several things about playing the bag. His help included a lot of little things which added up to a big difference in my play this spring, as compared to last. Also, Hank helped me at bat."[12]

Although Robinson was not a big-time slugger, he was a very good contact hitter. In 540 plate appearances in 1948, he struck out just 42 times. The flip side was that he went up to the plate swinging and didn't walk much, either, collecting just 36 base on balls. Fortunately for Robinson, he was surrounded in the batting order by hitters that other teams' pitchers had to respect. The Indians were strong in the heart of the order and there was not really anyone to pitch around. Boudreau did shuffle the order often enough, trying to milk Robinson, Keltner, Gordon, Doby, and his own batting ability for maximum pop.

Greenberg said that Robinson had improved as a hitter, but wouldn't take the credit, attributing it to the player's work ethic more than anything.

"I didn't help Eddie," Greenberg said. "He helped himself. You can tell a young ball player things, but if he doesn't cooperate, nothing is accomplished. He's a good boy and rounds out our infield very nicely. Eddie isn't a great fielder, but he's much better than adequate and getting better all the time. Ed has good power at the plate. You'll notice that he usually gets a piece of the ball—a good piece. They don't very often strike him out. He usually hits the ball somewhere."[13]

It is impossible to see the future, even when the savviest of baseball men try to read it when analyzing young players. In Robinson's case he was a somewhat late bloomer because of the war and injuries. He seemed to blossom in '48 just when the Indians needed him most, but they didn't keep him around long after that. However, as a player and administrator, Robinson ended up spending sixty-five years in the sport and reached the heights of a general manager. Greenberg was correct in that Robinson was still getting better. He made four All-Star teams, hit more than 20 home runs in a season four times, and collected at least 100 RBI in a season three times. But none of those accomplishments were recorded while wearing a Cleveland uniform.

Still, although he played for a couple of pennant winners with the New York Yankees, Robinson did not win another World Series in his career and his early days in the majors and the 1948 season with Cleveland represented the high points of his playing career.

"Getting sold to the Indians was a glorious day in my baseball career," Robinson said. ". . . I got into my first Major League game in Cleveland Municipal Stadium against the Philadelphia Athletics. I'll never forget Lou Boudreau . . . telling me to get up there and pinch-hit against Luman Harris. I was shaking when I went up to the plate."[14]

Many years after his first meeting with Doby—and Doby's recollection that Robinson was one of his Indians teammates who did not embrace him in a friendly fashion—Robinson was very generous in his description of Doby and in praising his role as a pioneer in American society.

"Looking back on it, I admire and respect Jackie Robinson tremendously because it took a great amount of courage to be the first black player in Triple-A and in the big leagues," Eddie Robinson said. "Jackie handled it well. In my opinion, Jackie and Larry Doby, my future teammate in Cleveland, and the first black player in the American League, are right there with Dr. Martin Luther King in advancing the cause of African Americans."[15]

Although such things never surfaced in any kind of notable way while he was playing for the Indians, when looking back on his career in another way years later, Robinson said that he never felt that Boudreau believed in him.

"Cleveland's manager was the twenty-eight-year-old Lou Boudreau, who didn't seem to like me from the start and never talked to me or gave me any encouragement," Robinson said. "He didn't seem to be happy to have me join the team. He may not have known how to encourage young players because of his own youth, but from the beginning we just didn't hit it off. Unfortunately, we had a strained relationship until I left the Indians."[16]

Robinson felt much more warmth towards Bill Veeck. Veeck, as he did to so many ball players, either promised extra rewards to underpaid players if they came through, or spontaneously gave them bonuses. Robinson was making all of $3,500 as a player and said Veeck told him if he did well that he would take care of him. Veeck presented Robinson with a $5,000 bonus, a stunning payoff out of the goodness of his heart given that exceeded Robinson's salary.

"That's just the kind of big-hearted guy he was," Robinson said. "He was always available to the players. Any time a player had a problem or something he wanted to talk about, he could talk to Bill. If it was a money issue, Bill took care of his ball player."[17]

In 1948, Robinson, Joe Gordon, trainer Lefty Weisman, and catcher Jim Hegan formed a singing quartet. They provided amusement for the rest of the team while exercising their vocal chords while waiting for trains to take them on road trips, when the players hung out in bars, or when they were at the ballpark. They even went public during rain delays, entertaining soaked fans over the Cleveland Stadium public address system.

"We weren't bad," Robinson said. "We sang all the good old harmony songs like, 'Wedding Bells (Are Breaking Up That Old Gang Of Mine).'"[18] Unfortunately, no music videos survive of the ensemble's work together.

Whether Robinson worried about whether or not Boudreau liked him or not, he was in the lineup for good in '48 and as the season wore on, the Indians stayed at or near the front of the pack in the American League, shedding contenders one by one. Probably the biggest reason of all was Boudreau. He was proving to be the manager that Veeck wanted him to be, but also enjoying the finest season of his Hall of Fame career on the field. "The Good Kid" was the great player in '48.

Boudreau was a seven-time All-Star who batted more than .300 four times in his career. He won the American League batting title with a .327 average in 1944, but batted a career-high .355 in 1948. He also hit a career high in home runs (18) and RBI (106). And on top of that, his fielding was out of sight. The Baseball Writers' Association of America voted Boudreau the American League's MVP. At the end of the calendar year, *Sport* magazine collected ballots from a cross-section of experts and they voted Boudreau the athlete of the year across all sports for his performance with the Indians. Boudreau gathered 22 first-place votes, while runner-up Joe DiMaggio had two. No other players received a first-place vote.

Spurred by his touchy talks with Veeck, Boudreau believed all along that if he was going to hang onto his managerial position after 1948, the Indians would have to at least win the pennant and probably the World Series. He never forgot that Veeck tried to trade him to the St. Louis Browns and that the new owner did not have complete faith in his leadership skills. Boudreau very much believed he had to prove himself beyond anything he had shown before. There was no better way to help the Indians in the win column than to play better than ever at shortstop.

Muddy Ruel, one of the experienced coaches Boudreau and Veeck surrounded him with, had nothing but praise for Boudreau's managerial instincts and bold moves.

"A showboat? Not that fellow," Ruel said. "He put himself on the spot too often. He was just too big a man to fail. The moves he made weren't for any personal aggrandizement. He was trying to win."[19]

Indians ace Bob Feller said Boudreau seemed like a self-made player to him. Feller's first impression of Boudreau's skills when he showed up for one game in 1938 for the varsity was not a positive one, though he laughed about it later.

"Lou had two left feet and threw [poorly]," Feller said. "I wondered what scout signed this guy and then I found out it was the same one [Cy Slapnicka] that signed me. He really was a great athlete and a great friend."[20]

Feller appreciated the allegiance that Boudreau showed to him during the 1948 season. Feller had been the franchise for more than a decade, the ace of the staff, the most unbeatable hurler the Indians could send to the mound. Then in 1948 he was struggling, putting up that shaky 9–11 record halfway through the year when the team was vying for a pennant. Feller, normally supremely confident, was being criticized from unexpected sources, his previous backers querying what was going on. But Boudreau never wavered in his support for Feller and his backing kept him in the rotation and paid off.

"I remember in 1948," Feller said, "Lou said, 'We're going to sink or swim with Feller.' I was having a rough season and after he said that I won 10 of my last 12 games. He instilled a confidence in his players they never forgot."[21]

While the Indians finished July at 53–38, they immediately went on a tear in August that they thought might shake up the American League race. Adding Satchel Paige to the staff was a big factor, but Feller caught fire after his slow start and just about everyone on the roster played better. By August 6, the Indians were on a six-game winning streak and were 20 games over .500 for the season. Their attendance by August 1 was over 1,440,000 for the season, and they were on pace to set a new mark. After one defeat against the Yankees, the Indians won three more games in a row and were 8–1 for August. Cleveland had another eight-game winning streak in August, and finished the month with a 75–50 record.

Standing at 25 games above .500 was terrific and represented playing about as well as the Indians could play. There was one problem, however. On August 31, the Yankees' record was 75–49, the Boston Red Sox' record was 76–48, and even the Philadelphia Athletics were still in the hunt at 73–54.

Trading off the league lead with Philadelphia early and then taking over first place going into June, the Indians had maintained the top spot in the AL longer than anyone else, but as the pivotal month of September began, they were in third place. It was hard to believe they could play that well and not be ahead. During that era the prevailing wisdom was that the team in first place after Labor Day would win the pennant. On Labor Day, the Indians were in third and had fallen farther behind the Yankees and Red Sox.

"There's not much chance left now," Veeck said. "It will take a miracle for us to win."[22]

That pessimism seemed both harsh and premature, but Boudreau admitted much later that his thinking tracked Veeck's. He felt his club was in trouble and might not be able to overtake Boston's four-and-a-half-game lead and New York's three-game lead. But the season was not over. There were still three weeks of games remaining on the schedule and that was plenty of time to mount a run.

Chapter Twelve notes on pages 289–291.

# 13

## FELLER AND PAIGE LEAD SURGE

---

**B**OB FELLER HAD waited a career to play on a Cleveland Indians team that could win the pennant. For several years he was the main (and sometimes only) beacon of light for the team. He was the most dominating pitcher of his era, compared to the all-time greats long enough until it was conceded that he was one of the all-time greats.

Then in 1948, for just about the first time in his life, when batters stood in against Feller they didn't seem to fear him. The fastball that had once been unscientifically clocked at more than 100 mph in a test was not moving as swiftly as it had. Hitters were catching up to his best stuff. It pained Feller to no end that he was selected to the All-Star team more based on reputation than performance and that at one point during the season he was 9–11.

Several months into the season he was not being looked at as the No. 1 starter on the Indians. In this particular year he trailed Bob Lemon and upstart rookie Gene Bearden in reliability—not that Feller was in any danger of being taken out of the rotation. Manager Lou Boudreau made it clear that Feller was his guy and he was sticking with him. Boudreau had faith that Feller would right himself and start winning.

"If ever a championship represented what managers and coaches call a team effort, 1948 was that season," Feller said. "We seemed to get help from everybody. We led both leagues in hitting, as well as fielding. The pitchers did their share, too. Cleveland was the leader in 10 of the 12 pitching departments, with Bearden leading the league with the best earned run average. I led the league in strikeouts for the seventh time—also the last.

"Bearden and Bob Lemon both had better overall seasons than I did in '48. I started slowly and by midseason I wasn't even a .500 pitcher. With the team having a good first half, I knew we had a legitimate shot at the pennant, but I had to be of more help in the second half."[1]

While Feller was ahead of his time in marketing himself based on his popularity in the game, latter-day baseball fans might be surprised to hear that he was so good and so transcended the sport that his picture appeared on the cover of a Wheaties box and that he also had a candy bar named after him long before Reggie Jackson did.

"Getting on the front of a Wheaties box is a child's dream," Feller said. "It symbolizes the recognition of the general public that you're a star. I never dreamed, when I signed my professional contract at age sixteen, that I would ever be on a Wheaties box, even though I had eaten lots of Wheaties as a young boy. In fact, I was fortunate enough to appear on Wheaties boxes many times in my career. I signed a contract with General Mills the same year that Shirley Temple did. She got $10,000 and I got $2,500. Of course, I wasn't cute, I couldn't sing or tap dance, and I didn't have curly hair."[2]

Feller said it was also every kid's dream growing up as a baseball player to appear on his own baseball card and that he remembered some of the earliest times they were packaged with chewing gum rather than tobacco. Feller said he was thrilled when the Euclid Candy Company of Brooklyn made a deal with him for the "Bob Feller Bar."

"The bar was similar to the Baby Ruth bar," Feller said. "It had a chewy center of caramel and peanuts, covered in chocolate."[3] Feller said that he was proud to have a candy bar named after him and that he saved wrappers that were preserved in his museum in Van Meter, Iowa.

Feller was well aware of the dispute that concerned the Baby Ruth bar. Although just about everyone, Babe Ruth included, was positive the candy bar was named after the Yankees' slugger when it appeared for sale in 1921, somehow the Curtiss Candy Company sought to convince the world it was actually named after former President Grover Cleveland's daughter, Ruth. Since Cleveland had been out of the White House for nearly three decades and Ruth had been dead for seventeen years, and especially seeing as Babe Ruth was the most prominent athlete in America, it was a hard sell. But the manufacturers got away with it, turning over zero royalties to the baseball player.

Most seasons, Feller was a good enough player to have both Wheaties and a chocolate bar named after him. And while his season didn't start off that way, he was once again at the top of his game down the stretch.

On August 6, Feller was shelled, giving up 10 hits and seven runs, but won his 11th game of the year. Perhaps it was a signal that his luck was changing because it took luck to win the 9–7 game against the Yankees after being hit that hard. On August

15, Feller scattered 11 hits, but surrendered just two runs in besting the White Sox for a complete game and his 12th victory. On September 1, Feller evened his record at 14–14 with a masterful performance against the Philadelphia A's. He fanned nine, gave up six hits, and Cleveland won, 6–1.

In the latter stages of the season, the Indians got excellent mound work from spot starters who hadn't been key figures in the team's plans in the early going. Bob Muncrief went 5–4; Steve Gromek improved to 7–2; Sam Zoldak, another of Veeck's pick-ups, contributed, as did reliever Ed Klieman, when Russ Christopher wasn't handling the bullpen load. Paige was magnificent, living up to the billing he had brought to the majors from his youthful years in the Negro Leagues and while barnstorming. This was all part of the "team effort" that Feller cited. Yes, it is a cliché, but it was also true during this season.

Gromek was a 6-foot-2, 180-pound right-hander who had been with the Indians since 1941 as a twenty-one-year-old with mixed success. Gromek's best years occurred in 1944 when he finished 10–9 with a 2.56 earned run average and in 1945 when he broke out with a 19–9 record and a 2.55 ERA. However, in the two years preceding the 1948 pennant race, Gromek had regressed, falling to 5–15 in 1946 and 3–5 in 1947. That's why Boudreau was not counting on him for the '48 season. That was also why when Gromek regained his best form, it was a bit of a pleasant surprise. By the time the regular season ended, he had posted a 9–3 record with a 2.84 earned run average in 130 innings. He was a very valuable player when the Indians needed him the most.

The earner of just $3,000 when he made his first Indians roster, Gromek's 19-win campaign boosted him hugely to $15,000. Originally, Gromek was just a filler player on the roster and he dressed the part, never bothering to dress up. When Boudreau informed him he was moving into the rotation on a regular basis in 1944, he did so by telling him, "Wear a shirt and tie from now on because you're one of my starters."[4]

Ed Klieman was a hot-shot in the minors and won 23 games for Baltimore in the International League before the Indians called him up in 1943 for a late-season start against the Boston Red Sox. Klieman lost the game to Boston, 1–0, pitching a complete game.

"The biggest thrill of my career was getting called up by the Indians and starting against the Red Sox," he said.[5] He lost 1–0 and he never could break into the Indians' starting rotation. In 1948, he was coming off a 5–4 record with 17 saves out of the bullpen for Cleveland's fourth-place '47 club.

In 1948, Klieman was more of a middle relief guy, finishing 3–2 with just four saves, but a 2.60 earned run average. He came out of the pen to finish Paige's first Major League start and eventually bounced around the American League for a couple of years after departing from the Indians.

"I did a lot better against Ted Williams than a lot of 'em did," Klieman said. "But I had trouble with the last-place teams, especially the St. Louis Browns. The toughest hitter I faced was Tommy Henrich of the Yankees."[6, 7]

While Tris Speaker was tutoring Larry Doby and Bill McKechnie was counseling Boudreau, pitching coach Mel Harder was working wonders with the staff. Only Feller had his moments when he struggled, but relievers and spot starters like Paige, Klieman, Gromek, Russ Christopher, and rare find Gene Bearden, as well as Bob Lemon were pitching as well or better than they ever had and ever would in the future. Some of the credit has to go to Harder, who was an Indians icon.

Harder was born in 1909 in Nebraska, joined the Indians in 1928, and pitched for Cleveland for 20 seasons, ending in 1947 when he was thirty-seven with a 6–4 record. During his tenure on the mound he won 223 games and made four All-Star teams. He threw 13 total innings in All-Star play and did not allow a run.

Long after he was a fuzzy-faced rookie, Harder, who broke into the majors weighing 140 pounds, told stories about his early days in the league in the 1920s, about not only facing Babe Ruth, Lou Gehrig, and Ty Cobb at the plate, but the way the veterans on the Indians led him around.

"The older players would invite me to a bootlegger's joint on Woodland and I would drink one or two beers after each game," Harder said.[8] Well, that's what he admitted to, anyway, but then said that's how he gained weight. The extra poundage had to represent more than a beer or two swigged. Harder spent sixteen years as Cleveland's pitching coach following directly after his 20-season playing career and was praised by such hurlers as Feller, Lemon, and later Early Wynn.

Even though pitchers always seemed to improve when they consulted Harder, he was low key and often turned the compliments back on the givers.

"I didn't do it," he said. "It was easy to spot the men who had the good arms and determination. They wanted to become good pitchers and were always asking questions."[9]

It also helps to have solid catching and a sharp receiver who can handle a staff. The 1948 Indians did so in Jim Hegan (with Joe Tipton as his back-up). Catchers do more than simply hold up their glove as a target. They talk to pitchers, give them encouragement, put down the signs, and call the game. More than managers or coaches, once the game begins, they are in constant contact with the thrower who holds the ball and starts the action.

Despite losing three full years of his career to World War II service, Hegan spent 17 years in the majors, most of them with Cleveland. He was unsure of his status in Boudreau's scheme at the start of the 1948 season, but he had been an All-Star for the Indians in 1947 despite hitting just .249. That was testimony to his brilliant fielding. Hegan caught 144 games in 1948, slugging 14 home runs and driving in 61 runs, although his batting average was still only .248. Yet his fielding percentage was .990 and in his lengthy career Hegan committed just 87 errors in 1,666 games. Because he routinely caught more than 100 games a season Hegan acquired the nickname "Man of Steel."

The glove made Hegan, who was from Lynn, Massachusetts, not far from the Red Sox's Fenway Park. He never was known for his bat, but his reputation for wise handling of pitchers earned him five All-Star selections even with mediocre offensive numbers. The concern about Hegan during spring training of 1948 was his failure to sign a new contract based on his belief he should be paid more. Hegan resented Boudreau taking over pitch-calling duties for a while, too.

For a period of time Boudreau and Hegan gave one another the silent treatment except for required discussions about specific games or plays. By the end of the season, though, Boudreau was raving about Hegan in public.

"Jim Hegan is the finest catcher and one of the finest fellows in baseball," Boudreau said. "As much or more than any man, he was responsible for what we did."[10]

Years later, Hegan, who stayed in the game as a coach and scout with the Yankees and Detroit Tigers for twenty years, deflected credit for the 1948 success.

"Anybody with a good pitching staff is a contender all the time," Hegan said. "Pitching and defense keep you in the ball game. I don't think I did anything more than any other player in 1948 to help us win. Everybody pitched in."[11] There he was, a good catcher, again having the back of his pitching staff.

Baseball men never stopped complimenting the ease and smoothness that Hegan brought to his work behind the plate and it was his fielding that kept him in the game for so long.

"If he'd hit even .280 lifetime he'd have been a shoo-in for the Hall of Fame," said Al Rosen, who spent several years as a Hegan teammate. Birdie Tebbetts, another catcher and eventual manager, said of Hegan, "As far as I'm concerned you start and end the discussion of catchers with him."[12]

Of course, with Hegan behind the plate for 144 games, the Indians barely had need for a back-up in 1948. Usually a receiver's body does not hold up the way that Hegan's did that season, so emergency help is necessary on the roster. It's just that Boudreau chose to ride Hegan in '48 and Hegan was pleased to be in the line up nearly every day.

Cleveland's insurance policy was Joe Tipton. Tipton had the somewhat thankless task of being the Indians' relief catcher in 1948, though he was almost never used. A twenty-six-year-old rookie from McCaysville, Georgia, Tipton appeared in 47 games, but had just 97 plate appearances all season. To his credit, despite being rusty at the plate most of the time, Tipton batted .289.

Tipton, who also drove in 13 runs in his limited playing time, called Boudreau and Veeck, "two wonderful people" and said the highlight of his seven-year Major League career was "just being part of the 1948 Cleveland Indians."[13]

Tipton's Indians tenure may have turned out differently. Although Boudreau admitted that Hegan was the best catcher in the American League, when he and Hegan were at tense logger-heads, Boudreau and Veeck were willing to pursue a trade for him if it would bring the team reliable outfield help. They were prepared to count on Tipton as the No. 1 receiver. Instead, Hegan stayed and the outfielders that Boudreau were sorting through produced.

Once Paige showed he could start and succeed despite possessing the body of a forty-two-year-old and the wear and tear on his arm of a veteran, he won Boudreau's confidence as the Indians tried to overtake and dispense with the Yankees and Red Sox. On August 11, Paige pitched two and two-thirds innings of relief when Bob Lemon won his 15th game in game one of a doubleheader.

On August 12, the Indians improved their record to 63–42 with an astounding 26–3 victory over the St. Louis Browns. The joke in Cleveland was that the Indians were three-touchdown favorites—and exceeded the point spread. Cleveland scored nine runs in the first inning, four in the third, four in the fifth and three in the six and seventh. The Indians clouted a ridiculous 29 hits. Gene Bearden coasted through seven innings, allowing just one run and, of all people, Bob Feller pitched two innings in relief to get the save. The Indians had 55 at-bats with Hal Peck clubbing four hits and scoring four runs. Almost unimag-inably, Bearden also contributed four hits, four runs, and four RBI in what must have been one of the best hitting shows ever put on by a starting pitcher. Dale Mitchell, Lou Boudreau, Joe Gordon, and Jim Hegan each added three hits. The numbers were just staggering and, of course, flukish, as the Indians had lost to the Browns the day before, 8–4.

A day after the massacre, Paige pitched a complete-game, five-hit shutout of the White Sox to raise his record to 4–1. One week later, Paige shut out the White Sox again, this time on three hits with five strikeouts, capturing a 1–0 decision. Paige upped his record to 6–1 ten days later, and each time he showed the type of slippery stuff he had displayed for years, Veeck was gleeful. He was happy for himself and for his team, but he was also thrilled for Paige, to whom this second act in life was a gift and only months earlier seemed unlikely to take place.

Indeed, Veeck had come through, waiting for the right moment to summon Paige to the majors where on the biggest of stages it was his turn to come through long after he felt he had been dumped along the wayside by the sport. Paige had already become a folk hero among African Americans, and each time he pitched and handled men two decades his junior he embarrassed the baseball establishment for not recognizing his greatness years earlier.

Paige probably did not throw a heater as fast as he had in his 20s or 30s, but he was nearly 6-foot-4 and still as lean as a beanpole, with a seemingly never-tiring elastic arm. Paige's age was always a joking issue, but that overlooked the point that Paige was ageless. He was in the thick of a pennant race and helping the Cleveland Indians every time he took the mound.

"The odds against Satchel Paige's becoming a household name were about a million to one," said John "Buck" O'Neil, who met Paige in 1935, teamed with him in the Negro Leagues, and managed him with the Kansas City Monarchs. Although lack of such accurate mechanisms stymied measurement of the fastest of the fast pitchers from Cy Young and Walter Johnson to beyond, O'Neil cited a 103 mph clocking for Paige.[14]

Even when Paige was supremely excited about joining the Indians, he controlled his expressions—both facially and verbally—indicating he had no reason to be nervous about this long-awaited ascension to the majors. "Plate's the same size, isn't it?" he said, his way of letting everyone in listening range know that he was not fazed.[15]

The biggest problem that Paige had in adjusting to pitching in the American League was the perplexed reactions by umpires to his "hesitation" pitch. Paige had long employed his slow-motion toss, but while he had the freedom to use it at will in exhibitions, in the majors the motion looked suspiciously like a balk. It may or may not have been, but umpires didn't know how to call it and AL President Will Harridge stepped in, trying to figure out the best way to handle things. In the end he ruled that Paige could not use the weapon or else have it called a balk if there were men on base. Both Paige and Veeck insisted the pitch was legal, but they lost the argument.

Paige commented, "I guess Mr. Harridge didn't want me to show up those boys who were young enough to be my sons."[16]

Paige had been baffling hitters young enough to be his sons for quite some time, so why should his time with the Indians be any different?

In his way, Paige had become an overnight sensation with the general baseball public. On August 3, Paige's start against the Washington Senators attracted a night game record crowd of 72,434 customers. His start against the White Sox at Comiskey Park in Chicago on August 13 attracted a night record crowd there of 51,013.

At times Paige used a wind-up like a windmill, or cranking the engine on an old-style car, the type Paige may have been old enough to see, according to many.

When Paige was 5–1 and his earned run average was 1.33, Veeck couldn't help himself. He chose that moment to retaliate against the *Sporting News'* original haughty editorial criticizing him for signing Paige. Veeck made his reply in a telegram, writing to J. G. Taylor Spink, "Paige Pitching—No runs, three hits. Definitely in line for the *Sporting News* Rookie of the Year Award. Regards, Bill Veeck."[17] Likely if makers of cartoons were on the premises when Spink received the message he would have been portrayed as having steam coming out his ears.

The one thing that annoyed Paige was how sportswriters repeatedly referred to him as "Satchelfoots," a nickname briefly used in his past that Paige despised and now had been dredged up. He did not, as some wrote, have size 16 feet, but only size 11. As Paige reminded anyone paying attention, he pitched with his right arm, not his feet.

Amazingly, it took roughly a month for Paige, the oldest and sagest player around, to become a fresh-faced sensation, just by being himself. He cracked jokes, told stories, won games, and kept people guessing about his age. Fans ate it up. It turned out that the Paige act so long confined to the hinterlands, might well have played on Broadway all along.

Chapter Thirteen notes on pages 291–292.

# 14

## EARLY SEPTEMBER—MAKING A RUN

**IF A TEAM** in the baseball world is not safely over .500 and playing well by the beginning of September, they're probably already looking ahead to next season. September marks the beginning of the football season, the beginning of the school year in most locales, and the beginning of autumn leaves falling in colder climates.

It also marks the end of the baseball season for most teams in the American and National League, the ones that are not pennant-winners and October hopefuls.

In 1948, it was still bunched at the top of the AL standings, with the Cleveland Indians, Boston Red Sox, New York Yankees, and Philadelphia Athletics grouped in the first division of the eight-team league. For the baseball fan who has followed the sport since 1969 when Major League ball added playoff tiers, it may be difficult to recall that up until then, only one team in each league still harbored championship hopes by October.

Pennant winners advanced directly from the regular-season finish into the World Series. There was no such thing as the American League Championship Series or the National League Championship Series and ball players' only reference to phrases such as "wild card" came from playing card games in the back of the train during road trips. So in 1948 as the season's 154-game schedule was playing out, it was all or nothing. Teams had to finish first or wait until spring training to resume play.

Pretty much since Babe Ruth first suited up for the Yankees in 1920 following his trade from the Boston Red Sox, New York had been the team to beat in the American League. Ruth begat Lou Gehrig, who begat Joe DiMaggio, and the Yankees had other stars to back them up. Only the interruption of World War II, when so many players entered the Armed Services, was the natural rhythm of the AL disrupted. The Yankees did not win the pennant every year in the mid-to-late 1940s.

In 1944, the Browns won the only pennant in the franchise's long history while in St. Louis. In 1945, the Detroit Tigers captured the AL flag. In 1946, the Red Sox won their first pennant since 1918. In 1947, the Yankees won their first pennant and World Series in four years, an eternity by Bronx standards of the era. What that meant in 1948 was that for a little while, the rest of the American League could compete with the Yankees, and dismiss their feeling that they owned the pennant by birthright. As September of 1948 dawned, four teams believed they had a legitimate chance to win the AL crown.

Going into September 1, having played 125 games, the American League standings were as follows:

| Team | Wins | Losses | Winning % | Games Behind |
|------|------|--------|-----------|--------------|
| Boston Red Sox | 77 | 48 | .616 | – |
| New York Yankees | 76 | 49 | .608 | 1.0 |
| Cleveland Indians | 76 | 50 | .603 | 1.5 |
| Philadelphia Athletics | 73 | 55 | .570 | 5.5 |

There were too many teams to worry about. Indians manager Lou Boudreau knew his team had to keep playing well, but also hope that some of the other teams slumped.

Cleveland met the Athletics on September 1, and before the game Philadelphia manager Connie Mack seemed to recognize his team's precarious place in the standings.

"If the Clevelanders can go back from the East no worse than two games out of first place, they should win out with the kind of schedule they have left," Mack said.[1]

The schedule was fairly kind to the Indians for the rest of September. They had just one game scheduled against the Yankees and one against the Red Sox. The remaining Cleveland games were against weaker clubs. Meanwhile, the A's had 11 games left against New York and Boston.

Cleveland bested Philadelphia 8–1 that night with Bob Feller going the distance for the win. He was backed by 10 hits: two apiece produced by Dale Mitchell, Joe Gordon, and Eddie Robinson. Out of synch for much of the year, Feller was pulling himself together for a strong stretch run with the complete game accented by nine strikeouts.

The Indians next hit the road, with three against the almost-always-lowly Browns and two more against the not-very-good White Sox. The schedule led coach Bill McKechnie to expound on what might occur as the days of the season dwindled.

"It is not the first division teams that decide pennant races," McKechnie said. "It is the second division that holds the key to any championship in this sport."[2]

By that, McKechnie meant the good teams had to beat the bad teams in order to stay competitive at the front. If they gave away games against lesser squads they would squander their chances. Tris Speaker, who was growing more intrigued as the season wore on, chimed in as well, saying the Indians really should dominate the White Sox, but had to be careful of the Browns.

"The Browns can score runs," Speaker said, "and this means the Cleveland pitching must be steady throughout the games. Unlike the White Sox, the Browns can come from behind and get back into a ball game. The Indians play a pair in Chicago and they should beat the White Sox. Cleveland's pitching is so vastly superior to Chicago's and Cleveland's batting is better by 40 or 50 points."[3]

Bob Lemon threw a six-hit shutout on September 3 to win his 19th game of the season, 7–0, in the first match-up with the Browns as Eddie Robinson and Ken Keltner drove in two runs each. It was also Lemon's 10th shutout of the season and Tris Speaker, a man who recognized quality on the field when he saw it, was impressed.

"Bob could easily become the first man of these later years [since the introduction of the lively ball in the 1920s], to pitch a dozen shutouts," Speaker said. "He mixes up fastballs with a great curve and an occasional slider. He works smoothly and easily. You'd never guess he was in line for another shutout."[4]

However, proving McKechnie a prophet, Cleveland lost the next two games in a row, both by 4–3 scores, to St. Louis. It was not the showing that the Indians wanted or needed and seemed very costly at the time. Lemon's victory was in the first game of a doubleheader and the first 4–3 defeat was pinned on Sam Zoldak. Only Keltner, who struck three hits, was hot for the Indians. The second 4–3 loss was fairly similar. Satchel Paige was off, allowing three runs, but Klieman absorbed the defeat in relief.

On September 6 at Comiskey Park, the Indians lost their third game in a row. The White Sox prevailed, 3–1, topping Gene Bearden in game one of a doubleheader. Most frustrating for the Indians was that they stroked 10 hits (two each by Dale Mitchell and Lou Boudreau), but left men all over the bases. In the second game of the doubleheader, Cleveland stopped the bleeding with a 1–0 victory by Feller. The game was cut short to seven innings because of darkness and the Indians limped home from their road trip displeased by their recent results.[5]

On September 7, an off-day for the team, a headline in the *Cleveland Press* sports section read, "Tribe Fights For Life; Boudreau Fights For Job."[6] It was a pessimistic outlook with three weeks remaining in the regular season, but fit the general worried mood of the populace. The Indians had not had many good chances to cop a pennant since 1920 and after the game effort this season no one wanted to see it slip away this late in the game. The story suggested the Indians were sliding into oblivion and taking Boudreau with them.

In the same issue of the paper Speaker pointed out the main problem in his mind was that the Indians were not getting timely hitting.

"It strikes me that the Indians have been beating themselves in their recent games," Speaker said. "At least, they've done a pretty good job of wasting base hits. The Indians wasted eight of their 10 hits (in the 3–1 loss). They used two for their only run. The sportswriters write a lot about teams 'bunching their hits.' Believe me, it's a good idea. All the hitting in the world isn't any good unless you can bunch two or three blows to set up a rally."[7]

Whether it was good fortune, good timing, digging deep, or being pricked by critics, the last game of the road trip against the White Sox started something for the Indians. Just when they needed it most, they embarked on a seven-game winning streak. They needed to win and they went out and won and kept winning after the September 8 start of a series against the Detroit Tigers at Cleveland Stadium.

\* \* \*

One of owner Bill Veeck's famous promotions was scheduled near the beginning of a 16-game home stand. If ever a team had an opportunity to right itself by taking advantage of playing in the friendly confines of its own park, this was it. The second game against the Tigers was "Ken Keltner Night," honoring the team's long-time third baseman. Keltner had already banked 26 home runs, equal to his career best, and had been named to his seventh All-Star team in July. Among the various presents Keltner received was a new car.

Indians pitching was shaky for the opener versus the Tigers. Lemon was no threat to hurl a shutout this night, allowing five runs while walking eight men. His starting opponent, Fred Hutchinson, however, was not particularly sharp either, giving up 11 hits and seven runs in four innings. Paige relieved Lemon, but was also wild. This night the Indians' bats heeded Speaker's advice and did what was needed to out-last the Tigers, 8–7. Outfielder Larry Doby cracked four hits, scored a run, and drove in one. Catcher Jim Hegan had three hits and three RBI. Wally Judnich, playing first, also drove in three runs with two hits and Zoldak picked up the win in relief. The joking in the newspaper the day after the much-needed victory was that it was "Wally Judnich Night" the day before "Ken Keltner Night."

After that 14-hit showing the Indians were in third place, two games behind the Yankees, and four-and-a-half games behind the Red Sox. The Red Sox were beginning to look like the best team in the AL. Boston had made a breakthrough in 1946 with its first AL pennant since Babe Ruth wore red stockings—not blue pinstripes—and the core of the team was the same.

In Joe McCarthy, Boston was led by one of the greatest managers of all time, someone who had directed the Yankees to World Series supremacy several times earlier in his career. The Sox were a hard-hitting outfit and had better pitching than usual. It was not a rotation that would stand the test of time, but in 1948 was at its best.

That year, Jack Kramer went 18–5, Joe Dobson, 16–10, and usual ace Mel Parnell, 15–8; Ellis Kinder finished 10–7; Dave Ferriss was a spot starter who went 7–3; Earl Johnson was the best man out of the bullpen and finished 10–4. One of the other Red Sox pitchers that season was Denny Galehouse. Galehouse finished 8–8 as a fairly regular member of the rotation.

The Red Sox' real strength, though, was their ability to score runs. Boston collected 907 of them that season. There were really no weaknesses in the Boston lineup. Stan Spence in right hit a lousy .235, but added 12 home runs and 61 RBI and was a four-time All-Star. Spencer was surrounded in the order by catcher Birdie Tebbetts (.280), first baseman Billy Goodman (.310), Hall of Fame second baseman Bobby Doerr (.285), slugging shortstop Vern Stephens (who was the player Veeck nearly traded Boudreau for), third baseman Johnny Pesky (.281), center fielder Dom DiMaggio (.285), and of course the inimitable Ted Williams in left. Williams hit 25 home runs, drove in 127, walked 126 times, and batted .369 that season. One of the greatest hitters of all-time, Williams was known for having the keenest eyes this side of Superman's X-ray vision and never swung at a bad pitch. That's why his on-base percentage was .497.

For once it seemed as if the Red Sox may be tougher than the Yankees. But no one was completely writing the Yankees off in early September either. Joe DiMaggio was still at the top of his game and batted .320 that year. Yogi Berra hit .305, Tommy Henrich hit .308, and Johnny Lindell, filling the third outfield slot adjacent to DiMaggio and Henrich, batted .317.

Pitching-wise, these were the days when the rotation was led by Allie Reynolds, Ed Lopat, and Vic Raschi, but the Yankees were probably one starter short. Reynolds, obtained from Cleveland in that swap for Joe Gordon, finished 16–7 on the season. If Veeck had finagled Gordon out of New York without giving up Reynolds, the comparative strengths of the two teams might have been vastly different.

Due to a scheduling quirk the Indians did not have a full series against either the Red Sox or the Yankees during September of 1948. What the Indians had to do was trump the lesser teams, as McKechnie had said, and count on the two teams ahead of them in the standings to lose enough games for Cleveland to catch them.

"Ken Keltner Night" turned out well for the Indians, even though Keltner went 0-for-5. Before the game Keltner was presented with a Chevrolet station wagon, a radio-television-clock appliance, a washing machine, luggage, and a dog (a collie puppy) for his children.

The Indians also added Al Rosen and Ray Boone to the roster after the minor-league seasons ended. Rosen was named Most Valuable Player in the American Association. Boone got into the game as a pinch-hitter, but struck out.

The Cleveland-Detroit game on September 9 was a pitchers' duel between Bob Feller and Hal Newhouser, both later Hall of Famers. Newhouser gave up two runs in eight innings. Feller gave up one run in seven innings, but Paige failed him in relief, allowing the tying run.

The game went into extra innings, but Cleveland pulled it out, 3–2 after 13 innings, with Zoldak getting the win after throwing four-and-a-third innings of two-hit, no-run ball. Keltner did score the game-winning run on a single by first baseman Eddie Robinson. An injured thumb meant that Larry Doby could barely hold his bat and Boudreau removed him from the game in the eighth inning. The win moved the Indians to within one game of the second-place Yankees.

"We've just got to keep winning," Boudreau said of chasing the Red Sox. "Something is likely to give up there if we do."[8]

The Indians did keep winning, sweeping the Tigers, 10–1, the next day for a four-game winning streak. There's not much to complain about when your team wins by nine runs, and the Indians gave Boudreau a bigger present with the win than any that Keltner had received. Keltner and Boudreau each blasted three hits and Thurman Tucker, Joe Gordon, and starting pitcher Gene Bearden added two hits each in a 14-hit barrage that chased Dizzy Trout after only four innings. Bearden pitched a complete game for his 14th win, astounding fans anew with each marvelous exploit from a guy who was iffy to make the opening-day roster when spring training convened.

By all definitions, Bearden was the sensation of the 1948 season in the big leagues. Sportswriters couldn't get enough of his unlikely tale, always looking for angles to explain his inexplicable emergence to greatness. Boudreau called him a "self-starter" in terms of his workout ethic, which wasn't exactly gushing as far as compliments went. Sportswriters sought out a doctor that treated Bearden's war injuries.

"Unprofessionally, I would say he is a guy with a lot of guts," said Naval surgeon Dr. A. H. Weiland, who helped repair Bearden's very damaged knee. "Any bone fracture is serious, but one around the knee is the worst because the knee carries so much weight. I hear from Gene every once in a while and while his leg is now mechanically sound he tells me that on cold days he has to be careful when he starts warming up."[9]

The press also found Bearden's father for a chat. Henry Bearden had been a superior baseball player who might have found his way to the majors, the story went, but he gave up his pursuit of an athletic career in trade for job security as a railroad worker. He was proud of his son, but said that he didn't really show the signs he needed of becoming a big leaguer until he picked up that knuckleball that had all of baseball talking in 1948.

"I thought he had the stuff, and I knew he had the control," Henry Bearden said of Gene. "But it wasn't until years later, when he picked up his knuckleball under Casey Stengel at Oakland that he really arrived."[10]

As allowed by the rules once past September 1, the Indians enlarged their roster with call-ups from their minor-league system.

Teams that are out of the pennant race often give a good look to players that are likely to be up-and-comers. Those in the pennant race don't have much call for players who weren't good enough to make the season-long roster at a time when most games are tense. Besides Rosen and Boone, both on the cusp of top-notch Major League careers, they added catchers Ray Murray and Hank Rusz-kowski, and pitchers Ernie Groth, Bob Kuzava, Lyman Linde, Dick Rozek, and Mike Garcia. The Indians would have been a true juggernaut that season if Rosen and Garcia, future stars, were ready to play every day in '48. There was not actually much need for those players because every game the Indians played was of significant importance and they couldn't take a chance on untested talent. Mostly, the newcomers from the minors just made the dugout more crowded or were available in an emergency.

After sweeping the Tigers the Indians entertained the St. Louis Browns for what was supposed to be a four–game series, but turned into five because of a 3–3 tie—an encounter called off after 12 innings due to darkness. The Indians were looking for vengeance after their less-than-satisfactory visit to St. Louis two weeks earlier.

The series opener on September 11 was a 4–1 triumph for Cleveland, and Steve Gromek went the distance, permitting just four hits. Tucker and Gordon provided two hits worth of offensive support each. The next day, Lemon won his 20th game of the season in a 9–1 drubbing of the Browns highlighted by Allie Clark's three-hit, two-run game that was complemented by Keltner adding three hits. The 3–3 tie was the second game of a doubleheader on September 12, and despite a first-rate performance by Feller, the Indians couldn't shake the Browns before the umps decided it was time to go home.

After that long day most players were happy to get a good night's rest entering the series finale. It is doubtful, however, that many of those same players slept quite as well the next night, September 13, after what they witnessed on the field. The unexpected intruded on the game and the pennant race. No one could envision in advance a stunning mid-game development that transpired and if only briefly took everyone's minds off of sport.

Chapter Fourteen notes on page 292.

# 15

## TRAGEDY AND SUSPENSE

---

**D**ON BLACK STOOD in the batter's box in the home half of the second inning at Cleveland Stadium. The Indians' starting pitcher against the St. Louis Browns on that day, Monday afternoon, September 13, was not a member of the usual rotation.

After the emergence of Gene Bearden and Satchel Paige, if anything the Cleveland Indians of 1948 had more pitching than manager Lou Boudreau could squeeze into the schedule most of the time. Black was one of the pitchers who got the call infrequently, as a fill-in, and his record in 18 appearances—his 10th start—was 2–2. A six-year Major League veteran in his third season with the Indians, Black struggled most of the season and was not throwing like the hurler who in 1947 won 10 games and compiled a 3.92 earned run average. During this campaign, Black's ERA had climbed to 5.37. No team could afford to give much work to a pitcher who permitted more than five runs a game.

Given the circumstances, with the Indians in a hot pennant-race, Black was fortunate to get the start. In some ways he might have been pitching for his future, as well, since he was thirty-one and looking so vulnerable each time he took the mound. Part of the reason why Black wasn't more effective that season was a series of minor injuries to his arm, ankle, and toe, all of which inhibited comfortable throwing for a time.

A 6-foot, 185-pound right-hander from Salix, Iowa, Black was originally scouted and signed by the Philadelphia Athletics, for whom he pitched three seasons earlier in the 1940s, though mostly without distinction. His seasonal earned run average never dipped below 4.00 and he never put up a winning record—his best season for Philadelphia was 10–12 in 1944, a mark he matched in 1947. One of those victories was a very satisfying no-hitter over the Athletics.

An even bigger victory than the no-hitter, especially for Black's well-being, was the focus he brought to Alcoholics Anonymous and how it helped him. Although others knew some of the facts of the matter, Black made the choice to renounce his anonymity by saying that he had overcome his problem through membership in the group. The reason A's owner Connie Mack made Black expendable was his drinking, but Cleveland owner Bill Veeck took a different approach. He was the one who steered Black to AA and also as best he could watched over him to help prevent any relapses.

A year later, when Black had been sober for some time and was ready to announce the details of his battle with the bottle to the world, he said he would not have been able to pitch the masterpiece if not gaining help to fight his alcoholism.

"You can chalk that victory up for Alcoholics Anonymous," Black said.[1]

The day before Black's pitching turn against the Browns on September 13, his recovery from alcohol abuse was touted in a Sunday newspaper supplement called *American Weekly* that appeared in papers that belonged to the Hearst chain and was distributed nationwide. The story was partially about how Black was giving up his anonymity in order to help others.

In that story, Black was asked if he felt any temptation to go back to drinking, especially when things got tough in a game. A sarcastic comment made in the press box that Black probably would have given anything for a drink of bourbon when he was in a jam was rebuffed by him. "All I wanted in that situation was a fresh stick of chewing gum," he said. "Bourbon doesn't even tempt me. I'm living a new life. I'm beginning to appreciate friendships I almost ruined. Physically, I'm 100 percent improved."[2]

The irony of the timing of the release of the story was better grasped after the game because it was headlined, "Don Black's Greatest Victory." Before the end of that Monday ball game, that was no longer true. Black's greatest challenge was imminent and pressing and his greatest victory would require a different type of perseverance.

Going into the Browns game the Indians were 31 games over .500, but still trailed the streaking Boston Red Sox by two-and-a-half games in the American League standings.

Cleveland had won seven games in a row by September 12, the day before Black took the mound and his health became paramount in people's thoughts. The Indians were 84–53. Paige started a game on the 12th and seemed to lose his mastery. He lasted just four innings and although he did not get the loss, Boudreau seemed less sure of using him in big games after that. Cleveland won 6-4 and Russ Christopher notched his 16th save. It was clear as the season turned to its final weeks that

Christopher was going to be the main man out of the bullpen and he had earned that right.

As Black, a righty swinger, stepped up to the plate against the Browns' Bill Kennedy (who had started the season as a teammate with the Indians before being shuffled off to St. Louis in one of owner Bill Veeck's moves tinkering with the roster), he had no way of knowing that after two innings of shutout pitching, with three strikeouts recorded and two hits allowed, his day was almost done . . . and so was his career.

Within moments Black was fighting for his life, one of the few players ever to come close to dying in a Major League game. With no hint or warning, he collapsed to his knees at the plate as those around him gasped in horror. No one knew what happened and at the time no one understood what happened. They only knew that Don Black had been abruptly incapacitated in the middle of play.

At that point in the game the Indians led 1–0. For a team in a battle for first place, attendance was sparse that day, with only 7,008 paid admissions. That meant the ballpark was quiet, anyway, but library silence descended. Fans freaked out by the sight of a player so swiftly felled for no apparent reason were hushed and then broke into talk no louder than whispers.

Immediately, those with long memories in the press box, or long-time followers of the team, recalled the 1920 incident marking the only time a Major League player had been killed as a result of a play on the diamond. On August 16, 1920, Cleveland shortstop Ray Chapman was hit in the head by a pitch by the Yankees' Carl Mays, collapsed into a coma at home plate, and died twelve hours later.

Chapman was twenty-nine. That year, too, the Indians were embroiled in a suspenseful pennant race. Cleveland prevailed and won the World Series, its only championship on record as the 1948 club fought it out. The Black incident did not stem from a pitched ball, but as he was aided from the field and taken to a hospital, the parallels seemed strong. Shaken members of the Indians lost the game, 3–2, and then awaited word on Black's condition.

Black was transported from Cleveland Stadium to St. Vincent Charity Hospital where he was diagnosed with a cerebral hemorrhage suffered between swings of his bat and was initially listed in critical condition. The diagnosis was more specifically defined as an intracerbral hemorrhage, or stroke. He fell unconscious. From that point through the next day of his convalescence, Black was in and out of consciousness. Once he awoke and asked for a drink of lemonade. Another time he awoke, recognized his wife Joyce, squeezed her hand, and said, "Hi."[3]

Joyce Black had been in attendance at the Indians-Browns game and ran to her husband's side in the bowels of the stadium before he was taken by ambulance to the hospital. In the early going, while being transferred to the hospital, Joyce Black said Don was delirious, talking about baseball-related topics. "He kept muttering, 'I've got to win this one,'" she said, and "'We've got to win that pennant.'"[4]

Joyce Black doubted that the attack had anything to do with baseball. If that Monday had been an off day, as often occurs during the summer, she said Don would have been playing golf and he may well have suffered the same fate on a course. At the time of the hemorrhage, Black had faced two pitches from Kennedy and was carrying a 1–1 count at the plate.

After two pitches, Black stepped out of the batter's box, walked in a small circle at the plate, and then dropped to his knees as he addressed home plate umpire Bill Summers. "My God, Bill, what happened?" he said to Summers. Summers bent over Black and asked him what was wrong. Black replied that "it started on that last pitch to Pellagrini." Pellagrini was Ed Pellagrini, the St. Louis shortstop, whom Black had gotten out on a called third strike. "I put my hand on the back of his neck," Summers said. "He was trembling like a leaf. He was sick to his stomach and we thought that was the trouble."[5]

Black could not rise to his feet, but nor did he tumble over and lie down. He remained in a sort of hunch for several long minutes while others tried to help him. Black held his head, as if trying to assuage a pounding headache. Indians trainer Lefty Weisman and coach Bill McKechnie were the first to try and comfort him, and Weisman and fellow pitcher Bob Lemon helped lift him up and escorted Black off the field. Black was taken to the hospital as the game resumed. The first doctor reports about his condition touched on an aneurysm as an underlying cause. After the initial consultation the idea of brain surgery was abandoned as too risky.

Besides immediately watching over Black when he suffered his attack, Summers later expounded on how well he had been pitching for those first two innings.

"Don had wonderful stuff," Summers said. "A fine fastball and a good curve and slider. He was firing as hard as I have ever seen him."[6]

Black was conscious more often than not within a couple of days as fan letters and telegrams poured into the hospital to cheer him up. Doctors were quoted extensively. It was stated flat out immediately that he would not pitch again during the 1948 season, but that it was possible he would regain enough strength to pitch at a future date. He would likely not suffer from any paralysis due to the stroke.

When Black asked what date it was, he seemed surprised that it was mid-September, saying, "Gee, I've been cheated out of July and August."[7]

When Black was first admitted to the hospital, physicians gave him a 50–50 chance to live, so the fact that he was talking to his wife and nurses was viewed as a very positive sign. A week passed before any members of the Indians were allowed to visit Black, and trainer Weisman and pitcher Ed Klieman were the first ones in the door to see him. It was reported in the Cleveland newspapers that he recognized both of them, but little else was said about the drop-in.

After Black left the field, the game resumed. Lemon, who of course originally had been a position player, completed Black's at-bat, picking up where the count left off. Bob Muncrief was sent in to relieve him on the mound. Muncrief pitched four innings of shutout ball, turned the game over to Steve Gromek, but watched later as Sam Zoldak lost it.

September was the do-or-die month on the field, but the expression took on a different meaning when Black was stricken by the cerebral hemorrhage. He was coping with real life and death issues. The Indians had to regroup, focus on the daily games, and pull together.

By that point in the season the *Cleveland News* had hired on one-time Indians star Tris Speaker to speak his mind about the pennant race with short daily columns in the sports pages. The column was billed as "Speaker Speaks" and his byline read "Tris

Speaker, Manager, Cleveland's Only Pennant Winning Team, 1920." Coincidentally, on the day of the Black tragedy, when the team needed to reach into the bullpen to use six pitchers to get out of the game, Speaker had chosen to write a piece that was headlined, "Fine Relief Work Is Helping Indians."[8]

Penned immediately after the seven-game winning streak, Speaker said, "It's comforting to notice the role that relief pitching has played in it." He emphasized the work of Sam Zoldak and said "the big difference that effective relief pitching is making" made the winning streak a reality.[9]

Speaker's comment followed Zoldak's fireman job rescuing Paige and marked his third win in relief that week.

While Black remained in the hospital, making incremental improvements, the baseball season continued. The Indians had to keep on showing up for games every day and were trying to beat off the Red Sox and Yankees once and for all. It was unclear if they could do so.

Once again, showing why he was always regarded as a friend of the players and fans, on September 16, Bill Veeck announced that he would financially assist Black by donating to him the Indians' share of proceeds from a game played at Cleveland Stadium. "Don Black Night" was to be no routine ball game, either, on a day when fans otherwise likely would have been dished up a lowly team in the standings.

"I wanted to do this in the game with the Red Sox," Veeck said. "This way the fans will be donating to a worthy cause and get the finest attraction we have left."[10]

Veeck picked the Indians game versus the Red Sox, a very hot ticket game during the pennant race. The September 22 contest attracted 76,772 fans to a game Cleveland won. Veeck made a gift of $40,000 to Black. Also, the day before the game the *Cleveland Press* advertised the creation of something called the "Whammy Supreme," which was supposed to put a hex on the Red Sox. Described as a "good-luck charm," the item was in the shape of a pennant and had "Cleveland Indians—American League Champions, World Series, 1948" written on it. Hurriedly, 50,000 of the souvenirs were manufactured and put up for sale.[11]

As the Indians battled through the remainder of their schedule, Black remained in the hospital. He was not released until October and he never played baseball again. His final appearance in uniform was standing at the plate that sad mid-September day when he was stricken with the cerebral hemorrhage that nearly killed him.

Chapter Fifteen notes on page 293.

# 16

## ALL OUT FOR THE PENNANT

---

**M**AYBE IT WAS the severe trauma afflicting Don Black that established Bill Veeck's mood, but his expression of gloom about his Indians winning the American League pennant just a day after Black's injury didn't gibe with the facts of the race.

By nature, Veeck was an optimist who believed that things would work out. So it was surprising to hear him say on September 14 that Cleveland did not have much of a chance to claim the pennant when the Indians had 14 games left. On that day, the Indians had lost to the New York Yankees, 6–5, and their record was now 84–55. Ed Lopat out-pitched Bob Lemon for the victory, though Cleveland cut the margin to one run in the bottom of the ninth and received exceptional relief work from Satchel Paige. Allie Clark and Joe Gordon homered for Cleveland, but it wasn't enough.

No doubt Veeck was discouraged by New York's four-run seventh that clinched the game. Bobby Brown bashed four hits and Joe DiMaggio contributed two. That left the Yankees at 85–52. The Boston Red Sox's mark was 87–50.

"Not much chance left now," Veeck said. "It will take a miracle." Bigger miracles than this had confronted teams in the past that had prevailed, so Veeck's pronouncement was quite short-sighted. The odds may have favored Boston, but the Indians were far from mathematically eliminated with two weeks of play remaining. "Well, we've got the nucleus of a good team. Until this happened I thought we were going to win. But now it looks like we've got to look to the future."[1]

While most eyes were on the Indians at the ballpark, there were updates about Black that trickled out to fans. *Cleveland News* columnist Franklin Lewis seemed more optimistic about life than Veeck did. Well aware of the severity of Black's state, Lewis sought to strike a hopeful tone in a story, telling how some athletes, with their incredible will, overcome physical setbacks and return to their former glory.

"All I know is that Black is an athlete and athletes, the guys we write about all the time, turn some of the sharpest physical corners you ever saw just about the time they are supposed to give up," Lewis wrote. ". . . they do come back, Don. They have."[2]

The defeat by the Yankees was discouraging, but Cleveland still had seven more games in a row at home against the Washington Senators, the fading Philadelphia Athletics, and then a single game against the league-leading Red Sox.

A short update of Black's condition was issued, one that might produce mixed emotions. The good news was that he was feeling better since being admitted to the hospital, but the bad news was that he was still struggling. He was not lapsing into unconsciousness much a few days after the stroke, but was still listed on the hospital's danger list. The Indians were on the danger list, too, in quite a different manner. While a day off brought grim faces to the park for the start of a three-game set with the Senators on September 16, good news was given when Larry Doby's thumb injury had improved and he was now ready to play. Manager Lou Boudreau picked Gene Bearden, his hottest pitcher, to throw the opener. Also, while the Indians were resting, the Red Sox were being trounced, 17–10, by the Chicago White Sox.

If there was anything wrong with Doby's hand that a band-aid wouldn't protect, it was not noticeable. Doby was assigned to the sixth spot in the batting order and by the time he got to the plate in the home half of the first inning, some of his teammates had already passed through with great success. Dale Mitchell led off the game with a hit and three ducks were on the pond when Doby stepped into the batter's box against Senator hurler Sid Hudson. A Doby grand-slam sparked a five-run inning and the Indians bested Washington, 6–3. Bearden went the distance for his 15th win of his rookie season.

Afterwards, Boudreau made it clear that he was not thinking the way Veeck was thinking. He believed very strongly the Indians could still win the pennant, never mind in the future. "We'll never give up," Boudreau said, "and my only fear is that we'll run out of games too soon."[3]

Boudreau was talking a big game and he was very much trying to be a manager who made all of the right calls down the stretch. However, as a player, the man who had led the team in hitting all season was in a spiraling slump and was desperately trying to regain his stroke. He was 0-for-4 in the Senators game, but at least his teammates got the necessary hits.

Bob Feller gave himself a talking to and pulled himself together since falling below .500 in the first half of the season, regaining his All-Star form. In the second contest against the Senators he dominated, turning in a complete game, 11-strikeout performance in a 4–1 victory. That lifted his seasonal record to 16–14, and he was 7–3 since his 9–11 start. Catcher Jim Hegan and third baseman Ken Keltner had two hits apiece to ignite the offense. Feller was making a run at resuming his rightful place as team ace.

After pitching mostly in late relief in recent weeks, Sam Zoldak got the nod for the third contest with the Senators and he pushed his record to 11–10 with a complete-game five-hitter in a 10–1 Indians romp. Mitchell sprayed four hits, Wally Judnich added two, and Boudreau burst out of his slump with two hits and three RBI as he smacked his 14th homer of the year.

So the Indians swept the Senators, something very high on their to-do list. Cleveland had to keep winning, but it wouldn't matter if the Red Sox and Yankees did as well. After pausing on the shore of Lake Erie for that single game, the Yankees did not; they lost three out of their next five games. Boston hit a mid-month stretch when it went 2–4. Neither could be considered full-fledged collapses, but the losses allowed Cleveland to gain a little bit of ground. As Boudreau said, though, would the Indians run out of games before they could catch the leaders?

Regardless, the Indians had to keep winning. That was paramount. The next obstacle was a three-game series at Cleveland Stadium against the Philadelphia Athletics, which had surprisingly hung tight in the race all season. While they had dropped back slightly in early September, they'd started to surge again. The Athletics were not completely out of the race yet, even if they were the only ones who had faith. At the least the A's were capable of being spoilers, and that was what Cleveland had to watch out for. It wouldn't do to have one eye on the out-of-town scoreboard while blowing games to Philadelphia. Sure enough, Philadelphia arrived in Cleveland riding a five-game winning streak and carrying an 83–61 mark. It really was a four-team race, one of only a handful in baseball history with only about 10 days remaining in the regular season.

On September 19, the Indians and A's hunkered down for a doubleheader, both teams hungry for critical victories with the clock ticking down on the season. Erstwhile outfielder-turned-star pitcher Bob Lemon was on the mound for the Indians against Philadelphia right-hander Carl Scheib, who was in the midst of what would be his best season in an 11-year career. Scheib sported a 13–7 record entering the contest.

For most of the game the Indians picked away at Scheib, collecting a hit here, a hit there, but being kept off the scoreboard even as they left runners on. Lemon left in favor of reliever Russ Christopher after seven and two-thirds innings and the game knotted 3–3. However, in what was a crucial rally, the Indians scored twice in the bottom of the ninth off of Scheib to win the game, 5–3. Knocking out his second hit of the game, a Larry Doby walk-off blast won it after Joe Gordon collected his 28th homer of the season in the second.

Boudreau gave the ball to Steve Gromek for the nightcap and he was brilliant against Dick Fowler. Fowler, like Scheib, was having the best year of his career with 15 wins, but the Indians beat him, 2–0, as Gromek twirled a three-hit shutout.

More than 75,000 fans turned out for the doubleheader, allowing the Indians to set a new American League attendance record of 2,300,893. The previous league mark was 2,265,512, set by the Yankees in 1946. Interestingly, the Yankees and Red

Sox were both on pace to break the old record, too, illustrating that there's nothing like a wild pennant race to keep fans' juices flowing. Veeck, who had contributed in so many ways to luring fans through the gates—from assembling the winning team to dreaming up giveaways and entertaining stunts—took the microphone and addressed the 75,382 fans to notify them about cracking the record.

"Thanks a million," Veeck said.[4] He was probably tempted to say thanks 2.3 million, but held back since it didn't roll off the tongue so readily.

While the Indians were thwarting the Athletics twice on September 19, the Red Sox were losing a doubleheader to the Tigers and the Yankees were splitting a doubleheader with the Browns. That left the standings so tight that a hopeful prison escapee might not have been able to wedge a nail file between the teams. Boston was 89–54, Cleveland was 89–55, and New York was 88–55. The losses pretty much killed Philadelphia. Just win, baby, was Cleveland's mantra, long before the Oakland Raiders' Al Davis adopted the slogan.

On September 20, the Indians had become front-page news in the *Cleveland Press*, their status explained with a headline reading, "Not A Hope, It's A Fact Now! Tribe's Back In Race, And How!" Forget Veeck's miracle proclamation, this was reality.

"A lot of people deserve credit for what happened today," Boudreau said of the doubleheader sweep.[5]

Boudreau was one of them. In the ninth inning of the first game versus the A's, Boudreau scooped up a grounder with a tough grab that started a double play when the game was still tied. In the second game he hit two home runs to back Gromek.

Tris Speaker nodded sagely at the results of Boudreau's mini-hitting rampage, saying that not even the thumb problem that somewhat mirrored Doby's injury should have kept the player-manager sidelined and he made the right call by staying in the lineup and swinging until he connected.

"A lot people thought he'd be better off taking a few days' rest," Speaker said. "But with a hitter like Lou, batting slumps don't last too long because he knows how to work his way out. Boudreau knew that in order to come out of a batting slump you've got to keep fighting in there. Well, Lou emerged from his slump Saturday. And his two home runs yesterday, giving him three homers in two days, furnished positive evidence of it. He looks now as if he'll continue hitting in his usual splendid style the rest of the season, despite the ailing thumb."[6]

The next day, the Indians squashed the A's for a third straight time, the sweep pretty much ruining Philadelphia's pennant chances. It was Cleveland's 90th win of the season, a 6–3 victory for Gene Bearden, who notched his 16th triumph of the season. It was not one of Bearden's best games, since he allowed 12 hits in six and two-thirds innings, but it was good enough. Christopher picked up his 17th save in relief. Joe Gordon was the big producer with three hits and three RBI while Jim Hegan and Dale Mitchell added two hits apiece as Cleveland built a 4–0 lead before Bearden was touched for a run.

Bearden and Christopher out-dueled Philadelphia's Lou Brissie, the author of a courageous comeback story that rivaled their own. Brissie, winner of a Purple Heart during World War II, endured a two-year layoff from the sport following his shattered tibia that required twenty-three operations to heal. In an unusual overlapping of moundsmen, all three had overcome phenomenal odds affecting their health to develop Major League careers. Brissie took the loss that day and finished 14–10, his best year in the majors. Following that defeat, the A's were 83–64, and they never got closer to first again. The losses to the Indians sent Philadelphia into a tailspin as they lost nine of their final 10 games. Ending up 84–70 was not indicative of how well the Athletics played until mid-September.

Cleveland's consecutive series sweeps of Washington and Philadelphia provided a six-game winning streak heading into a September 22 showdown against the Red Sox—the benefit game on "Don Black Night." The circumstances of Cleveland clicking in every phase of the game and claiming the six straight wins sent the city into a frenzy of pennant fever. This is when the "Whammy" pennant popped up for sale as a way of symbolically hissing at the incoming Red Sox. The *Cleveland Press* created a contest heralded on the top of its September 21 front page that as first prize offered tickets to every game of the 1948 World Series—regardless of where they were played. The way to win was to predict the minute, hour, and day the American League pennant was going to be clinched. Entrants were also requested to write in twenty-five words or less, "I hope the Indians win because . . ."[7]

Likely someone wrote that they hoped the Indians would win the pennant so the fan wouldn't have to go watch the Yankees play in another darned World Series.

Cleveland Stadium was going to be filled with more than 75,000 fans for "Don Black Night," and Boudreau chose Bob Feller to start the important game against the Sox. This was the last head-to-head meeting for the Indians against any other team with a chance to grab the pennant. Cleveland was personally responsible for crushing the A's. In the single game against New York, the Indians lost, and they wouldn't see the Yankees again. The Red Sox and Yankees still had to play one another, which could produce results to Cleveland's benefit. This one in Cleveland, though, was a take-control-of-your-own-destiny game. That day the Indians sat one half-game behind Boston in the standings and one-half game ahead of New York.

"We were playing the Red Sox and if we won we would be in a three-way tie," is what Feller said of "Don Black Night." "As if that and the Don Black cause didn't add up to enough drama, Joe McCarthy, the ex-Yankee who had become the Red Sox manager, told the reporters before the game that he was delighted I was pitching for the Indians. He said his team would 'knock his brains out' and said I was 'just another pitcher.'"[8]

It did seem like an odd thing for an experienced manager to utter on the eve of a huge game when about to face a pitcher whose record proved he was probably the best of the times. Naturally, Feller took the message personally and got a little bit ticked off. Not so angry, though, that he let it interfere with his work. And by that point in September his work was something to marvel at again, the way it had been for years before he began that season in a slump.

Feller pitched as well as ever against Boston's Joe Dobson, a 16-game winner. The Indians jumped on Dobson immediately, scoring three runs in the first and Feller, on his way to a complete game, allowed just three hits and two runs while striking out six men as he won his 17th game of the year. Dale Mitchell, who heated up as the weather cooled off, clouted three hits. Boudreau, no longer in a batting slump, stroked two hits, and Ken Keltner whacked three hits, scored two runs, and drove in two. In the first, Thurman Tucker walked, stole second, and was driven in by a Gordon single. Then Keltner hit a two-run homer. Nobody had more than one hit for the Red Sox and catcher Birdie Tebbetts' double was the only extra-base hit for Boston.

"I don't know what McCarthy had in mind," Feller said, "but it's a good thing he didn't bet his house payment on his prediction. We went right after the Red Sox and scored three runs in the first inning. That was all I needed. It was so cold I wore two jackets in the dugout between innings and took an extra three minutes to warm up before the game. Everybody was contributing."[9]

The defeat of Boston put the Indians at 91–55—in a dead heat with the Red Sox. The Yankees bested the White Sox and their record improved to 90–55. While the donnybrook continued in the American League, the Boston Braves were on the verge of clinching the National League pennant without as many theatrics. The Braves finished six-and-a-half games ahead of the Cardinals, so they had time to rest their pitchers and watch with bemusement from afar as the three AL clubs slugged it out for the right to play them in the World Series.

Riding a seven-game winning streak, the Indians had a day off before embarking for Detroit for a three-game series against the Tigers. Cleveland had eight regular-season games remaining and six of them were against Detroit. Meanwhile, Boston traveled to New York for a three-game series. A sweep by one or other of the teams would probably destroy the prospects of the loser.

As the Indians went off to Detroit, owner Bill Veeck and business manager Rudie Schaffer consulted and agreed that the team should print World Series tickets. It was a matter of expediency, just in case the Indians won the pennant. The club also announced its sales policy for the tickets, but refused to actually put them on sale yet. Schaffer said about 10,000 fans had already written to the Indians asking to put be on a World Series ticket list, but that the team had returned the applications.

"We can go ahead with the ticket sale when the pennant race is determined, or when we feel reasonably certain," Schaffer said."[10]

No sense jinxing the team, which surely the Indians front office would have been accused of if it chose to sell tickets too early and the team then failed to capture the AL crown.

The policy Schaffer and Veeck decided upon was to limit each application for tickets to four per purchase. In those good old days of comparatively cheap entertainment, the price of box seats was set at $8, the price of reserved seats at $6.25 and the price of bleacher tickets at $1. For the 2012 World Series at Detroit's Comerica Park, standing room only tickets sold for $325. Clearly, inflation has made a difference over nearly sixty-five years.

Boudreau probably didn't want to hear anything about ticket sales since he was focused on making the Series a reality. For a guy who was so gung-ho in revving up his troops earlier, Boudreau spoke more conservatively after the Indians handled the Red Sox.

"Now I think we've got a chance," Boudreau said. "Don't forget, the Red Sox play five of their eight remaining games at home." Despite getting critical wins from Gromek, Zoldak, and others in recent weeks, Boudreau gave serious thought to his rotation for the closing days of the season. "As a matter of fact it will be Lemon, Bearden, and Feller for the rest of the way with the possible exception of one game against the White Sox. Steve Gromek may pitch that."[11]

This was not the time to use untested September call-ups or the men at the back of the rotation. Boudreau's big three starters all season had been Lemon, Bearden, and Feller. No one blinked when he said he was going to ride them to the end. If they got tired they could rest over the winter. It was time to let the big guns carry the club on their shoulders. If the Indians lost with those three pitching, then so be it, they went down fighting with their best.

With just over a week and eight games left in the regular season it was possible that all three hurlers could end up as 20-game winners and if they did, the chances were good that they were going to lead the Cleveland Indians to the World Series.

Chapter Sixteen notes on pages 293–294.

# 17

## AL PENNANT IN INDIANS' SIGHTS

THE TALK AROUND Cleveland was all about the Indians—all about the prospect of winning the city's first pennant in twenty-eight years and bringing the World Series to town for the first time since 1920. If there was another topic on people's minds it was almost surely swiftly superseded by, "How 'bout them Indians?"

Yes, the Indians began printing those Series tickets and announced a plan to distribute them. Fans were told that unless their applications to buy tickets were sent in a self-addressed envelope and that they were postmarked no earlier than 12:01 a.m. on Tuesday, September 28, they would not be considered. The gold rush was on.

Bill Veeck made the political decision to allow a special, invited group of 5,000 people the privilege of being advance applicants. Veeck admitted that many on the list were prominent public officials such as city councilmen, but also included were fans that had bought tickets by mail in the past and might not easily be privy to up-to-date information about the ticket process because they lived farther away.

"In the event our Indians represent the American League in the fall classic," Veeck wrote in his heads-up letter, "we want to give you the opportunity of purchasing seats before placing tickets on general sale."[1]

At that moment Cleveland was an Indians town. Full page ads were running in newspapers from a local men's clothing store named Rosenblum's picturing third baseman Ken Keltner modeling suits. The cost of dressing up began at $45. The message was basically, *He wears them. You should, too!* Keltner's other suit, his Cleveland Indians uniform, was more important to most of the populace in the area. But the Indians were everywhere.

The *Cleveland Press* was touting its World Series ticket contest each day in a story at the very top of the front page. There was a big drop-off in the value of the three prizes offered, certainly psychologically. First prize was tickets to every World Series games wherever they were played. Second prize was $100. Third prize was $50. Who knows? Maybe some winner might prefer the bucks if the Indians didn't qualify for the Series. However, at the time, the Indians holding off the other contenders was foremost in fans' minds.

The Indians departed for Detroit and a three-game series against the Tigers. In some minds the Tigers may have underachieved in 1948 with a 74–72 record, but they were dangerous foes for the Indians at this point. Those with fair memories would recall that the Indians of 1940 traveled to Briggs Stadium for important games in September and were demolished in five out of six games. Detroit had the starting pitchers to bother Cleveland this time around, too, and the Tigers committed to Fred Hutchinson, Hal Newhouser, and Virgil Trucks for this trio of games. On any given day any of those moundsmen could be mesmerizing.

Boudreau said the present-day Indians would not have 1940 in their thoughts at all, if they were even aware of the eight-year-old debacle.

"That was a long time ago," Boudreau said. "How many of us remember it, that fold-up in 1940? There's nothing like that cooking in the minds of these fellows."[2] Boudreau was almost certainly correct, although he remembered the circumstances. Bob Feller and Ken Keltner were also around then, but there was no reason to believe ancient history would affect their performances in Detroit.

The September 24 opener in Detroit was close all the way though, and both starting pitchers, Bob Lemon and Hutchinson, pitched well, but not overpoweringly. Detroit prevailed in this one by a final of 4–3. Hutchinson pitched a complete game to raise his record to 13–10. Lemon came out after six and one-third innings, leaving completion duties to Sam Zoldak. Lemon absorbed the loss, bringing his record to 20–13. Keltner, with three hits, and Larry Doby with two, did most of the work for Cleveland, but it wasn't enough.

Dick Wakefield, Detroit's left fielder, did the most damage for the winning side with two hits. Pre-game, he happened to attract attention from visiting reporters who cornered him and he said, "This must be important to draw all you guys." The scribes said they had not made the pilgrimage to Detroit to invest in new 1949 automobiles. The event did seem to be more important in Cleveland, New York, and Boston, however, because just 10,464 Detroit citizens turned out to watch.[3]

Meanwhile, at Yankee Stadium, New York banged around Boston starter Ellis Kinder and rode the relief work of Joe Page to a 9–6 victory. Five Boston players, Ted Williams, Dom DiMaggio, Stan Spence, Billy Goodman, and Johnny Pesky each swatted two hits, and it still wasn't enough to conquer the Yankees. New York benefited from a three-run homer off of the bat from one of its less-heralded players, third baseman Billy Johnson.

After the results from the two games that night, readers of the league standings were faced with some fascinating numbers. The Cleveland Indians, New York Yankees, and Boston Red Sox all had identical records of 91–56 with seven games to go that would carry into early October.

So everything and everyone was tied up with a week to play. The Indians' winning streak was broken, but Boudreau did not sound panicked when the final score was tabulated.

"We'll still win," he proclaimed. Nearby, in another part of the clubhouse, coach Bill McKechnie made the identical pronouncement. No doubt was being expressed on the Cleveland side.[4] If anyone seemed nervous about the loss to the Tigers it wasn't the dugout brain trust.

Tris Speaker was still surveying the action from his perch as a guest newspaper columnist and he did not remark about similarities to 1940 as much as to 1920 when he was in charge and led the Indians to their previous pennant.

"The common expression I hear in every press box these days is 'This certainly is a big ball game today,'" Speaker said. "Well, they all are in this kind of race. You sit out every inning of every game and even as cold as it was here [Detroit] yesterday when the Indians were losing to the Tigers 4–3, we were all sweating out the afternoon. I thought I'd left most of this behind me twenty-eight years ago, but apparently there's not much new under the sun, or in baseball." Speaker then recalled something that a cynic may have said could have been wiped from his memory. In a crucial game in the late stages of the 1920 pennant run, the Indians faced the Chicago White Sox and "Shoeless Joe" Jackson hit a screaming shot deep to right-center field. Speaker nabbed the ball with a thrust of his glove and by laying out his body horizontally. Alas for him, he crashed hard into a concrete outfield wall and knocked himself unconscious. Speaker said he didn't wake up for several minutes, but he hung on to the ball for the out and gave his team a three-and-a-half-game lead in the race.

"I wasn't crashing into any walls yesterday," he added, "but I might as well have been. I couldn't have been more nervous or worrisome. It sure looks like we're playing 1920 all over again."[5]

The next day, in round two, the Indians climbed all over five Tigers pitchers, starting with Trucks, who took the loss to fall to 13–13. Cleveland piled on 14 hits to accumulate nine runs in a 9–3 win. Bearden came through for his 17th victory and pitched a complete game. Eddie Robinson smacked three hits and drove in two runs. Dale Mitchell, Boudreau, Keltner, and Jim Hegan all added two hits each. Cleveland was up 2–0 when a five-run fifth inning put things out of reach.

In New York, the Red Sox took the second of three scheduled games from the Yankees, 7–2, as Jack Kramer went the distance for his 17th win. Kramer stifled the Yanks on seven hits and only one earned run as his teammates reached Allie Reynolds for five hits and five runs in five innings as he was driven to the showers. With all of the vaunted hitters in the Boston lineup it was back-up outfielder Wally Moses, nearing the end of his career as he was a couple of weeks shy of his thirty-eighth birthday, who did the most offensive damage. Playing right field, Moses, who approached .300 lifetime, went 2-for-3 and scored three runs. Boston was up 5–0 by the end of the fourth inning.

The third game in the Indians-Tigers series pitted two future Hall of Famers in Feller for Cleveland and Newhouser, a two-time Most Valuable Player award winner, for Detroit. The hurlers matched one another through two innings, but Cleveland broke into the lead in the third when second baseman Joe Gordon came up with a runner on and belted a two-run homer. The Indians added another run in the fourth and one in the seventh. The Tigers could barely scratch Feller's best stuff.

Cleveland backed Feller with 10 hits, two from Jim Hegan. Feller, who went all of the way, surrendered just five hits and one run while striking out nine. Cleveland captured the game and the series, 4–1. After his early problems Feller's record stood at 18–14. The Indians were returning to Cleveland with a 93–56 mark and with all of their remaining regular-season games at Cleveland Stadium.

The Yankees rebounded in the third game of the Boston series at Yankee Stadium, winning 6–2. That left Boston at 92–57, a game behind the Indians, but also headed to Fenway Park to play out their regular season at home. After their clutch win, propelled by pitcher Tommy Byrne's complete-game five-hitter that out-shone Boston's combination of Mel Parnell, Denny Galehouse, and Dave Ferriss, New York was tied with the Red Sox, also at 92–57, and trailed the Indians by a game.

As if his team was not enough of an attraction—and it was a big enough lure to set a new attendance record—Bill Veeck never ran short of promotional ideas, even in the midst of one of the hottest pennant races in history. Thus began the scheduling of what was considered to be one of the greatest promotional gambits in the creative Veeck's ownership career.

The Indians had already featured a "Ken Keltner Night," honoring the third baseman with gifts for his many years of service to the team. They had also featured a "Don Black Night," raising money to help cover the pitcher's hospital bills. Some Cleveland residents suggested there should be a "Bill Veeck Night," too, in order to honor the man who had rebuilt the franchise so swiftly and manufactured this pennant-contending team.

However, one average citizen, who resided in nearby Lakewood, Ohio, essentially said, *Enough already*. Instead of giving these reward nights to players and team figures that made more money and already received more attention as members of the esteemed profession of baseball, why not have a special night for a fan?

The citizen in question was named Joe Earley, and he wrote a letter to the editor that was printed in the *Cleveland Press* advancing his alternative idea. "Now they want a 'Bill Veeck Night,'" Earley wrote. "Let's have a 'Joe Earley Night.' I pay my rent and my landlord spends it on things that keep business stimulated. I keep the gas station attendant in business by buying gas regularly. I keep the milkman in clover by buying milk. He uses trucks and tires and as a result big industry is kept going. The paper boy delivers the paper, wears out a pair of shoes occasionally and the shoemaker wins. A lot of people depend on me [and you] so let us all get together and send in your contributions for that car for 'Good Old Joe Earley Night.'"[6]

As anyone who ever met Bill Veeck probably sensed from the moment the letter was printed, Veeck swooned over the idea at first reading, probably fell harder than he did for either of his wives. Of course Veeck embraced the proposal. And of course he added to it when he scheduled "Good Old Joe Earley Night" for real.

Earley's letter appeared in the *Press* on September 9. He was a World War II veteran, naturally enough an Indians fan, and worked as a night watchman at an automobile plant. Earley had written his letter tongue-in-cheek, not expecting much response other than a chuckle or two from those who spotted it in the paper. Much to his surprise, he was buried with phone calls from readers who sought him out and also began sending him money. Earley promptly announced that he was going to donate any money that came his way to the local Cancer Fund. Earley's wife June said it was all a joke and said, "If it's a good laugh for everybody, it's a good thing."[7]

That was hardly the last of the matter, though. Veeck took over and scheduled "Good Old Joe Earley Night" for September 28 at the Indians-Chicago White Sox game at Cleveland Stadium and took on the role of master of ceremonies himself. The day before his big night, Earley had a guest appearance on a popular local radio show called *The Ohio Story*, a fifteen-minute program. It was also revealed that another Joe Earley existed, though this one was from Vermont. He happened to be in Cleveland on business and walked right into the hullabaloo featuring his name.

Veeck embraced the original Joe Earley and the idea espoused in his newspaper letter. The plan was to honor the average Joe, the Everyman fan. And since many of those everyday fans were also everywomen fans, Veeck also called the evening "Princess Aloha Orchid Night." Veeck rented a plane and had 20,000 Princess Aloha orchids flown to Cleveland from Hawaii and presented to the first 20,000 women to enter the park. But, as they said on the quiz shows, that's not all.

Veeck, who loved this kind of stuff as much as P. T. Barnum, took the field to welcome everyone before the game and then began pointing to fans at random seated around the stadium to present them with gifts that included 50-pound blocks of ice, live turkeys and guinea pigs, rabbits, and fruits and vegetables by the bushel. No one knew what to make of the prize consisting of three stepladders.

The extravaganza had the 60,405 fans laughing in the aisles. Then Veeck got down to the not-so-serious business of bestowing gifts on the man who started it all—Good Old Joe Earley. Citing Early's inspiration for the special night, Veeck informed the crowd that Early deserved special presents. He said that Early was being given a new house by the Indians styled in "early American architecture."[8] Veeck waved his hand and out on the field rolled a flat-bed truck holding a poorly constructed out-house on board.

That was just the beginning. Joe Earley also got the car he coveted—sort of. The vehicle presented to him was a circus car, but instead of a football team's worth of clowns climbing out, a gaggle of female models poured from the small car. The horn was honked and the bumpers fell off. Several gag gifts followed and the fans ate it up. When chickens and other livestock were trotted out, Earley, who lived in an urban apartment, had a moment of alarm. "My gosh," he said, "you must have made some arrangements."[9]

Eventually, Earley was presented with several more "real" valuable prizes, including a new 1949 Ford convertible, several appliances, including a television set and a dish washer, luggage, and a new dog. One of the neat awards for baseball fan Joe was a lifetime pass to American League ballparks. The average Joe made out very well on the night he imagined, but never believed would come to pass. He seemed a bit overwhelmed by his good fortune once he was ushered off the stage, impressed that the mayor, Tom Burke, knew his name, and extremely thankful for Veeck's generosity, though also a bit bewildered by some of it.

"I thank Bill Veeck and this outfit," Earley said, "and the newspaper and radio people. My gosh, what am I going to do with that livestock. Think it really belongs to me?"[10]

Wife June certainly seemed to think so. "Listen, Joe," she said, "I don't know much about farms, but I know that a cow needs milking."[11]

Earley was also treated to dinner at the stadium before the game with team vice president Hank Greenberg and other Indians officials, and he was up all night from excitement. When he went to collect his new car loaded down with gifts the next day, he discovered that the keys he had been handed did not include the ignition key.

"How do I go about thanking everybody for such a thing?" Earley said. "Wonder if they really mean that 'the livestock's down at the Stadium with the rest of the things?' I got to hire a truck. What do you do with a cow in the city?"[12]

Indeed, the *Sporting News* subsequently commented that, "All in all it was a great night for John Q. Cleveland."[13] For once the Bible of the sport did not seem to think that Veeck acted with too much frivolity and facetiousness with one of his promotions. Apparently the *Sporting News* thought it was more appropriate to honor the fans of the game than Satchel Paige.

Joe Earley fared better than anyone else in the stands that night, but the other Indians fans identified with the event and realized Bill Veeck was thanking all of them.

Then, to cap the night's entertainment, the Indians clobbered the White Sox, 11–0. If the team was in any way distracted from its business by the pre-game shenanigans, there was no hint of it. The Indians scored three runs in the first inning, another in the second, an additional run in the fourth, and then poured across six runs in the fifth. They drilled Chicago pitching, notably starter and loser Bill Wight, for 13 hits. Allie Clark, who had missed half of the season with injury, was the leading figure in the slaughter, rapping out four hits while accumulating three runs scored and three RBI. Mitchell, Doby, Keltner, and Boudreau each stroked two hits.

"We're hitting," said Indians coach Muddy Ruel, "That's the big thing. We're hitting."[14]

On the mound, Gene Bearden just kept on spinning his magic, holding the White Sox to four hits in the shutout as he nabbed his 18th victory. The rookie had been outstanding all season and was still doing it in the clutch, in the heat of a pennant race under pressure. He struck out seven and upped his record to 18–7. That gave the Indians their 10th win in 11 games. They owned September.

The Red Sox were back in Fenway Park for a game against the Washington Senators, but veteran Ray Scarborough was on his game for Washington as he picked up his 14th victory while holding the Sox to six hits and two runs in the 4–2 decision. Boston's Joe Dobson was lifted by manager Joe McCarthy after one and one-third innings after permitting five hits and four runs. It was the time of year when managers had little patience with starters who were experiencing an off-day.

New York was on the road, throwing 19-game winner Vic Raschi at the Philadelphia A's. Playing for pride at this point, the Athletics handled New York, 5–2. Carl Scheib was reached for 11 hits, but went all of the way, benefiting by stranding too many Yankees on the base paths.

Joe Earley was not the only one who went home happy. Cleveland's record was 94–56, Boston's was 92–58, and New York's was also 92–58. The Indians were in first place and held a two-game advantage over both of its closest pursuers and they had just four games to play.

Chapter Seventeen notes on pages 294–295.

# 18

## STRETCH RUN

---

**THE INDIANS HAD** turned Cleveland into a town of believers with their September run, and clobbering the White Sox was like an exclamation point. The Indians returned to the park the next day and bested Chicago again, this time by a score of 5–2.

For one of the rare occasions during their surge, the Indians fell behind early, 2–0, in the second inning as Bob Feller took the ball attempting to give his team its 95th win of the season. Feller's and Cleveland's Septembers were parallel achievements. When the Indians scored three runs in the bottom of the sixth inning and added two more in the seventh, he was home free.

Feller spread around 10 hits, but gave up just the two runs, as he posted his 19th win of the season. Reaching that total had seemed remote only a couple of months before. From 9–11, Feller rebounded with a 10–3 skein. He may have been the old man of the staff, but Feller was pitching as well as ever when the Indians needed him the most. This time they used him on short rest and Feller was a tad off his game. After the slow start, however, he settled down and easily out-pitched Chicago's Frank Papish, who was 2–8 on the year.

Like most successful pitchers of his generation and before, Feller was a workhorse. En route to his 266 victories, Feller led the American League in innings pitched five times, all five prior to the 1948 season. His streak ended that season, but he still pitched 280 1/3 innings. As the years went by, the five-pitcher starting rotation with four days of rest became routine and it was a big deal with sportswriters whenever a pitcher was used on "short rest." Feller thought the issue had been overblown and didn't mind pitching a day earlier than originally scheduled.

"Four-day versus five-day rotation," he said. "This has become a controversy that depends on how much stamina the pitcher has within him. I worked on a farm and was used to manual labor, so I had a lot of stamina. There is no reason why a pitcher without an injury cannot pitch with three days' rest. I don't believe in five-day rotations. If you're on a four-game schedule you can do wind sprints and work out in-between starts, with your big workout in the middle day of the schedule. If you're on a five-game schedule, then your workout can be every other day, but not the day before."[1]

A lot of people were still talking about the 11–0 shellacking of the White Sox as well. Columnists who not long before had considered the Indians' pennant threats to be drying up, were now handing them the flag. *Plain Dealer* sports editor Gordon Cobbledick was one of the pontificators. ". . . this one may have been the biggest of the big," he wrote. "Not only was it the game that put the Tribe two in front with only four to go, but it could have been the one that made the Red Sox and Yankees ask, 'What's the use?'"[2]

The Red Sox had two games remaining against the Washington Senators and Boston and New York closed out the regular season with two games against one another. They might well knock each other off giving Cleveland clear title to the pennant, or things could break so that one team was eliminated and the other caught the Indians.

Meanwhile, in Cleveland, fans did not seem to think much of the chances of either the Red Sox or Yankees, convinced their Indians were going to annex the pennant. To prove their faith they sent applications to the team for World Series tickets in stunning numbers. The Indians had impressed the baseball world all season by periodically cramming crowds of more than 75,000 people into Cleveland Stadium. The building, which opened in 1931, listed a baseball capacity of 74,000-plus, but had exceeded that number.

As promised, as the season neared its end, the Indians introduced a procedure to allow fans to write in for Series tickets after a certain date. The fans listened, but many must have been standing next to their mail box at 12:01 a.m. to start filing. It took only a few days for owner Bill Veeck to pronounce his team swamped. The inundation of applications passed an estimated one million. So many fans sought tickets that Veeck figured out that Cleveland Stadium could be bulging with 85,000 people whenever the Indians played a Series game.

The phrase "standing room only" was invented for situations like these and Veeck intended to not only sell every seat, but to allow for considerable standing room.

"We'll even sell standing room in the grandstands," he said, "and maybe number the bleacher tickets."[3]

If the Indians qualified as the American League representative for the Series and the Series lasted a while, the Indians would host three home games at Cleveland Stadium with a theoretical ticket total of 198,000. Veeck knew his staff was overwhelmed from the first mail delivery in the legal time frame and immediately began looking for up to forty part-time workers to help with the task of sorting applications. The massive number of applications made Veeck rethink his original policy announcement of letting an applicant seek four tickets for a game. Instead, he reduced the maximum ticket request to two tickets in order to accommodate more fans.

"The volume of requests has exceeded all expectations," Veeck said.[4]

After Feller and Gene Bearden stymied the White Sox, Boudreau's late-season commitment to the small number of pitchers appeared sound. Fans were gushing over Bearden's skills. The unknown of the spring might have been the most popular player on this popular team as autumn took over the calendar. Feller was satisfied that he had turned around his slow start and turned into a major contributor. Bearden was too shy to accept much credit after winning his 18th game. It was a remarkable ride for Bearden. If Boudreau had sent him out to the minors in the spring there wouldn't have been a peep. Instead Boudreau took the gamble to keep Bearden and give him every chance to succeed.

Almost from his first opportunity, Bearden had been extraordinary. His knuckler completely confused American League hitters and time after time he pitched big games, stacking up the wins when the team needed him. No one would begrudge a bow or two from Bearden, but he didn't bother, instead praising veteran catcher Jim Hegan as the important part of their duet.

"There's the guy who's responsible," Bearden said of his backstop. "He's the best I've ever thrown to, and in my opinion, the best in the business. Jim knows what pitch to call and if you can give him that one you don't have any trouble. My control was [on] tonight and I could put it where he wanted it."[5]

Again, although qualifying for the Series was not official, Major League Baseball asked the Indians to submit a list of twenty-five players for its postseason roster. There was one surprise in the group. Since Don Black was out following his cerebral hemorrhage, the Indians were allowed to add one player who had not been on the roster prior to August 31. The team nominated Al Rosen and Rosen, the back-up third baseman and star in waiting, was approved.

The remainder of the World Series roster, if it came to that, featured the regular-season regulars. No one else was eliminated due to injury. The approved roster had:

| Pitchers | Infielders | Outfielders | Catchers |
|---|---|---|---|
| Bob Feller (19–15) | Lou Boudreau (.355) | Dale Mitchell (.336) | Jim Hegan (.248) |
| Bob Lemon (20–14) | Eddie Robinson (.254) | Larry Doby (.301) | Joe Tipton (.289) |
| Gene Bearden (20–7) | Joe Gordon (.280) | Thurman Tucker (.260) | |
| Satchel Paige (6–1) | Ken Keltner (.297) | Allie Clark (.310) | |
| Sam Zoldak (9–6) | John Berardino (.190) | Bob Kennedy (.301) | |
| Russ Christopher (3–2) | Ray Boone (.400) | Hal Peck (.286) | |
| Steve Gromek (9–3) | Walt Judnich (.257) | | |
| Ed Klieman (3–2) | | | |
| Bob Muncrief (5–4) | | | |

Some had been hurt earlier in the season, but everyone was healthy in September. Boone, like Rosen, had been called up later in the summer and had not seen much action. Rosen was surprised to be included on the list and was very pleased that he might have a chance to play in the World Series even before having a full rookie year.

"Just heard about it a few minutes ago," Rosen said after the Indians romp over the White Sox, "and still can hardly believe it's true."[6]

Ticket sales were exploding, the roster was set, and everybody in northeast Ohio was delirious. Now all the Indians had to do was win the darned pennant to make their first World Series in three decades a reality.

Then Cleveland went out and lost the opener of a two-game set to the Detroit Tigers, 5–3. Lemon got the start and pitched fairly well, but he surrendered four runs, three of them earned in eight and one-third innings while looking exhausted. He took the loss, dropping his record to 20–14, and Christopher and Zoldak pitched in relief. This time Cleveland could not handle Virgil Trucks, who was probably getting tired of being pushed around by the Indians. Mitchell, Doby, and Boudreau managed two hits apiece, but it wasn't enough to hold off the Tigers.

"This was what the pessimist meant when he said, 'Don't count your World Series tickets until the pennant is hatched,'" was the lead sentence in the lead story in the *Cleveland Plain Dealer* after the Indians lost that one to Detroit.[7]

On September 30, the Red Sox used a five-run fifth inning and 15 hits to top Washington, 7–3, for Mel Parnell's 15th victory. Boston's offense was keyed by three hits each stroked by Dom DiMaggio and Johnny Pesky while Ted Williams, Stan Spence, and Birdie Tebbitts all had two apiece. The Yankees out-lasted the Athletics, 9–7, in a slugfest with Bobby Brown, Yogi Berra, and Charlie Silvera providing the fireworks.

The regular season was scheduled to run into October for its final weekend, and while the Boston Braves prepared to host Game 1 of the 1948 World Series, they had no idea who would show up to occupy the American League dugout.

After the loss to the Tigers, the Indians' record was 95–57, The Yankees were 94–58, and the Red Sox were 94–58. The best case scenario for the Indians was to beat Detroit two straight. Then it would not matter what was happening at Fenway Park between the Red Sox and Yankees. Two straight wins and Cleveland owned the pennant. But if Boston or New York won two straight and the Indians lost, there would be a two-way tie. If the Indians lost both games and teams at Fenway split there would be a three-way tie for first place. That would be something new and different. In the years since the AL was founded in 1901, there had not been a tie for the American League pennant, never mind a three-way tie.

On Saturday, October 2, the Indians and Tigers met again. Cleveland started Bearden, going after his 19th win. Detroit started Lou Kretlow, who was going after his third. The Tigers must not have understood that 1948 was a year of destiny for Bearden. The game was scoreless until the bottom of the fourth inning when the Indians erupted for five runs on their way to a crucial 8–0 victory. Amazingly, Bearden had done it again, throwing an eight-hit shutout with incredible pressure on him.

Nobody came up bigger in the batting order than Larry Doby, who smashed four hits and scored two runs. Joe Gordon and Eddie Robinson contributed two hits each, but once the Indians broke out halfway through the game, the contest was no longer close. It was a huge win for the Indians with one day left in the season. They could do no worse than tie for the pennant and with a day remaining could grab the flag outright.

In Boston, the Red Sox ruined the Yankees' day, winning 5–1. Ted Williams went 2-for-2 with two runs scored and two RBI. On the mound, Jack Kramer handcuffed the feared Yankees batting order and out-pitched Tommy Byrne. New York mustered only five hits. For once the American League pennant was not going to hang in Yankee Stadium. One could almost hear the rest of the league singing, "Ding dong the witch is dead."

Cleveland controlled its own fate. By beating the Tigers, the Indians could clinch their first pennant in twenty-eight years. Bob Feller, chasing his 20th victory, was going to get the ball from Lou Boudreau. There was no more appropriate person than Feller to represent Cleveland with the pennant on the line. The Tigers were leaning on Hal Newhouser, with 20 wins already in the bank, to prevent Feller from achieving his goal.

This day, Rapid Robert did not have his good stuff. The Tigers battered him for five hits and four runs in two and one-third innings before he was lifted and the Indians ran out the game with the help of five additional pitchers. Newhouser was in command, allowing just five hits, and Detroit won, 7–1, gathering 15 hits.

Feller suffered through a demoralizing day, never pitching to his potential. Cleveland Stadium held 74,181 fans watching gloomily as the Indians were barely in the contest.

"On the last day of the season, October 3, Lou gave me a chance to win the pennant for my team," Feller said. "A win over Detroit at home and we'd be the American League Champions, the team with a chance to beat the other Boston team, the Braves, in the World Series. We didn't want an all-Boston Series. But it was the kind of day that pitchers dread, and their managers, too. I had nothing when the game started and nothing when I left it two and a third innings later. I gave up five hits and three walks, didn't strike out a man, and was unable to do what I wanted to do most—win the pennant for my team.

"I was completing my tenth season as an Indian and had won 175 games for them, but I lost the one I wanted most."[8]

In Boston, the Yankees couldn't win it, but if the Red Sox did, they would tie the Indians. Red Sox manager Joe McCarthy turned to Jack Kramer for the start and New York started Bob Porterfield. Neither was particularly sharp on a day when there were 26 hits at Fenway Park. Most of them belonged to the Red Sox, though, and so did the majority of the runs. Boston won, 10–5, and by finishing with four straight triumphs the Red Sox gained a share of first place.

It was 1946 before Major League Baseball witnessed its first pennant tie in either league. That year the Brooklyn Dodgers and St. Louis Cardinals each finished the regular season with 96–58 records. That was the only precedent, but during that time period the leagues operated more or less independently. The Dodgers-Cardinals playoff called for a best-two-out-of-three series. However, when the Indians and Red Sox tied in the AL, it was decided that a one-game playoff would suffice. In both instances the players' statistics counted as part of their regular-season records. St. Louis won its playoff in two straight games.

Odds-makers quickly established the Red Sox as 6/5 favorites to win the playoff game and set up an all-Boston World Series with the Braves. The Indians packed for a long stay, counting on the win over the Red Sox to propel them into a Series against the Braves that would begin in Boston.

What was completely unknown was who the Indians would send to the mound for one of the biggest games in team history. The main throwers, Feller, Lemon, and Bearden, had all taken their turn within the last few days. Never mind a four-day rest or a three-day rest. Which one of the trio gave Cleveland the best chance to win even if his arm was a little bit sore and tired?

That call was going to be up to player-manager Lou Boudreau to make. Boudreau dropped no hints about his choice after the loss to Detroit when the reality of another game against Boston reared up.

"No one's going to know the pitcher until he walks out to take his warm-up pitches," Boudreau said.[9]

For sure Boudreau didn't mind clouding the issue for the Red Sox. But he was also probably in the dark until he consulted with the hurlers themselves to hear how they were feeling. Heck, given the iffiness of their status, perhaps Boudreau wouldn't know who was going to pitch for his club the next day until someone volunteered.

It was a one-game season, Cleveland against Boston. Definitely nail-biting time if you were a fan of either team. Indians fans had been waiting twenty-eight years for a pennant and a World Series title. Boston fans just enjoyed a pennant in 1946, but they hadn't toasted a world champion in thirty years.

Chapter Eighteen notes on page 295.

# 19

## ONE FOR ALL THE MARBLES

**O**NE THING ABOUT the Indians playing the Red Sox in a winner-take-all game: Lou Boudreau was the man who invented the Ted Williams shift.

Anyone who was playing against the Boston Red Sox between 1939 and 1960 needed to be conscious of Williams' spot in the batting order. For all the firepower in the lineup, no one was more feared among Boston players than the "Splendid Splinter." Williams was the scourge of the American League. He not only was the last man to hit .400 with his .406 average of 1941, he hit for power (521 lifetime homers) and may have had the best eyesight in the history of the sport. Williams had such a discerning eye for where the ball was headed after the pitch left the thrower's hand that he could pick up the stitches rotating. Mr. Williams' 20/10 vision was one reason he almost never swung at a ball outside of the strike zone and ended up with more than 2,000 walks in his career.

A couple of years earlier, Boudreau (like most of the AL) wearied of Williams bashing in the brains of his club and invented a defense that more resembled a basketball team's zone than a traditional baseball placement of players throughout the field. Williams was notorious for hitting the ball to right field. When he hit the ball out of the park, well, there was nothing you could do about that. If it was going to fly, it was going to fly.

But Boudreau theorized that some of Williams' hard-hit grounders past first or second base might be stopped by an additional fielder shifted over to the right side of the infield, and that some of his scorching line drives might be hit right at fielders rather than between them if that side of the field was more densely populated with fielders.

Already managing the Indians in 1946, Boudreau came up with a plan to take some of the offensive sting out of Williams' bat. The first-baseman hugged the right field foul line; the right-fielder played a little closer to the line; the second baseman was jerked out of the infield altogether and positioned behind the first-baseman as a second right fielder; the shortstop moved into the slot where the second baseman usually played; the third-baseman moved all of the way over behind second base and the center fielder played a shallow right-center; the left fielder was the only defensive man on the left side of the field and he was drawn in to the equivalent of a very deep shortstop position; the right side of the infield was as crowded as a New York subway station at rush hour.

This was the scheme that Boudreau introduced on July 14, 1946. He drew this plan up on a blackboard in the clubhouse between games of a doubleheader. Whether Boudreau knew it or not, other teams in the 1920s had tried to defense hitter Cy Williams of the Chicago Cubs in the same general fashion. Later, in 1946, St. Louis manager Eddie Dyer employed the

Williams shift in the World Series against Boston, but rather than being a strong believer in its potential effectiveness, he was hoping more that it would play with Williams' mind.

Recalling what inspired him to design the new defense for Ted Williams, Boudreau explained that he had had a great game, going 5-for-5 with four doubles and a home run, but that Cleveland lost the opening game of the doubleheader because Williams went 4-for-5 with three home runs. Boston won, 11–10.

"My French blood was all stirred up," Boudreau said. "So was my French vocabulary. I was angry, upset, and determined to stop Williams. "I held a meeting between games and told my players, 'Any time Williams comes up with the bases empty and you hear me yell, "Yo!" this is what I want you to do, And I diagrammed the shift on a chalkboard."[1]

The players stared at Boudreau agape at the creative positioning and didn't react well at first.

"Most of them laughed because they thought I was kidding," Boudreau said. "I assured them I wasn't. One of them said, 'Hell, Lou, he'll just bunt.' I said, 'Fine. I hope he does.' And I did." Whoever made that locker room comment didn't know Williams. Williams was not likely to bunt.[2]

His second time up, the circumstances Boudreau outlined was in place, so he yelled, "Yo!", and the shift was on. As everyone scurried around the field, Williams watched the shenanigans, stepped out of the batter's box, and talked to umpire Bill Summers. "What the hell is going on out there? They can't do that." Summers said that they could do that if they wanted. Williams did not bunt. The ump said Williams cursed and laughed. Then Williams grounded out to Boudreau playing where the second baseman usually was. Later in the game when the shift was on again and the bases empty, Williams walked. After the game when asked about the crazy fielding lineup, Williams told sportswriters that if every team started playing him that way he would start batting right-handed. Boudreau's response? That "would have been fine with me."[3]

Boudreau was banking that Williams, a man of rigid habit and temperament, would be unable—or unwilling—to adjust his hitting to take advantage of the wide-open spaces on the left side. He was also hoping that his pride would play a role in his belief he could beat the shift.

The fact that Boston and Cleveland would meet in the first American League playoff meant that inevitably the Indians must contain Williams and either the shift would be employed or the topic would be fodder for sportswriters' discussion.

By 1948, the "Ted Williams Shift" had not become an epidemic and it did not seem to have dented Williams' career very much, either. That season, Williams won the fourth of his six AL batting titles with a .369 average. He smacked 25 home runs, drove in 127 runs, and walked 126 times. Whatever the other teams were doing, it was not keeping him off the bases.

Still, Boudreau believed in it, even though he modified the location of his defensive players at times. "As long as Williams was stubborn enough to challenge it, which he did most of the time, the shift helped us," Boudreau said. "Our charts showed that we were 37 percent more successful when we used the shift against Williams than when we didn't."[4] And that was before Bill James started his numbers tinkering.

If Williams had bunted for a hit on his first time or two facing the shift, creating singles for himself, there is a chance the shift would have been abandoned immediately. He also was known to slam line drives off the Green Monster in Fenway Park, the great and tall wall in left field. However, the shift could not be employed with men on base, especially on second, because the runner would steal third without opposition and Williams, who did have great bat control, probably would have adjusted his swing to drive the runner in.

"I didn't hit to left field," Williams said, "but I hit to left-center more than most people thought. The defense, even though they moved it around, they still covered left center a little bit. But the big area for me was from second to first. The second baseman out on the grass, he was the culprit."[5]

Ted Williams' bat versus Lou Boudreau's brain was to be one storyline in the extraordinarily important game to both franchises.

The other main issue was who was going to pitch. The choice, because the teams had played their hearts out just to reach the playoff game through the weekend, was not an easy one. The best pitchers for each club were tired. The crucial pick by the manager on who to send to the mound might well determine the outcome of the season. Boudreau had already told Cleveland sportswriters he didn't know who he would start. The question for Boston was just about as murky.

There were headlines in the Cleveland newspapers keeping fans apprised of the World Series–ticket sweepstakes, basically concluding that those who applied had a one-in-eight chance of obtaining ducats for the big games—if they ever took place.

After Cleveland finished in a tie with Boston, that ended the Indians home season and produced a final tabulation on a new baseball attendance record for the regular season. Putting a smile on owner Bill Veeck's face was the turnstile count of 2,620,627.

As the Indians caught a train from Union Terminal to Boston, they got word that the Red Sox odds had increased to 7.5/5 favorites to capture the flag.

After the Indians gained their tie, coach Bill McKechnie expressed supreme optimism about the outcome of the game against Boston. His wife informed him that she wanted to go to the World Series and he told her to pack. "Get your things together," he said. "You're going to Boston tonight and you aren't coming back till Friday."[6]

Even though Boudreau had declined to name his starting pitcher and probably didn't even know yet, the Cleveland sportswriters tried angle after angle to get him to talk and tell them whose arm the season rested on.

"Tell you what I'll do," Boudreau said. "I'll give the man who guesses my starting pitcher two tickets to the World Series."[7] Boudreau hinted that he might make changes in his starting lineup, too, but didn't say who or what.

In Boston, manager Joe McCarthy was being peppered with the same question by his city's beat men. Who was going to pitch for the Sox? McCarthy said that he was probably going to start either southpaw Mel Parnell or Ellis Kinder. Parnell was in his first full season and finished 15–8 as he was maturing into one of the best left-handers in team history. Righty Kinder was thirty-three, had been around a few more blocks than Parnell, and carried a 10–7 record.

When the Indians arrived in Boston, those who picked up a copy of the *Boston Globe* were greeted by a clever headline describing their loss to the Tigers on Sunday, the day before. It read "The Prince And The Poppers." That referred to Detroit pitcher Hal Newhouser, whose nickname was "The Prince."

The poppers referred to the Indians' weak hitting. A Cleveland reporter out and about on the streets leading up to the game said that nobody in Boston was talking about anything except the big game. He noted that the locals were going around saying, "This is the kill." It was clear the fans expected the Red Sox to win.[8]

Boudreau really did know who he was going to start, but wanted to keep it secret. Before the Indians left for Boston, the manager called a team meeting to discuss the next day's starting pitcher.

"I told the players that because it meant as much to them as it did to me, I wanted everybody to have some input as to which pitcher we should start," Boudreau said later. "Nobody volunteered, so I said my choice was Gene Bearden. There were a few oohs and aahs, but that's all. I acknowledged that Bearden had pitched the day before and would be working with only two days' rest, but that he was the best we had at that time, better than Feller, better than Lemon, and better than Steve Gromek." What stuck in Boudreau's mind was that Bearden was a knuckleball pitcher and thus his arm was less likely to be tired from recent work than the other hurlers'. He said that Johnny Berardino was the only one to question the choice of Bearden, saying, "You can't pitch a left-hander in Fenway Park."[9]

While there was no real dissension, talk continued for about ten minutes. Then Joe Gordon took command with the final statement. "Lou," he said, "we went along with your choice for 154 games and finished in a tie. There's not a man in this room, who two weeks ago, wouldn't have settled for a tie. I'm sure we can go along with you for another game."[10]

The players did keep the secret, even as reporters tried to pry information from them on the train ride east. It was a strong show of faith in a rookie pitcher who had been an unknown six months earlier, but no one complained about Boudreau's analysis either. At that point in the season Bearden was the staff ace, out-pitching even future Hall of Famers, the two Bobs, Lemon and Feller. Boudreau later said that he wanted to keep Bearden out of the limelight because he didn't want him to be wearied by the constant demand for interviews if it was known he was going to be the starter and Bearden needed all of the slumber he could get anyway.

"I didn't want him to do anything but rest," Boudreau said, "and I didn't want him to worry. I should have known him better. He could have posed all night for photographers and still won today. He's got what it takes."[11]

For the playoff, Boudreau posted a starting lineup that had Bearden pitching, Jim Hegan catching, Allie Clark, not Eddie Robinson, at first (though he inserted Robinson later), Joe Gordon at second, himself at short, Ken Keltner at third, Dale Mitchell in left, Larry Doby in center, and Bob Kennedy in right.

Boston's starting lineup included Birdie Tebbetts catching, Billy Goodman at first, Bobby Doerr at second, Vern Stephens at short, Johnny Pesky at third, Ted Williams in left, Dom DiMaggio in center, and Stan Spence in right. The shocker was the man on the mound. It was not Parnell or Kinder, nor 18-game winner Jack Kramer or 16-game winner Joe Dobson. McCarthy started righty Denny Galehouse, who was 8–8 on the season. Among those who believed the Red Sox were cursed when they traded Babe Ruth to the New York Yankees, and painfully review all of the mistakes and near-misses of the franchise in pennant races and playoffs before the club won a Series in 2004, this was one of those inexplicable decisions that haunted them.

Galehouse won a World Series game for the St. Louis Browns in 1944, but was nearing the end of his career—the final decision of his playing days was this playoff game versus Cleveland. As 33,957 fans watched in dismay in Fenway Park, the Indians slowly and methodically dismantled Galehouse's offerings.

What began as a close game—for three innings—was broken open by Cleveland in the fourth inning with four runs. As Bearden mowed down the tough hitters in the Boston lineup, Galehouse seemed more and more vulnerable and was gone before the end of the fourth to be relieved by Kinder. Unfortunately for Kinder and the Sox, he was also treated rudely by the Indian bats. In a remarkable showing on two days rest, Bearden won his 20th game of the season. Although Lemon and Feller both warmed up in case of emergency, Bearden pitched a complete game, yielded just five hits and presided over an 8–3 win.

Boudreau was as magnificent with the bat that day as Bearden was on the mound. Boudreau went 4-for-4, drove in two runs, and scored three. Keltner added three hits and drove in three. The Indians pummeled Boston pitching for 13 hits to earn their place in the World Series. Boudreau started the key four-run rally with a single to right. Gordon hit a hard grounder to left past Pesky. Keltner followed with a three-run homer into the screen above the Green Monster in left field.

When Bearden recorded the final out in the late afternoon, his teammates mobbed him and carried him off the Fenway field on their shoulders, a fitting tribute to a man who won the most important games of the season at the very end of it to become the difference-maker between an almost-season and a pennant-winning one. In fact, their celebration was so energetic the Indians tore some of Bearden's clothes off his body. Final standings: First place, Cleveland Indians, 97–58; Second place, Boston Red Sox, 96–59.

The Indians won their pennant in Boston, but because it was a playoff game, they had little time to savor it. Not only did they not have time to return to Cleveland for any kind of celebration with their fans, they had to stay right where they were in the city of the vanquished opponent to get ready to play the other team from Boston: the Braves. Back in Cleveland, however, the fans went wild, some shouting in the streets, "The Indians won the pennant!" Ohio Governor Thomas J. Herbert sent a congratulatory telegram to Bill Veeck. People partied in the streets with strangers in downtown Cleveland.

Even though there was no team on hand for a parade, office workers threw open their windows and floated ticker tape into the streets as if an official celebration had been organized. A local Congressman, George Bender, was walking through the street chiming a bell to honor the Indians, a bell he had used to gain attention at a Republican National Convention. An opposition party member commented that Bender could probably be convinced "to introduce legislation making Lou Boudreau secretary of state."[12] He was probably right—and Boudreau would probably have been chosen without difficulty.

The biggest party may have taken place in the Indians clubhouse. Long-time trainer Lefty Weisman had beer poured over his head and he began crying because he said he had been waiting "a long time for this. I've been waiting twenty-seven years." Coach Bill McKechnie, a championship manager, was told that it looked as if he had never had such an experience. "It never gets old son," he said. "It never gets old." Feller exulted over Bearden's efforts and thinking back to how he had lost the last regular-season game only a day earlier said, "That Bearden. What a man! He got me off the hook again, didn't he?"[13]

Beating Boston was one of the greatest victories in Cleveland Indians history and the sweet triumph was good for at least a night's worth of celebrating before the team turned to the next task. Bearden was feted and toasted. It was not for almost twenty years that a hidden story about the win came to light, revealed by Boudreau. In 1967, Boudreau let out a behind-the-scenes tale of something that occurred on the bench during the contest.

"During the early innings of the game, the most nervous man on our bench was trainer Harold [Lefty] Weisman," Boudreau said in Chicago during his latter days as a broadcaster. "He kept walking up and down the long dugout in Fenway Park carrying his little black bag—standard equipment for all trainers. Finally, it got so bad I yelled to him, 'Take a seat and let everybody concentrate on the game. You're making me as nervous as you are.' Whenever Lefty did sit down it was always next to Bearden, but I never paid any attention to that."[14]

After the game, Weisman went up to Boudreau and apologized to him for being a dugout distraction. He startled Boudreau by telling him the real reason he was going back and forth and then sitting with Bearden during the home half of the innings when Boston was at bat.

"'I was slipping Gene brandy between innings and I didn't want you and the players to catch on to what I was doing,'" Weisman said. "'He was nervous and I figured the brandy was the best possible tonic for his nerves. I only did it for the good of the team. I hope you aren't too upset.'" Weisman had a secret compartment in his doctor bag where he hid the brandy.

Boudreau kept quiet about the incident for nineteen years and said he wasn't really sure how he would have responded if he had known what was going on when it was going on. "I've known countless cases of players drinking off the field," he said, "but this is the first time I ever knew of a player drinking on the bench during the game—and it was one of the most important games of my life. Maybe it's best I didn't learn about the situation until it was all over. Bearden pitched one of the greatest games of his career."[15]

The incident was a better kept secret than who was going to pitch that day—and one that was kept under wraps far longer.

Chapter Nineteen notes on page 296.

# 20

# THE WORLD SERIES AT LAST

**T**HE BOSTON BRAVES had clinched the National League pennant with a week to go in the regular season and watched with studied interest as the Indians and Red Sox fought it out for the American League pennant. Many baseball people were rooting for an all-Boston series. It seemed as if it would not only be a good one, but add a certain flavor if two teams from the same city battled it out for the world championship.

Boston's record was 91–62 and the Braves finished 6.5 games ahead of the St. Louis Cardinals under manager Billy Southworth, who had led the Cardinals to considerable glory earlier in the 1940s. Southworth, a .297-hitting outfielder as a player, led St. Louis to three pennants and two World Series titles in the first half of the 1940s as a manager. When he joined the Braves, his guidance produced the team's first pennant since 1914.

Southworth was appointed leader of the Braves in 1946 and knew he had a good team in spring training of 1948. Known as "Billy The Kid," Southworth raved about his top two pitchers, Warren Spahn and Johnny Sain. He was right about their talents, but the Braves seemed otherwise chronically short on starters. The phrase "Spahn and Sain and Pray for Rain," was coined to describe the Boston rotation.

"We had quite a climb to face," Southworth said of the Braves' steady improvement since 1946. "It was a jump we couldn't make in one or two years. But we have been moving up. I can promise you you'll have a much better ball club in 1948 than we had in 1947. I know we'll be better. And maybe a lot better with just a little luck."[1]

Hesitant to creep too far out on a limb, Southworth couched his optimism in carefully chosen words. But the Braves got their luck and were a lot better.

Sain, later regarded as perhaps the best pitching coach of all time, led the staff with a 24–15 record. Southpaw Spahn had an off-year for him with a 15–12 record, but Spahn was in the early stages of a career that would make him the winningest left-hander of all time with 363 victories. Newcomer Bill Voiselle was 13–13 and blossoming Vern Bickford went 11–5.

Just a few years later the Braves would be blessed with some of the greatest sluggers the game had ever known: Hank Aaron and Eddie Mathews, complemented by Joe Adcock. But none of them had arrived on the scene and these Braves had to scrap harder for runs. Third baseman Bob Elliott, with 23 homers and 100 RBI, was their biggest offensive gun. Right fielder Tommy Holmes batted .323, but with only six homers. Left fielder Jeff Heath bashed 20 home runs and batted .319, but the team was staggered when he incurred a broken leg near the end of the season that caused him to miss the Series.

Since the American League season ended with a one-game playoff, the build-up time for the Series was measured in hours, not days. Boudreau had announced he was dedicating the playoff game to the hurting Don Black and word came to Boston that Black had been able to listen to the contest on the radio. He even stood up for the first time since suffering the cerebral hemorrhage on September 13.

"Tell the boys to keep slugging," Black said from his hospital room. "Tell 'em I'm rooting for them, too. Lord, I'd love to be in there pitching."[2]

After beating the Red Sox, the Indians had a party at the Kenmore Hotel and Boudreau toasted Black. Actually, even before that shindig, the all-for-one and one-for-all theme was on display. When the Indians made the last out against the Red Sox, Bill Veeck climbed out of the box seat on the third-base side where he had watched the contest and ran across the diamond to catch up with his men. Veeck, hobbled by his artificial leg, wasn't very speedy. But he caught up to the team as it entered the tunnel to the clubhouse.

Inside the locker room Veeck and Boudreau embraced, a sign of healing from their initial rift when Veeck bought the team in 1946 and wanted to replace Boudreau as manager. Veeck was afforded the chance to speak to the team, but for a talkative man, he was very brief.

"I have only one word to say," said Veeck, who must have meant that the count began then. "Thanks."[3]

Game 1 of the Series was scheduled for October 6 at Braves Field, seemingly minutes after the Indians clinched the pennant against the Red Sox. Sportswriters had to cram their game stories reporting on the Indians–Red Sox scrap into the same papers as their Series previews.

One thing was certain: Gene Bearden was not going to pitch the opener. Giddy from his success in the playoff, Bearden talked as if he had pitched in a zone, barely realizing he was holding Ted Williams at bay and thinking the game had one more inning to run when his teammates mobbed him on the mound.

"I'll bet I was the most surprised person in the ballpark," Bearden said. "I didn't even know what inning it was."[4] Talk about becoming yesterday's news in a hurry: Good job, Gene, now get out of the way, we've got a World Series to play.

Boudreau chose Feller to start the opener against Sain. Feller had been the face of the franchise since his ascension to the majors in 1936 and had been waiting a dozen years for the opportunity to pitch in the World Series. Today was his day. Feller built up a good sweat after the victory over the Red Sox and pronounced himself ready for the Braves.

"The chance has been a long time coming," Feller said. "I certainly don't want to muff it now. I was afraid the damage had been done Sunday by Detroit. You don't always get a second opportunity."[5]

Boudreau, who had batted .355 during the regular season, was coming through in the clutch in the Indians' biggest games at the end of the season, in the playoff against the Red Sox, and in the World Series. Before the first Series game, though, Boudreau was almost laid out flat by a severe cold. He had nearly lost his voice, which probably wouldn't have bothered him much if that situation got him out of talking to the sportswriters.

Sain had just completed his third straight 20-win campaign for Boston—a total of 65 victories—and in those decisions he had completed 60 of the starts. He was rarely in need of relief and he usually sounded quite sane when he spoke, as in someone who talked common sense. Certainly he did not seem edgy on the eve of the Series.

"If you were pitching to a machine you could work until you brought every type of pitch to perfection," Sain said. "But batters aren't machines. You fool a man with a certain pitch one day and the next he belts it out of the park. It's just another ball game. I'll go to bed around midnight. That's what I usually do. No point in changing my habits for the World Series."[6]

The 40,135 fans that filled Braves Field saw a phenomenal pitching duel between Sain and Feller. Feller felt he needed redemption because of his loss to the Tigers on the last day of the regular season. Ordinarily, the job he did against the Braves would have been good enough, but it wasn't an average pitching day. Feller permitted just two hits, one to Holmes, and one to Boston left fielder Marv Rickert, a lesser-known four-year veteran. But the Braves pushed across one run in the eighth inning and defeated Cleveland, 1–0.

"When the game started I was as ready as I've ever been in my life," Feller said. "This was what all of us wanted, what we had worked for, and what I had been dreaming about since I was a boy on the farm in Van Meter. I couldn't blow this chance. Missing out on a chance to win in the World Series isn't like messing something up during the season. There's always a next season, but you never know if there's another World Series in your future. You have to go out and do the job right now."[7]

The fact was that Feller did rise to the occasion, did pitch great ball, and was doing his job. He retired the first 11 Braves before issuing a walk and gave up his first hit in the fifth inning. Then Feller set down the next nine hitters in order.

"By the time the Braves came up in the bottom half of the eighth inning, Sain and I had posted 15 zeroes on the scoreboard at Braves Field," Feller said. "Then I did exactly what a pitcher is not supposed to do in that situation. I walked the first hitter in the inning."[8]

Boston pinch-ran Phil Masi for Bill Salkeld, the recipient of the walk, and Mike McCormick bunted him to second with a sacrifice. Boudreau went to the mound and told Feller to intentionally walk Eddie Stanky. Feller didn't want to do it, believing he could get the hustling player out. But Boudreau insisted, thinking that Sain, the next batter up, could be induced to hit into a double play. Sain flew out to right instead. With Tommy Holmes up, Boudreau called for a pickoff attempt of Masi at second, a play the Indians had worked on for a long time.

Feller whirled and threw to Boudreau, who slapped the tag on Masi. Out, for sure, the Indians felt. Safe, called the umpire.

"We caught Masi napping," Feller said. "Unfortunately, we caught the umpire, Bill Stewart of the National League, doing the same thing. Lou put the tag on Masi as he slid back into the bag. Lou tagged Masi out by two feet."[9] Outraged by the call, Feller looked on helplessly as Holmes swatted the ball down the left field line to bring Masi home with the game's only run.

The Masi call lingered and bothered the Indians. They knew they were right and the ump was wrong. *Cleveland Press* beat writer Frank Gibbons said the view from the press box was conclusive that Masi was out. He wrote that "Masi was not only out, but that he might as well have been out to lunch." His description, and the Indians' comments, made it seem as if Masi had been fooled as thoroughly by the pickoff as the audience watching a magic show. "We aren't complaining," said Boudreau, who of course was, "but two men were napping on that play, Masi and Stewart."[10]

Feller really couldn't have pitched much better. He threw just 85 pitches in the complete game and Holmes described what was always viewed as Feller's second-best pitch as out of this world. "Bob Feller showed me the greatest curve ball I have ever seen since I started playing baseball," Holmes said. "We had heard a lot of Feller and his great fastball. We had been told he was the fastest man in the majors. But he surprised us. He had his curve along with great deception."[11]

Sain was simply better that day, throwing a four-hit shutout with six strikeouts and no walks. Feller walked three. Four different players collected singles for the Indians, but Sain snuffed out any hint of a rally. For Cleveland it was like striking a wet match against a stone and being unable to light a fire.

The controversy over the Masi play at second aside, Sain was masterful and the Indians might not have scored upon him if he had kept throwing into the 14th inning.

"I'll never forget the brilliant pitching as offered by our Johnny Sain," said manager Billy Southworth. "Sain knew what he was in for when facing Bob Feller. So he went all out as he had previously this season on so many occasions . . . Cleveland saw some great pitching. I am confident now that the Braves have the kind of pitching that will be able to cope with the power possessed by the American Leaguers."[12]

Sain, better than anyone else, realized how hard he had to work to best Feller that day. In the clubhouse after the game photographers begged him to smile, but he didn't feel like grinning, more like recuperating from the tension.

"I told the photographers, if a couple of breaks had gone the other way you guys would be in the other locker room taking pictures of Bobby Feller," Sain said. "The game was too close to smile. It was just the greatest thrill of my life beating Bob Feller and the Cleveland Indians, 1–0 in the opening game of the 1948 World Series. But ball players can't get as excited as I was, they'd never be able to get their work done. For the fans, OK, but not the ball players. It was a tremendous game, really close. And it was important. Public interest made this a big game, the biggest game I've ever pitched in."[13]

There was not much time to worry about what happened because Game 2 was scheduled for the next day at Braves Field. Cleveland went with Bob Lemon as the starter and the Braves, as was predictable, sent Warren Spahn to the hill. Manager Southworth said Spahn was probably the only guy still in the majors he believed could win 30 games in a season. Spahn, who won 20 or more games in a season thirteen times, was not at his best that year and that carried over to the World Series.

Spahn was the best pitcher of his era, succeeding Feller and leading into Sandy Koufax and Juan Marichal. He grew up in Buffalo, spent about ten seconds in the majors in 1942, and then did not play again in the majors until 1946, his ball playing interrupted by World War II service. He fought at the Battle of the Bulge and was a war hero, earning a Purple Heart, but when he got his chance as he ripened into his late 20s, Spahn became a baseball hero, too. He had a notably high leg kick, great control, and was an innings eater. Spahn became a 17-time All-Star.

However, even the best of pitchers have days when the curve doesn't curve and things go haywire. The Indians jumped on Spahn in this game, knocking him out of the box in the fifth inning after allowing six hits and three runs. Meanwhile, Lemon was at his sharpest. He surrendered just one run—an unearned one—and threw a complete game for Cleveland's 4–1 victory that knotted the Series. The Braves took a one-run lead in the first, but errors by Alvin Dark (two) and Bob Elliott complicated Spahn's outing as the Indians took the lead in the fourth inning.

Lou Boudreau and Larry Doby contributed two hits each for the Indians while the Braves matched the Cleveland total with eight, including two each by McCormick and first baseman Earl Torgeson.

Holmes, who had knocked in the winning run in the first game, said it was his fault that the Braves didn't beat Lemon as well as Feller in the second game.

"We have nobody but ourselves to name for losing the second game of the World Series," Holmes said. "We had our chance in the first four innings to knock Bob Lemon out of the game, but we couldn't hit in the pinches. Three times I had a chance to possibly send Lemon to the showers, but each time he got me on a sinker ball. I left four men stranded on the bases when a hit would have meant runs."[14]

Two games into the Series and Alvin Dark had two errors at short and Bob Elliott had three at third and they were complaining about the grooming of their home park's infield. Football games had been played on the field in recent weeks and left divots and other problems. Elliott showed off bruises on his arm and leg where bad bounces got him.

"It's spongy as a powder puff along the bases and the holes," Elliott said.[15]

The groundskeepers would have some time to work on that lumpy field because the World Series was shifting to Cleveland for Game 3—the first Series game in the city on the shore of Lake Erie in twenty-eight years. Indians fans had been in a tizzy since the moment the team clinched the pennant by beating the Red Sox. Now, finally, the big-game action was coming back to them at Cleveland Stadium. Boudreau had been in an Indians uniform for years, but this was the first time he was able to represent Cleveland in a World Series. The town let the players know how it felt about them.

"It seemed the entire city was going wild over us," Boudreau said.[16]

That's exactly what the city was doing. Cleveland was in a frenzy over its Indians.

Chapter Twenty notes on pages 296–297.

# 21

## THE BRIGHT LIGHTS IN CLEVELAND

**N**OW THAT THE circus had shifted to Cleveland, the city was responding in like fashion to the arrival of the Big Top and the lions and tigers and bears, oh my. Some $1 bleacher seats were going to be made available to fans and a fellow named Richard McLaughlin decided he would be first in line.

Some forty-eight hours before what was expected to be a brief sale, McLaughlin pitched a tent in front of Gate E at Cleveland Stadium to ensure that he would be a winner. He even ended up writing about his quest in a newspaper.

"Under the law of squatters' rights I guess that makes me first man in line to get the first bleacher seat," McLaughlin proclaimed. "At least, I don't see any other screwballs around here who might want to stake a prior claim. There are thousands of baseball fans lined up at the various gates to each side of my tent, all waiting for the reserved seats they ordered by mail last week. But there were only a few in line at 8 a.m. when my wife dropped me and all my paraphernalia off at Gate E, shook her head sadly as if to say 'The old man's stripped his gear,' and departed."[1]

McLaughlin set up a new home for himself, his tent measuring seven feet by nine feet. He would have a couple-days wait, but he didn't expect to be lonely. In fact, he very much expected things would liven up as the bleacher-seat sale time approached.

"It ought to be a lot of fun that night, chewing the fat with all the other characters crazy enough to give up a night's sleep at home just to see a World Series game. Just a World Series game? What'm I saying? It'll be the first one in Cleveland in twenty-eight years, won't it? The Indians are going to win, aren't they?"[2]

After the million-or-so people applied for tickets to World Series games in Cleveland, it turned out that not everybody who was granted tickets could make it. On the eve of Game 3, the Indians front office found itself holding 193 unclaimed tickets. So team workers began telephoning fans who had written in, but had not been lucky enough to receive tickets requested, and at the last minute they devoured the leftovers.

Those fortunate few were able to make late plans to attend. They were also the envy of the many that had been shut out more emphatically than the Indians themselves by the Braves in Game 1.

Concurrent with this development rumors spread through town that there had been widespread theft of tickets and that many had disappeared between the Indians' offices and the intended recipients, but the story was debunked by the team and postal authorities. There were also a number of reports of scalping. In some cases the story went, those who had scalped tickets, paying over face value, were in turn scalping them to others with deeper pockets for even more money.

Meanwhile, the Indians themselves, the object of the devotion, hadn't been seen in town since the preceding weekend when they lost the regular-season finale and headed to Boston for the American League playoff game. Their return from Boston came via special train and when they arrived at Union Terminal, the players were greeted and hailed by a large crowd. Then the team was loaded into convertible automobiles to be escorted downtown in a welcome parade.

The favorite fan of the summer, Good Old Joe Earley, was resurrected with his own newspaper commentary and disclosed that as lucky a guy as he had been in September he was out of luck in October—not owning World Series tickets.

"Well, here I am," he said, "the richest poor man in town. I have everything I need—a television set, two radios, three automobiles—BUT I HAVEN'T GOT A TICKET TO THE WORLD SERIES. Two weeks ago I was a great guy. Bill Veeck led me out to home plate. The bands were playing and all the people were hollering, 'There he is . . . Good Old Joe Earley.' So here I am today 'covering' the World Series for the *Press*, and the way it looks now, I won't even be able to get into the ballpark. You know, the worst part about this thing is that all my friends think I'm a big shot and that I can wave a magic wand and produce ducats. When I tell 'em I haven't even got any for myself, they just sneer. So it looks now that the halo is gone from the brow of Good Old Joe. It's been replaced by a dark cloud of gloom."[3]

After Feller and Lemon pitched the two games for Cleveland in Boston, there was no mystery about who would start Game 3. The well-rested Gene Bearden was the man for the Indians. Boston countered with Vern Bickford.

As game time approached, Indians fans that were still on the prowl for tickets were willing to dig deeper into their wallets. Scalpers were asking for and getting prices that hit $25 to $60 for a seat. Any of the 70,306 fans who ended up with tix got their money's worth, though. Actually, despite that announced attendance, local papers reported that there may have been more in the building. Standing room only tickets were sold before the first pitch for each Indians home game and the gate swelled and swelled beyond 80,000 on some days. As the tens of thousands of fans entered Cleveland Stadium they were serenaded by bands that owner Bill Veeck had hired for the occasion to keep the festive atmosphere lively.

It was announced that more than 500 sportswriters were accredited for the games, at a time when the World Series was indisputably the biggest sporting event in the country (with the possible exception of some heavyweight title bouts). This Series was also televised nationally, the first attempt to do so. ABC, CBS, NBC, and DuMont combined to offer coverage under the umbrella of the Mutual Broadcasting System, and Gillette, the razor company, sponsored the coverage. At the time there were about a million television sets owned in the United States, so in some cities TVs were set up in public places for fans to watch. In Boston, 100 television sets were arranged on the Boston Common and photographs were taken of fans wearing heavy coats standing and watching the screens.

Red Barber, the smooth-talking radio announcer, handled the main play-by-play responsibilities. Famed for his radio work for the Cincinnati Reds, Brooklyn Dodgers, and New York Yankees, Barber used to tell his listeners he was broadcasting from "the catbird seat." Tom Hussey of Boston and Van Patrick of Cleveland assisted Barber.

When sales commenced, Richard McLaughlin did score his bleacher tickets, but Joe Earley could not beg a ticket from any source and, while he was trying to do that, he lost out on the bleacher sale so he didn't get into the stadium for Game 3 at all. He reported that he sat on a bench in a park listening on the radio—and his radio went dead.

Inside the stadium the Indians fans booed mightily when Bill Stewart—the umpire who made the ill-fated call at second base on the attempted pickoff play—was introduced as the home-plate ump. Eventually, the shouting and harassment of Stewart grew so loud that he was given police protection while in the city. Bearden neither ran out of gas or magic in his consistently brilliant rookie year, adding to his accomplishment of a 20-game-victory regular season. The right-hander pitched a complete-game, five-hit shutout as the Indians won the contest, 2–0. Braves manager Billy Southworth was quick with the hook in Bickford's case, removing him after three and a third innings when he permitted five hits and two runs, with one being unearned.

Although Bickford walked five, he wasn't hit all over the lot. The Indians scored one run in the third and one in the fifth and that was it. Bickford was relieved by Bill Voiselle, who threw three and two-thirds innings of one-hit shutout ball. Voiselle, who hailed from Ninety-Six, South Carolina, wore 96 on his uniform.

Lou Boudreau had compiled an extraordinary year as a player and manager of the Indians and was never held in higher esteem. A local realtor took out a newspaper ad to thank Boudreau for the wonderful season—but he also made sure to put in a plug for his product, too, incorporating houses for sale into the ad. Rather amazingly, Bearden also accounted for two of the Indians' hits besides controlling the opposition. Bearden, his knuckleball, and his bat loomed over all. It was early yet in the Series with Cleveland up 2–1, but within days Boudreau was calling the world championship round "Bearden's Series."[4]

If Bearden was rested before he began, even with the tension of the situation, he barely had time to burn up too many calories. The time of his shutout was one hour and thirty-six minutes. That's a fast game in any era. Bearden at no time seemed to have jitters—by that point in the season he probably had lived through enough challenges to be unfazed by anything. Bearden was so sure of himself that he even threw the knuckler on 3–2 counts as an out pitch.

The Braves' Tommy Holmes said that Bearden's knuckleball "was the most effective such pitch I've swung at. Bearden also showed us a good slider, and his pitching motion was a little tricky."[5]

By this point in the season, too, Bearden not only believed his arm capable of performing any feats, but his teammates did as well. After winning Game 3 to give the Indians the Series lead, he predicted that the his Tribe would win the remaining games in Cleveland and not have to be bothered with a return trip to Boston. Aware that Bob Lemon and Bob Feller were waiting their turns in the rotation, Bearden pretty much proclaimed his work finished for 1948.

"Nope, don't think I'll have to pitch again," he said. "That's right, don't think we'll be back in Boston either. Don't get me wrong, though. I'll be ready to go tomorrow if Lou needs me. I'm not tired now. You don't get tired if you're in shape."[6]

Boudreau said the next day's contest would be the important one—a chance to go up 3–1 in the Series. After the first three games his pitchers were not only throwing well, but none of them had made an error and outfielder Larry Doby was leading the club with a .363 average. Doby had improved mightily since the year before.

For Game 4, Boudreau gave the nod to Steve Gromek, who had been a hot pitcher of late. Gromek finished the regular season with a 9–3 record and a 2.84 earned run average. Boston countered with Johnny Sain again. This time attendance was announced at 81,897, a new mark. So many people were in the ballpark there was hardly anyone left in the vicinity to watch on TV or listen to the radio.

Gromek was twenty-eight in 1948. He had lost favor in 1947 when he finished just 3–5 primarily because of a knee problem, but was a 19-game-winner in 1945. He regained his old stuff in 1948 and ended up as the fourth man in the Indians rotation behind Feller, Lemon, and Bearden, who each won at least 19. After Boudreau anointed Gromek to hurl the fourth game he was asked who might pitch the following Monday, which would be a Game 7, if necessary. Boudreau made clear his thinking that it would not be necessary by responding, "Nobody!"[7]

Sain was the best the Braves had at the time and he was coming off a sensational opening-game performance. But could he keep it up? Could Gromek? The choice of Gromek over either Feller or Lemon was analyzed as a gamble for Boudreau by the scribes, but Gromek had pitched as well as anyone on the staff besides Bearden in the second half of September, whatever he had been asked to do as a starter or a reliever. The problem in the first game was not with Feller, but with the bats against Sain.

Wondering just how overpowering Sain could be, the atmosphere on a 62-degree afternoon at Cleveland Stadium was upbeat after the first inning when the Indians took a 1–0 lead and added a second run in the third. Sain was still very sharp, but this time Gromek was a little better.

Sain allowed five hits and two runs and walked nobody. Gromek gave up seven hits, but only one run in the seventh. The key blow of the game was a Larry Doby home run in the third that went down as the game-winner. Gromek had not expected to pitch in Game 4. Like almost everyone else following the sport, he figured Boudreau would give the ball to Feller. Then, in the locker room, Boudreau announced his plan to the team.

"I almost fell off my chair," Gromek said. "Feller was Feller in those days. I was a bundle of nerves before the game. I couldn't wait to get started. After that I was fine. I had great stuff."[8]

He did, but it still took a mighty shot off the bat of center fielder Doby to best Sain. In the aftermath of the game, a grinning Gromek grabbed Doby and gave him a huge hug. A photographer snapped the picture of the two men in a warm embrace and the picture zoomed around the country. The scene was also shown on television. The photo itself was big news because Gromek was white and Doby was black and there had never been such a shot in professional sports where the races mixed so positively and warmly.

This was Gromek's biggest day in the sport—he retired in 1957 with 123 wins—but he remained even more famous for the hug photo with Doby for the rest of his life, even in his obituary. The hug was a spontaneous act that Gromek never felt was a big deal, only normal behavior between happy teammates, which in the country's racial climate of 1948 was newsworthy.

"Color was never an issue with me," said Gromek, who was born in Hamtramck, Michigan, and as a youth played baseball in Detroit against players of all races. "Doby won the game for me. I was happy. I always got along well with him. He won a lot of games for me with his bat and glove."[9]

The purity of the moment, the obvious acceptance, and the casual feeling that Gromek was just doing what he would have done if another white player had hit the homer made the moment all the more special for Doby, who had not always felt such warmth from the other Indians in his days with the team.

Doby appreciated the photo and its implications more than most fans ever realized. Later, when he listed his prized possessions from sports, whether they were trophies or plaques, Doby cited the Gromek photograph, the act of brotherhood implicit in the picture with both men joyfully celebrating a shared moment.

"That's the one I like the best," Doby said years later. "It was exciting to me then, and it's still exciting to me now. The picture was more rewarding and happy for me than actually hitting that home run. It was such a scuffle for me, after being involved in all that segregation, going through all I had to go through, until that picture. The picture finally showed a moment of a man showing his feelings for me."[10]

No one will argue that the photograph was as significant a step towards Civil Rights in the United States as Jackie Robinson breaking the color barrier, or Doby himself breaking the color barrier in the American League, never mind the work of Dr. Martin Luther King. Yet the photograph was still a symbol. In the context of another episode of America at its best, it was a small step for mankind. When Gromek returned to his neighborhood in Michigan after the Series, he discovered that not everyone thought the way he did. He lost a friend over the issue, a man who thought Gromek had been too effusive in his expression of warmth towards Doby. Gromek shrugged off the lost companion as someone not worth keeping as a friend, but that illustrated the mood of much of the country on race at the time.

When Gromek died at age eighty-two in 2002, his obituary included a comment from Doby about the picture. Doby said he would "always cherish that photograph and the memory of Gromek hugging me and me hugging him because it proved that emotions can be put into a form not based on color."[11]

Gromek and Doby made a big memory for the entire Indians nation by teaming up to win a World Series game. Together, in the locker room, they teamed again with a small deed that in stature might have been of more import.

When the celebration subsided, the Indians were leading the Boston Braves, three games to one in a best-four-out of-seven series, and they had another game to play at home in front of the roaring throng of Ohio fans that daily shook Cleveland Stadium to its foundation.

One more game, one more victory, that's all the Indians needed to salve the misery accumulated over twenty-eight unhappy finishes. And they had the best player in team history ready to take the mound and win it. Bob Feller was hungry to get the call and polish off Boston to provide his home city with the biggest sports triumph it ever experienced.

It was almost impossible to measure such an intangible as to how much Feller wanted to deliver a World Series trophy to Cleveland. All Feller had to do was pitch better than the two-hitter he twirled in the opener. Not much to ask.

Chapter Twenty-One notes on page 298.

# 22

# DISAPPOINTMENT AND JUBILATION

**C**LEVELAND WAS READY for the title. With the Indians ahead 3–1 and Bob Feller taking the mound, confetti and other symbols of victory were gathered, ready to be unleashed with the pent-up emotions of nearly thirty years.

October 10 figured to go down as one of the best days in Cleveland history. Feller was the trusted ace of the staff, and Billy Southworth picked Nelson Potter to go up against him, hoping to turn to Warren Spahn for a sixth game. It was an incredible risk. Without Potter, far down on the depth chart amongst Braves starters, performing well, there would be no sixth game.

Potter was thirty-six and had started the season with the St. Louis Browns. He had drifted to the Athletics, and finally to the Braves. It was not a completely outrageous selection by Southworth—somewhat akin to Boudreau employing Gromek—because Potter had gone 5–2 down the stretch for Boston with a 2.33 earned run average.

Nobody was more pleased to get the start than Feller. This was what he had always imagined: Rapid Robert taking the hill to win the world championship for his Indians. Although Cleveland Stadium was so full that it was about to bust at its seams, more fans poured into the building for Game 5 than ever before. When the Indians stopped counting, after the standing-room-only crowd filled every crevice with a view, it was announced that there were 86,288 in the house.

The fans were in a party mood, ready to bear witness to the great championship achieved. The only problem was that the most important person in the building with the biggest role to play in making that happen did not feel right.

"It was another one of those days when a pitcher just doesn't have his good stuff," Feller said. "I was escaping from jams most of the game, but not often enough."[1]

There's nothing like the sight of opposing batters smacking the ball all over the yard to hush a home crowd and it got quiet enough in Cleveland Stadium to hear the thwacks when Boston batters put good wood on the ball and sprayed it to all fields. The chief culprit in the early going was Braves third baseman Bob Elliott. Elliott had committed a couple of costly errors in the field in Boston, but made up for the miscues at the plate in Game 5.

Boston reached Feller for three runs in the top of the first and after three innings the Braves had a 4–1 lead and Elliott already had two Series home runs on his resume. However, in the fourth inning, Southworth's Potter experiment failed and Cleveland roared back with a four-run inning for a one-run Indians lead. That chased Potter and brought in emergency reliever Warren Spahn, who was being saved for the later start. Naturally enough,

Southworth made the move as early as practical because without stemming the bleeding there would be no Game 6. The 86,000-plus came alive again with noise, virtually shaking the stadium in support of the Indians.

Feller was relieved and with a 5–4 lead it was like starting the game over. Just pull it together, he told himself, and we can be the champs.

"I went into the fifth inning with that attitude," Feller said. "I set the Braves down 1-2-3 and struck out [Marv] Rickert to start the sixth. But then the Braves started scoring again."[2]

Boston tied the game with a single run in the sixth, but that wasn't the major problem. Before the seventh inning ended, the Braves had put up six more runs, chased Feller, Ed Klieman (who didn't get any of the three hitters out he faced), Russ Christopher, and Satchel Paige. It was one of the biggest baseball disappointments of Feller's career. He couldn't deliver when he wanted to the most and instead was hit hard. Spahn tossed five and two-thirds innings of one-hit relief and permitted just three balls to be hit to the outfield.

Until his relief appearance as the fourth pitcher of the inning, Paige had been the forgotten man of the World Series. He had sat in the bullpen biding his time, wishing he would get the call to play. Initially he hoped to get a start. That wasn't going to happen. Then he just hoped he could get into a game and play a meaningful role. Years later, Paige explained his thoughts during this time.

"I felt sick," he said. "I felt low as anybody felt. I just sat in the bullpen hoping and hoping. Why? All I could ask myself. Why?"[3]

Fans did chant his name when it seemed the Indians were in need of relief, but manager Lou Boudreau was deaf to the call.

For a time it seemed there would be a better chance that Joe Earley would get into a Series game than Paige.

Paige was just about reconciled to being a Series-long spectator when he was inserted into the ball game. This was significant not only for Paige, but for history. He became the first African American to pitch in a World Series game. Paige tossed two-thirds of an inning to mercifully end the seventh for the Indians. He allowed no hits, walks, or runs and then was lifted for Bob Muncrief in the eighth.

There were men on base and the Indians trailed 11–5 when Paige strolled to the mound to the cheers of the Indians fans. Spahn was at the plate and hit a sacrifice fly. Then Paige set down Tommy Holmes on a grounder. None of this was accomplished without umpires three times whistling Paige to stop his motion because they claimed his wind-up was illegal. When Paige finished his stint, the fans gave him a huge ovation.

But the day ended as a downer for Indians backers. Soundly thrashed, with their Series lead cut to 3–2, the Indians now had to return to Boston for Game 6. They could have clinched the championship at home, and now they had to worry about tamping down the Braves' newfound energy and enthusiasm. Boston had fresh confidence and after taking the last game did not seem to believe that winning two more was either out of the question or going to be very difficult.

At the least the Braves had survived to play another day and that in itself was a pretty big deal. The Series wasn't over till it was over. As long as they had a pulse, the Braves had a chance.

"What a relief to get some runs," Southworth said, "and pitching, too. Gosh, we really exploded. Yes, we're right back in this Series. Bill Voiselle's the boy who will even it up tomorrow and Johnny Sain will sew it up Tuesday."[4]

There were no days off between games as the teams moved from city to city. Boudreau was coming back with his 20-game-winner Bob Lemon. The game was played on Monday in Boston, and it was the Monday that Boudreau had previously remarked that "Nobody" was starting. The Indians did not clinch the way he had hoped, so Boudreau needed somebody after all.

In the much smaller Braves Field, attendance was 40,103 for the next round. Southworth did indeed start Voiselle. Voiselle had gone 13–13 for the Braves that season. Earlier in the 1940s he won 21 games in a season for the New York Giants. He had been around, had some success, made an All-Star team. A rangy right-hander who stood 6-foot-4, Voiselle was being asked to pitch the best game of his life, yet he was also one of the pitchers lumped together in the "Pray for Rain" category in the Spahn and Sain poem.

The Indians scored one run in the third inning to take the lead and the Braves tied it 1–1 in the fourth. Cleveland countered with two runs in the sixth and a run in the eighth and, with a 4–1 lead, the players could sense victory on the biggest stage in the sport. But in the late going Lemon faltered, allowing two runs before Boudreau lifted him after seven and one-third innings. Southworth replaced Voiselle after seven solid innings of three-run ball and inserted Spahn to pitch again on short rest. Although he struck out four in two innings, Spahn was touched for the last run.

When Boudreau visited Lemon on the mound in the eighth it wasn't just to chat. It was to pat him on the back and send him to the showers. The bases were loaded and Boudreau was hoping

Cleveland could get out of danger unscathed. Boudreau waved in Gene Bearden. Once again, Cleveland was going to ride the man that brought them to the dance. Bearden had won the huge playoff game over Boston; he had already won a Series game; he won 20 in the regular season. The knuckleball artist had transformed his place on the squad from barely making the team in the spring to the man the Indians and city looked to in order to end twenty-eight years of professional frustration.

It was up to Bearden to end the suspense in Game 6 by shutting down the Braves without a hit, and especially not a run. The scheduled hitter was Rickert, who had already hit one homer in the Series. But Southworth pinch-hit for him, sending in Clint Conatser. The change was made because Bearden threw left-handed and Rickert hit lefty. Conatser, who batted .271 in a limited big-league career, swung from the right side of the plate. He swung hard from the right side, too, and connected solidly with a Bearden pitch. The ball sailed deep to center where Indians center field Thurman Tucker hauled it in. However, the out scored Tommy Holmes from third, a run charged to Lemon.

Southworth went to his bench again, subbing in Phil Masi as a pinch-hitter for Bill Salkeld. Masi doubled and Earl Torgeson scored, charging another run to Lemon. So far the insertion of Bearden wasn't looking like the wisest strategy Boudreau ever devised. The next batter, Mike McCormick, hit a blistering grounder up the middle that was earmarked for a high-speed ride through the infield for another hit. Only Bearden stuck out his glove, stabbed the ball, and threw to first to end the inning and the threat. It was a close call, but the Indians still led, 4–3.

Cleveland did not add to its total and in the bottom of the ninth the Braves were on the cusp of elimination. Eddie Stanky led off and in a bad signal for Cleveland, walked to start the inning. That meant the tying run was on base. Spahn was due up, but no one expected the pitcher to hit in this situation. Southworth pinch-hit Sibby Sisti for Spahn. He also sent in Connie Ryan, a fast runner, to take Stanky's place on first base.

Sisti attempted to lay down a bunt to move Ryan into scoring position, but he did not get good wood on the ball and popped it in the air. Ryan was running on contact and Indians catcher Jim Hegan not only caught Sisti's bunt try, but nailed Ryan off base for a double play. Hegan had to lunge for the short pop before whipping the ball to Eddie Robinson at first. Braves leadoff man Tommy Holmes came to the plate seeking to prolong the Series, but he hit a fly ball to left field, caught by Bob Kennedy, who had come into the game as a defensive replacement for Dale Mitchell.

Kennedy squeezed his glove tightly around the ball as the third out ended the World Series with the Indians at long last champs. Kennedy gave the last-out ball to Bearden, who saved it in a special place for the rest of his life.

Although they had won the title on a foreign field and the crowd reaction was subdued, the Indians shed all inhibitions for their celebration. Yes, it would have been nicer to win in Cleveland, but hey, it was still the World Series. It was revealed after the game that Lemon had started with a sore arm. The night before he underwent heat treatments on his right arm and the morning of the game he was given a lengthy massage by trainer Lefty Weisman.

Bearden was not particularly surprised to be summoned when things started looking shaky for the Indians.

"Lou told me before the game, 'If we get in trouble, it's you,'" Bearden said, "and I told him I'd be ready any time."[5]

Elliott, who had reached Feller for two home runs the game before, stayed hot and punched out three hits. But the Indians received two hits each from Doby and Robinson and Joe Gordon homered in the sixth off Voiselle. There was no doubt who the star of the Series was: Gene Bearden, also the star of the playoff game, and the unexpected star of the season.

"He won the pennant and the World Series for us," said Bob Feller years later. "If it had not been for Gene Bearden Cleveland would not have a world championship since 1920."[6]

And just what did Bearden do with that game ball that Kennedy caught and presented to him? It did not reside in his living room where he could gaze at it every day. The ball lived somewhere else for its own protection, the capstone to Bearden's and Cleveland's greatest baseball season.

"It's in a bank vault," he said.[7]

The Indians franchise might have encapsulated the entire 1948 season and placed it in a bank vault if it could have. The players, too, might have been tempted to do some extra banking since their winner's share of $6,772 per man was a record at the time.

In the Indians clubhouse Coach Bill McKechnie kissed manager Lou Boudreau. Boudreau addressed the team.

"I want to tell you fellows something," Boudreau said, "something that's deep from my heart. I want to tell you how grateful I am for your loyalty. You have conducted yourselves like gentlemen on and off the field. You have been absolutely magnificent."[8]

Bill Veeck threw the team a party after Game 6, but after a little while it was noticed that neither Larry Doby nor Satchel Paige, the two African American players, were in attendance. Rather than let the matter run its course, players formed search parties for the men, found them, and brought them to the event. That was also a statement for racial togetherness on the team, doing something that players had to go out of their way to do.

That was only Party No. 1. Party No. 2 began a few hours later on the train back to Cleveland. No one slept. Everyone drank champagne, spraying it everywhere. The Indians behaved like fraternity boys but, if there were any complaints, they were limited. The team pretty much wrecked the dining car. Yet Veeck took a boys-will-be-boys attitude towards the entire chapter and willingly forked over about $3,000 to the railroad to cover damages. Jim Hegan and Doby sang songs together. Johnny Berardino tried to make a speech, but tangled in his chair and fell into his steak and gravy.

On the train Gordon toasted Boudreau.

"To the greatest leatherman I ever saw," Gordon said, "to the damnedest clutch hitter that ever lived, to a doggone good manager, Lou."[9]

The gang walked right off the train and right into a parade organized for the Indians' benefit. Clothes soaked in champagne, the team was hustled through the mob of thousands that gathered at Union Terminal to welcome them home at Public Square and right into convertibles waiting for a parade down Euclid Avenue. The fans had been deprived of a true pennant parade and made up for that with this whiz-bang extravaganza. Confetti flew from office building windows. There were reports of roses strewn in the team's path. Supporters also released balloons from the downtown buildings as part of the merriment and they filled the sky. Fans shouted and waved and players waved back along the five-mile route.

Rookie third baseman Al Rosen, who was going to become a fixture in Cleveland, was astounded by the scene.

"Man, I never want to play baseball in any other city," he said. "This Cleveland is marvelous."[10]

While Mayor Tom Burke guessed there were around 400,000 on hand, it was estimated by the local newspapers that 200,000 people turned out to cheer the champion Indians. Boudreau rode in the lead vehicle. He was the toast of his team and now he was the toast of the town. The hardest thing to believe was that the long journey was over. Spring training seemed like another century. Back then Gene Bearden was a stranger, Larry Doby a sub-.200 hitter trying to make the club, Satchel Paige was still a legend in the mists, and Boudreau was eyed as a manager on a tightrope.

Now the Cleveland Indians were World Series champs for the first time in twenty-eight years. This title was bigger, the major living link in Tris Speaker aside, because TV didn't exist, radio was in its infancy, attendance was much lower, newspaper coverage shallower, and the players as a group less compelling. This time the Indians had done it, won it, with an amazing cast of characters, set the all-time attendance record as Bill Veeck made sure they got some laughs along the way, and made a grateful Cleveland king of the baseball universe. In the city by the lake, the year 1948 would live forever as the sweetest summer of them all.

Chapter Twenty-Two notes on pages 298–299.

# EPILOGUE

**T**HE **INDIANS IMMEDIATELY** scattered for winter after the parade honoring them as World Series champs. They left Cleveland with a glow from their achievements of the 1948 season and already started thinking about how they should be able to repeat as champions the following year.

Only next year was considerably different. The same three teams finished at the top of the American League standings in 1949, but not in the same order. The Yankees began their new dynastic run that brought them ten pennants in the next twelve years, edging the poor Red Sox by one game. The Indians finished 89–65, eight games behind the Yankees.

One of the main reasons Cleveland faltered was that Gene Bearden was no longer the miracle man. In 1948, everything Bearden touched turned to gold. In 1949, everything Bearden touched turned to copper. He finished 8–8 with a 5.10 earned run average after leading the American League with a 2.43 ERA the year before. In fact, Bearden was never again a prominent player.

Reliever Russ Christopher finished the 1948 season with a 3–2 record and 17 saves. But the man whom Bill Veeck rescued from the scrap heap of unwanted players never played in the majors again. His heart trouble reared up before the 1949 season, Christopher had heart surgery in early 1951 and dreamed of a comeback, but didn't make one. He was only thirty-seven when he died in 1954.

Almost none of the position players, with the possible exception of Larry Doby, whose average dropped (but whose other stats improved), were as good as they had been in 1948. That included player-manager Lou Boudreau, who had been chosen Most Valuable Player in the AL.

Within a few seasons the makeup of the Indians changed drastically. Bill Veeck sold the team and re-emerged as owner of the St. Louis Browns, where in 1951 he pulled off his most famous stunt—bringing a 3-foot-7-inch tall batter up to bat. He took Satchel Paige with him to St. Louis and Paige made an All-Star team.

By 1950, Boudreau was playing out the end of his career in Boston, never reaching All-Star heights again as a player, or matching his accomplishments as a manager, despite leadership jobs with the Red Sox, Kansas City Athletics, and Chicago Cubs. He was elected to the Hall of Fame, however, in 1970, and enjoyed a long broadcasting career, mostly with the Chicago Cubs.

A seven-time All-Star, Doby won two American League home-run titles and became the second African American manager in baseball history after Frank Robinson. Doby was elected to the Hall of Fame in 1998.

Joe Gordon, a nine-time All-Star, was elected to the Hall of Fame in 2009. He also became a manager who led the Indians between 1958 and 1960, and also the Tigers, Kansas City A's, and Kansas City Royals. In 1960, Gordon was involved in perhaps the strangest trade in big-league history when the Indians and Tigers swapped managers, sending Gordon to Detroit for Tigers manager Jimmy Dykes.

Bob Lemon won 22 games in 1949 and won 207 games as a pitcher. With a winning percentage of .618, Lemon was named to the Hall of Fame in 1976.

Although his days of dominance were over, Bob Feller kept pitching through the 1956 season, winning 266 games in all. He remains the most popular Indian in team history and a statue of Feller—much bigger than life—decorates an entrance to Progressive Field, where the Indians play today. Feller was chosen for the Hall of Fame in 1962.

Joining his players in the Hall in 1991 was Bill Veeck. After owning the Indians, Veeck owned the Browns and then the Chicago White Sox twice. It was Veeck who hired Doby to be his manager in the 1970s. Veeck also maintained close relations with Paige over the years. He not only counted on him to fill a rotation spot with St. Louis, later in the 1950s when Veeck owned the then–minor league AAA Miami Marlins, he hired Paige to pitch there. At the time Paige was about fifty years old. It was no surprise to either Veeck or Paige that Old Satch pitched very well.

In 1971, Paige became the first African American star of the Negro Leagues to be inducted into the Hall of Fame.

As a team, the new-look Indians of 1954 turned in one of the finest regular seasons of all time. Cleveland finished 111–43 and bested an outstanding 103-win Yankees team by eight games. Doby led the team in homers with 32. Bob Lemon won 23 games that year. Feller was 13–3. Al Rosen batted .300 and drove in more than 100 runs.

Then the Indians were stunned in the World Series by the New York Giants. That was the Series when Willie Mays made his famous long-run, over-the-shoulder catch of a Vic Wertz drive at the Polo Grounds. Cleveland was shockingly swept, 4–0.

The next time the Indians reached the World Series was 1995, when they fell to the Atlanta Braves, 4–2. In 1997 they fought back to the Series, but lost to the upstart Florida Marlins 4–3.

Since 1948 the Indians have won three American League pennants, but lost in the World Series each time. The season of '48 remains the most recent season in which Cleveland claimed a world championship in baseball. For a time in the 1990s the Indians were about as good as any team in the game and they were so popular in Cleveland that they set a baseball record for the most sellouts in a row (a record since broken by the Boston Red Sox). The Indians sold out every home game between June 15, 1995, and April 4, 2001, a total of 455 games.

In more recent years, the Indians did not fare so well on the field or at the gate. In 2013, with management committed to a serious revamping, the team hired Terry Francona, a two-time World-Series-winning manager with Boston, and began rebuilding the roster with an eye to winning another Series. It had been sixty-five years and counting and the Indians aspired to match the achievement of the 1948 Indians.

Veeck, Boudreau, Paige, Gordon, Bearden, Lemon, Doby, Keltner, Gromek, Mitchell, Christopher, and almost everyone involved in that season have passed away. Their accomplishments live on.

# ACKNOWLEDGMENTS

**T**HE **AUTHOR WISHES** to thank the research staff at the National Baseball Hall of Fame Library and executive director Tim Wiles for their help, as well as photo archivist Pat Kelly.

In addition, thanks to the Cleveland Public Library reference department staff for all its assistance with this project.

# NOTES

## Chapter 1: 1946–1947

[1] Veeck, Bill and Linn, Ed, *Veeck--As In Wreck*, (Chicago, University of Chicago Press, 1962/2001). P. 88.

[2] Veeck and Linn, ibid. P. 88.

[3] The trade that included Bearden also had Cleveland receiving Hal Peck and Al Gettel in exchange for Sherm Lollar and Ray Mack.

[4] Veeck and Linn, ibid. P. 144

[5] Stengel managed the Boston Braves (nicknamed the Bees from 1938–40) from 1938–42, and took over in '43 for Bob Coleman, after the Braves started the season with a 21–25 record.

[6] Boudreau, Lou and Schneider, Russell, *Lou Boudreau: Covering All The Bases*, (Champaign, Illinois, Sagamore Publishing, 1993). P. 81.

[7] Boudreau and Schneider, ibid. P. 82.

[8] This was the highest attendance the team had had in twenty-six years, when they drew 912,832 fans in 1920, a year in which they won the World Series.

[9] Veeck and Linn, ibid. P. 124.

[10] Veeck and Linn, ibid. P. 104.

[11] 1936: 54–100; 1938: 45–105; 1939: 45–106, 1940: 50–103; 1941: 43–111, 1942: 42–109; 1945: 46–108.

[12] *United Press*, "Indians Sign Newark Negro For First Base," *New York World-Telegram*, July 3, 1947.

[13] *United Press*, "Larry Doby, Ace Negro Infielder, Signs Contract With Cleveland," *New York Times*, July 4, 1947.

[14] *United Press*, Larry Doby, ibid.

[15] *United Press*, Larry Doby, ibid.

[16] Parrott, Harold, *The Lords Of Baseball*, (Atlanta, Longstreet Press, 1976/2001), P. 284.

## Chapter 2: Spring Training

[1] *Cleveland Press*, "Greenberg Plays First For Tribe Scrubs Today," *Cleveland Press*, March 21, 1948.

[2] Gibbons, Frank, "Boudreau Hopes For Greenberg Decision After Trial Today," *Cleveland Press*, March 23, 1948.

[3] Robinson, Eddie and Rogers, C. Paul III, *Lucky Me: My Sixty-Five Years In Baseball*, (Dallas, Southern Methodist University Press, 2011). P. 15.

[4] After announcing his retirement in 1947, Greenberg took the role as the Indians' farm system director. After two years in that role, he became the team's general manager and part-owner, along with Bill Veeck.

[5] In the six years that Berardino was on the Browns (1939–42, 46–47), the team had a combined record of 387–534 (.420 winning percentage).

[6] *Associated Press, New York Times*, "Will Quit Baseball For Career In Films," November 25, 1947.

[7] Christine, Bill, *Los Angeles Times*, "Futility Infielder," April 21, 1994.

[8] Gibbons, Frank, "Everything Gets Mixed Up For Mitchell At Tucson," *Cleveland Press*, March 2, 1948.

[9] Lustig, Dennis, *Cleveland Plain Dealer*, "Whatever Happened To Hank Edwards," July 12, 1970.

[10] In 2,231 career at-bats, Tucker hit only 9 home runs, with only 2 coming as an Indian.

[11] The *Telegraph Herald*, January 28, 1948, P. 11.

[12] Lustig, Dennis, *Cleveland Plain Dealer*, "Whatever Happened To Thurman Tucker," February 1, 1974.

[13] *Cleveland Press*, "Hal Peck Has Had The Breaks . . . And Most Of Them Were Bad," July 9, 1949.

[14] Seeley led the American League in strikeouts four times during his seven-year career (1944: 99; 1945: 97; 1946: 101; 1948: 102).

[15] Yonkers, Bob, *Cleveland Press*, "Five-Foot-Ten, 215-Pounder Hit 33 in I-I-I," date missing, Baseball Hall of Fame Library files.

[16] *Cleveland Plain Dealer*, "Will Farm Doby Or Start Him Regularly," March 23, 1948.

[17] Gibbons, Frank, "Mitchell's Injury Gives Clark Chance For Outfield Berth," *Cleveland Press*, March 5, 1948.

[18] Both Aaron (2003) and Bret (1998, 2001,10 03) made it to All-Star games during their playing careers.

[19] *Cleveland Press*, "Storm Ties Up City," March 11, 1948.

[20] Snyder, John, *Indians Journal*, Clerisy Press, Cincinnati, Ohio, 2008. Pg. 261.

[21] Gibbons, Frank, "Two Tribe Hurling Jobs Seen Open," *Cleveland Press*, March 11, 1948.

[22] Ledden, Jack, *South Bend Tribune*, "Gettel, Sophisticated Farmer, Faces Tigers," June, 1947. (Baseball Hall of Fame Library archives).

[23] Jones, Harry, *Sporting News*, "Tribe's War-Mangled Bearden Hid Injuries Behind Big Curve," May 19, 1948.

## Chapter 3: Play Ball

[1] Gibbons, Frank, "Tribe's Cold Performance Makes Lou Hot; Quits Warming Bench," *Cleveland Press*, March 12, 1948.

[2] Gibbons, Frank, "Tucson 'Vacation' Made Hegan Madder," *Cleveland Press*, March 20, 1948.

[3] In thirteen seasons in the big leagues, Boone never once played a game at catcher.

[4] "Heavyweight Boudreau Won't Diet," *Cleveland Press*, March 5, 1948.

[5] Gibbons, Frank, "Boudreau To Continue To Switch," *Cleveland Press*, March 19, 1948.

[6] Cobbledick, Gordon, "Plain Dealing: Feller Stands Alone Today as Sports Attraction; Turnout in San Francisco is Tribute to Bob," *Cleveland Plain Dealer*, March 16, 1948.

[7] Gibbons, Frank, "Feller, Blasted, Says Arm 'Needs Time,'" *Cleveland Press*, March 22, 1948.

[8] Ibid.

[9] Interleague play wasn't introduced into Major League Baseball until 1997. Therefore, the only way two teams from opposite leagues would go against each other would have to be in the World Series.

[10] Feller, Bob and Gilbert, Bill, *Now Pitching Bob Feller*, (New York, Citadel Press, 1990/2002). P. 146.

[11] The designated hitter rule did not come into effect in the American League until 1973, which explains why Lemon hit during a game between two AL squads.

[12] Gibbons, Frank, "Pitching Plus Slugging Equal 1$^{st}$ Place For Tribe," *Cleveland Press*, April 24, 1948.

[13] *Cleveland Press*, "Majority of Fans Pick Tribe to Finish in Third Spot," April 25, 1948.

[14] McAuley, Ed, "Muncrief Is In Right Spot, Middle Name Is Cleveland," *Cleveland News*, March, 1948. (Missing day, Baseball Hall of Fame Library Archives).

[15] Jones, Harry, "Bob Muncrief Has Hopes For Good Year If He Can Escape Injury Jinx," *Cleveland Plain Dealer*, March 20, 1948.

[16] Dolgan, Bob, "Thin Man' To The Rescue," *Cleveland Plain Dealer*, August 16, 1998.

[17] Ibid.

## Chapter 4: The Boy Wonder

[1] ESPN.com, "Indians Legend Bob Feller Dies at 92," December 15, 2010.

[2] While Durocher was only a career .247 hitter in his seventeen seasons as a player, he would go on to win over 2,000 games as a manager (2,008 to be exact), which is currently 10th all-time in baseball history. He would be elected to the National Baseball Hall of Fame in 1994.

[3] Feller's regular season debut came on July 24, in which he pitched two innings, giving up one run on three hits and striking out two, helping the Indians beat the Philadelphia Athletics by a score of 16–3 and being awarded with the save. He would only have twenty more saves for his career.

[4] Feller, Bob and Gilbert, Bill, *Now Pitching Bob Feller*, (New York, Citadel Press, 1990/2002). P. 18.

[5] Ibid, P. 142.

[6] Feller, Virginia and Lebovitz, Hal, "Wife's-Eye View Of An Immortal: He's My Feller!" *Baseball Digest*, September, 1952.

[7] Ibid.

[8] Boudreau, Lou and Schneider, Russell, *Lou Boudreau: Covering All The Bases,* (Champaign, Illinois, Sagamore Publishing, 1993). P. 93.

[9] ESPN.com, ibid.

[10] Fitzgerald, Ed, "Bob Feller, Incorporated," *Sport Magazine*, June, 1947.

[11] McAuley, Ed, *Cleveland Press*, "The No-Hit Motif—They Made Feller Mad," May 1, 1946.

[12] Feller is currently 5th all-time in career walks (1,764), and issued over 100 base on balls in half of his Major League seasons (nine out of eighteen).

[13] Feeney, Mark, *Boston Globe*, "Bob Feller, 92, Hall Of Famer Had Blazing Fastball," December 16, 2010.

[14] Ibid.

[15] Ibid.

[16] In 87 at-bats, Williams had a .368 batting average against Feller, with 9 home runs, 26 RBI, 26 walks, and only 6 strikeouts.

[17] Feeney, Ibid.

# Chapter 5: Who's on First?

[1] Bearden appeared in only one game in 1947, pitching 0.1 innings while allowing three runs on two hits with one walk.

[2] Stump, Al, *Sport Magazine*, "Pop Lemon's Boy," June, 1950.

[3] Ibid.

[4] Ibid.

[5] Ibid.

[6] Dray, Bill, *Sports Collectors Digest*, "HOFer Bob Lemon Has Many Sweet Memories," August 9, 1991.

[7] Withers, Tom, *Associated Press/Albany Times-Union*, "Indians Pitching Great Harder Died At 93," October 21, 2002.

[8] Boudreau, Lou and Schneider, Russell, *Lou Boudreau: Covering All The Bases,* (Champaign, Illinois, Sagamore Publishing, 1993). P. 93.

[9] Ibid, P. 105.

[10] Moore, Joseph Thomas, *Pride Against Prejudice: The Biography of Larry Doby*, (New York, Praeger, 1988). P. 69.

## Chapter 6: The Pieces Fit Together

[1] Ledden, Jack, *South Bend Tribune*, "22-Game Hit String Ties Up Tribe Job For Rookie Mitchell," (National Baseball Hall of Fame Library Archives, date in 1947 missing).

[2] For his career, Mitchell had 45 stolen bases with a season high of 13, and was caught 47 times, giving him a success rate of .489.

[3] Ibid.

[4] Gibbons, Frank, "Tribe Garden Glistens In Dale-Light," *Baseball Digest*, January, 1949.

[5] Rumill, Ed, *Baseball Magazine*, "Cleveland Stars Overshadow Mitchell," April, 1949.

[6] Lebovitz, Hal, *Sporting News*, "'Watch Dale Go in '49'— Speaker," November 10, 1948.

[7] McAuley, Ed, *Sporting News*, "Mitchell, 3-Base King, Threatens Records," May 10, 1950.

[8] Veeck, Bill and Cobbledick, Gordon, *Saturday Evening Post*, "So You Want To Run A Ball Club," April 23, 1949.

[9] Robinson, Eddie and Rogers, C. Paul III, *Lucky Me: My Sixty-Five Years in Baseball*, (Dallas, Southern Methodist University Press, 2011), P. 54.

[10] O'Neil, Danny, "Feller Buys Babe Bat From Shoreline Couple," *Seattle Times*, July 4, 2001.

[11] Richman, Milton, *United Press International/Cleveland Press*, "Shadows Lengthen For Sam Zoldak and an Old Friend Has To Cry," August 13, 1966.

[12] Jones, Harry, *Cleveland Plain Dealer*, "Lemon Pitches No-Hit Victory, 2-0," July 1, 1948.

[13] *Cleveland Plain Dealer*, "Lemon Credits Teammates' Support For No-Hitter, Praises Mitchell, July 1, 1948.

[14] Ibid.

[15] Gibbons, Frank, "'I Was Afraid All The Way,' Says Lemon Of His No-Hitter," *Cleveland Press*, July 1, 1948.

[16] Ibid.

[17] McAuley, Ed, *Cleveland News*, "No-Hit Lemon Likes To Pitch—At Last," July 1, 1948.

[18] Lemon, Bob and Vass, George, *Baseball Digest*, "The Game I'll Never Forget," March, 1975.

## Chapter 7: The Good Kid

[1] Berkow, Ira, "Lou Boudreau, A Longtime Player-Manager And Hall of Fame Shortstop, Dies At 84," *New York Times*, August 11, 2001.

[2] Boudreau, Lou and Schneider, Russell, *Lou Boudreau: Covering All the Bases*, (Champaign, Illinois, Sagamore Publishing, 1993). P. 52.

[3] Ibid, P. 53.

[4] Ibid, P. 54.

5 Cobbledick, Gordon, "Youngest Player Ever To Direct Major Club Gets 2-Year Contract," *Cleveland Plain Dealer*, November 25, 1941.

6 Lebovitz, Hal, *The Best Of Hal Lebovitz: Great Sportswriting From Six Decades In Cleveland*, (Cleveland, Gray & Company, Publishers, 2004), P. 236.

7 Berkow, ibid.

8 Berkow, ibid.

9 Berkow, ibid.

10 Boudreau, Lou and Fitzgerald, Edward Earl, *The Lou Boudreau Story: Player-Manager*, (newspaper excerpt from Little, Brown & Co.), Cleveland News, May, 1949.

11 Dolgan, Bob, "Boudreau Hero Of '48," *Cleveland Plain Dealer*, May 24, 1998.

12 Ibid.

13 Ibid.

14 Boudreau and Schneider, ibid. P. 106.

15 Withers, Tom, "Boudreau Dead At 84," *Associated Press*/USA Today.com, August 10, 2001.

16 Ibid.

17 Merkin, Scott, "Family Recalls Very Special Life," *Chicago Tribune*, August 16, 2001.

## Chapter 8: Larry Doby—Underrated Star

1 Hutchinson, Dave, "Doby Relives Past, The Good And The Bad," *Newark Star-Ledger*, July 3, 1994.

2 Parker, Dan, "Jackie Robinson Now Has Company, Competition," *New York Daily Mirror*, July 4, 1947.

[3] Moore, Joseph Thomas, *Pride Against Prejudice: The Biography Of Larry Doby*, New York, Praeger Publishing, 1988). P. 41.

[4] Moore, ibid. P. 45.

[5] Moore, ibid. P. 46.

[6] Moore, ibid. P. 47.

[7] Moore, ibid. P. 48.

[8] Moore, ibid. P. 52.

[9] Israel, David, "Veeck Proves To Be Far Ahead Again By Picking Doby," *Chicago Tribune*, July 3, 1978.

[10] Jackson, John, "Doby Faced Adversity Without Publicity," *Bergen Record*, December 2, 1985.

[11] Ibid.

[12] Veeck, Bill and Linn, Ed, *Veeck--As In Wreck*, (Chicago, University of Chicago Press, 2001). P. 170.

[13] Smith, Claire, "Larry Doby, Who Broke A Color Barrier, Dies At 79," *New York Times*, June 20, 2003.

[14] Boudreau, Lou and Schneider, Russell, *Lou Boudreau: Covering All The Bases*, (Champaign, Illinois, Sagamore Publishing, 1993). P. 110.

## Chapter 9: The Methuselah of the Mound

[1] Holway, John, *Josh And Satch: The Life And Times Of Josh Gibson And Satchel Paige*, (Westport, Connecticut, Meckler Publishing, 1991), P. xii.

[2] Holway, ibid. P. 11–12.

[3] Tye, Larry, *Satchel: The Life And Times of an American Legend*, New York, Random House, 2009), P. 42.

[4] Tye, ibid. P. 95.

[5] Tye, ibid. P. 172.

[6] Tye, ibid. 173.

[7] Tye, ibid. 174.

[8] Ribowsky, Mark, *Don't Look Back: Satchel Paige in the Shadows of Baseball*, (New York, Simon & Schuster, 1994), P. 191.

[9] Donovan, Richard, *Time Ain't Gonna Mess With Me*, Collier's Magazine, June 13, 1953.

[10] Boudreau, Lou and Schneider, Russell, *Lou Boudreau: Covering All the Bases*, (Champaign, Illinois, Sagamore Publishing, 1993). P. 112.

[11] Boudreau and Schneider, ibid. P. 112–113.

[12] Boudreau and Schneider, ibid. P. 113.

[13] Boudreau and Schneider, ibid. P. 111–112.

[14] Dickson, Paul, *Bill Veeck: Baseball's Greatest Maverick*, (New York, Walker & Company, 2012), P. 145.

[15] Lebovitz, Hal, *Satchel Paige's Own Story*, (Westport, Connecticut, Meckler Publishing, 1948/1993). P. 64.

[16] Dickson, ibid. P. 147.

[17] *Associated Press*, "Satchel Paige Signs Contract With Cleveland," July 7, 1948.

[18] Ribowsky, ibid. P. 255.

[19] Spivey, Donald, *If You Were Only White: The Life of Leroy 'Satchel' Paige*, (Columbia, Missouri, University of Missouri Press, 2012), P. XV.

## Chapter 10: Help from Everywhere

[1] Lustig, Dennis, "Whatever Happened To Hal Peck?" *Cleveland Plain Dealer*, February 8, 1974.

[2] Lustig, Dennis, "Whatever Happened To Thurman Tucker?" *Cleveland Plain Dealer*, May 11, 1970.

[3] Judnich was acquired on November 20, 1947, along with Bob Muncrief, in exchange for Dick Kokos, Bryan Stephens, Joe Frazier, and $25,000.

[4] Feller, Bob and Gilbert, Bill, *Now Pitching, Bob Feller*, (New York, HarperPerennial, 1990), P. 153.

[5] Feller and Gilbert, ibid. P. 154.

[6] Frank, Stanley, "They're Just Wild About Boudreau," *Saturday Evening Post*, September, 1948.

## Chapter 11: The Knuckleball Magician

[1] Bearden, Gene and Lebovitz, Hal, "When It Came Time To Leave Home, I Cried," *Cleveland News*, January 20, 1949.

[2] Bearden, Gene and Lebovitz, Hal, "You Should Have Seen The One That Got Away," *Cleveland News*, January 24, 1949.

[3] Bearden was traded alongside Hal Peck and Al Gettel to the New York Yankees for catcher Sherm Lollar and second baseman Ray Mack. Lollar would appear in only 33 games with the Yankees over two years, posting a .214 batting average. Mack would only appear in one game for New York with zero at-bats.

[4] Bearden, Gene and Lebovitz, Hal, "Rookies Are Born To Sweat It Out," *Cleveland News*, February 3, 1949.

[5] Bearden and Lebovitz, ibid.

[6] Boudreau, Lou and Schneider, Russell, *Lou Boudreau: Covering All The Bases*, (Champaign, Illinois, Sagamore Publishing, 1993). P. 108.

[7] Bearden, Gene and Lebovitz, Hal, "DiMaggio Makes Life Miserable," *Cleveland Press*, (Date Missing), January, 1949.

[8] Boudreau, Lou and Schneider, Russell, "Lou Boudreau: Covering All The Bases," (Champaign, Illinois, Sagamore Publishing, 1993). P. 124.

[9] Bearden, Gene and Lebovitz, Hal, "DiMaggio Makes Life Miserable," *Cleveland Press*, (Date Missing), January, 1949.

[10] Lebovitz, Hal, "Gene Strikes Out Science," *Cleveland News*, October 5, 1948.

[11] Lebovitz, ibid.

[12] Lebovitz, ibid.

[13] Lebovitz, ibid.

[14] Spink, J.G.T., "Looping The Loops: Big Gene Blows 'Em Down," *Sporting News*, June 6, 1948.

[15] Fullerton, Hugh Jr., "Gene Protects Tattered Shirt," *Associated Press/Cleveland Plain Dealer*, October 5, 1948.

[16] (No byline), "Bearden Victories? In The Hat!" *Sporting News*, October 20, 1948.

[17] Lebovitz, Hal, "Gene Strikes Out Science," *Cleveland News*, October 5, 1948.

## Chapter 12: Top *This* Infield

[1] McAuley, Ed, "Cleveland Third Sacker Admitted Mistake, Never Complained Over Abuse Heaped on Him Due to Ill-Advised Compensation Plea; As Result, He Won Over Many Hecklers," September 30, 1940, *Cleveland News*.

[2] Albee, Dave, "Stopping Joe D's Streak Made Keltner Famous," *Associated Press*, June 30, 1991.

[3] Cramer, Richard Ben, *Joe DiMaggio: The Hero's Life*, (New York, Simon & Schuster, 2000). P. 186.

[4] Lustig, Dennis, "Whatever Happened To Ken Keltner?" *Cleveland Plain Dealer*, January 28, 1974.

[5] Joe Gordon led the Indians with 32 home runs and 124 runs batted in.

[6] Lubinger, Bill, "Indians Great Rosen Endured, Prevailed In The Face Of Bigotry," *Cleveland Plain Dealer*, October 12, 2010.

[7] "Joseph L. (Flash) Gordon," *Sporting News*, April 29, 1978.

[8] Ibid.

[9] Fitzgerald, Ed, "The Acrobatic Flash," *Sport Magazine*, July, 1949.

[10] Ibid.

[11] During the 1948 season, Clark played games at four different positions, including right field (44), left field (21), third base (5), and first base (1).

[12] Rumill, Ed, "Cleveland's 'Robbie' Masters Tough Breaks," *Baseball Magazine*, August, 1948.

[13] Ibid.

[14] Robinson, Eddie and Rogers, C. Paul III, *Lucky Me: My Sixty-Five Years in Baseball*, (Dallas, Southern Methodist University Press, 2011), P. 22–23.

[15] Ibid, P. 37.

[16] Ibid, P. 38.

[17] Ibid, P. 42.

[18] Ibid, P. 46.

[19] Middlesworth, Hal, "Mastermind Or Monster?" *Baseball Digest*, November-December, 1956.

[20] Merkin, Scott, "Family Recalls Very Special Life," *Chicago Tribune*, August 16, 2001.

[21] Withers, Tom, "Boudreau Dead At 84," *USA Today/Associated Press*, August 10, 2001.

[22] Boudreau, Lou and Schneider, Russell, *Lou Boudreau: Covering All the Bases*, (Champaign, Illinois, Sagamore Publishing, 1993). P. 118.

## Chapter 13: Feller and Paige Lead Surge

[1] Feller, Bob and Gilbert, Bill, *Now Pitching Bob Feller*, (New York, HarperPerennial, 1990), P. 156.

[2] Feller, Bob and Rocks, Burton, *Bob Feller's Little Black Book Of Baseball Wisdom*, (Chicago, Contemporary Books, 2001), P. 80.

[3] Feller and Rocks, ibid. P. 81.

[4] Dolgan, Bob, "A Racial Milestone," *Cleveland Plain Dealer*, April 26, 1998.

[5] Lustig, Dennis, "Whatever Happened To Eddie Klieman?" *Cleveland Plain Dealer*, February June 14, 1970.

[6] Lustig, Dennis, "Whatever Happened To Eddie Klieman?" *Cleveland Plain Dealer*, February 4, 1974.

[7] In 12 at-bats against Klieman, Ted Williams went 3–12 with 2 RBI, 4 walks, and a .250 batting average. Tommy Henrich went 5–11 against Klieman for his career with 2 RBI and a .455 batting average.

[8] Dolgan, Bob, "Legendary Indians Pitcher, Coach Dies," *Cleveland Plain Dealer*, October 21, 2002.

[9] Dolgan, ibid.

[10] Gibbons, Frank, "Hegan Calls the Pitches Now," *Baseball Digest*, January, 1949.

[11] Lustig, Dennis, "Whatever Happened To Jim Hegan?" *Cleveland Plain Dealer*, February 13, 1974.

[12] Gammons, Peter, "Great Person, Great Catcher," *Boston Globe*, July 20, 1984.

[13] Lustig, Dennis, "Whatever Happened To Joe Tipton?" *Cleveland Plain Dealer*, January 26, 1974.

[14] O'Neil, John "Buck," "Unforgettable Satchel Paige," *Reader's Digest*, April, 1984.

[15] O'Neil, ibid.

[16] Ribowsky, Mark, *Don't Look Back: Satchel Paige in the Shadows Of Baseball*, (New York, Simon & Schuster, 1994), P. 258.

[17] Ribowski, ibid, P. 262.

## Chapter 14: Early September—Making A Run

[1] Gibbons, Frank, "'Tribe's In, I Feller Can Beat Us Tonight,' Says Connie Mack," *Cleveland Press*, September 1, 1948.

[2] Lewis, Franklin, "McKechnie's Words: Weaker Teams Win Or Lose Pennants," *Cleveland Press*, September 3, 1948.

[3] Lewis, Franklin, ibid.

[4] Speaker, Tris, "Lemon's Shutouts Really Remarkable," *Cleveland News*, September 4, 1948.

[5] On their 16-game road trip from August 24 to September 6, the Indians finished with an 8–8 record.

[6] Gibbons, Frank, "Tribe Fights For Life; Boudreau Fights For Job," *Cleveland Press*, September 7, 1948.

[7] Speaker, Tris, "Failure To Bunch Hits Hurts Indians," *Cleveland Press*, September 7, 1948.

[8] Gibbons, Frank, "Doby Doubtful Starter As Tribe Nears Second," *Cleveland Press*, September 10, 1948.

[9] Katz, Wallace, "'Man Of Guts,' Says Doc," *Cleveland News*, October 9, 1948.

[10] Birtwell, Roger, "Sacrificed His Own Career On Diamond, Tutored Gene," *Sporting News*, October 20, 1948.

## Chapter 15: Tragedy and Suspense

[1] Cobbledick, Gordon, "Don Black's Greatest Victory," *American Weekly*, September 12, 1948.

[2] Cobbledick, ibid.

[3] Gibbons, Frank, "Don Black Holding On In Fight For Life," *Cleveland Press*, September 14, 1948.

[4] Gibbons, ibid.

[5] Gibbons, ibid.

[6] Gibbons, ibid.

[7] Daere, Marie, "Don Black Better, Talks With Nurse," *Cleveland Press*, September 15, 1948.

[8] Speaker, Tris, "Fine Relief Work Is Helping Indians," *Cleveland Press*, September 13, 1948.

[9] Speaker, ibid.

[10] Dickson, Paul, *Bill Veeck: Baseball's Greatest Maverick*, (New York, Walker and Company, 2012), P. 151.

[11] Dickson, ibid, P. 153.

## Chapter 16: All Out for the Pennant

[1] Gibbons, Frank, "'Not Much Chance Left Now,' Declares Veeck," *Cleveland Press*, September 15, 1948.

[2] Lewis, Franklin, "They Do Come Back! Black Case Recalls Campbell's Battles," *Cleveland Press*, September 15, 1948.

[3] Gibbons, Frank, "'We'll Never Give Up!' Boudreau's War Cry," *Cleveland Press*, September 17, 1948.

[4] "Tribe Sets Season Attendance Mark; May Reach 2 ½ Million," *Cleveland News*, September 20, 1948.

[5] Gibbons, Frank, "Not A Hope, It's A Fact Now! Tribe's Back In Race, And How!" *Cleveland Press*, September 20, 1948.

[6] Speaker, Tris, "Lou Fights His Way Out Of Slump," *Cleveland Press*, September 20, 1948.

[7] "Press Pennant Payoff," *Cleveland Press*, September 21, 1948.

[8] Feller, Bob and Gilbert, Bill, *Now Pitching, Bob Feller*, (New York, Citadel Press, 1990/2002). P. 157–158.

[9] Feller and Gilbert, ibid. P. 158.

[10] "Veeck Orders Series Tickets Printed; Price Set, Limit 4 Sets To Customer," *Cleveland Press*, September 23, 1948.

[11] Gibbons, Frank, "Feller, Lemon, Bearden Rest Of The Way— Boudreau," *Cleveland Press*, September 23, 1948.

## Chapter 17: AL Pennant in Indians' Sights

[1] "5000 Given Chance To Beat Rush For World Series Tickets," *Cleveland Press*, September 24, 1948.

[2] Gibbons, Frank, "'Spoiler' Title For '48 Season As Tribe Series Opens," *Cleveland Press*, September 24, 1948.

[3] Lewis, Franklin, "Indians Lethargic, Robinson Hitless As Streak Cracks," *Cleveland Press*, September 25, 1948.

[4] Gibbons, Frank, "'We'll Still Win,' Boudreau Predicts," *Cleveland Press*, September 25, 1948.

[5] Speaker, Tris, "Just Like 1920 All Over Again," *Cleveland Press*, September 25, 1948.

[6] Dickson, Paul, *Bill Veeck: Baseball's Greatest Maverick*, (New York, Walker and Company, 2012), P. 154.

[7] Holmes, Dan, "Bill Veeck's Night To End All Nights," Danholmes.com, September 1, 2007.

[8] Dickson, ibid. P. 155.

[9] Collier, Joe, "'Good Old Joe," Even Beats Shmoos; Gifts Range From Cars To Chickens," *Cleveland Press*, September 29, 1948.

[10] Collier, ibid.

[11] Collier, ibid.

[12] Collier, ibid.

[13] Collier, ibid.

[14] Gibbons, Frank, "Let's Face It—Savage Indians Sense The Kill," September 28, 1948.

## Chapter 18: Stretch Run

[1] Feller, Bob and Rocks, Burton, *Bob Feller's Little Black Book Of Baseball Wisdom*, (Chicago, Contemporary Books, 2001), P. 128.

[2] Cobbledick, Gordon, "Plain Dealing: Indians' Savage Attack Against White Sox Could Have Been The Convincer For Red Sox and Yankees," *Cleveland Plain Dealer*, September 29, 1948.

[3] "Fans Apply For One Million Tickets," *Cleveland Press*, September 28, 1948.

[4] Ibid.

[5] Heaton, Charles, "Bearden Calls Hegan Best In Game After ChiSox Draw Blanks," *Cleveland Plain Dealer*, September 29, 1948.

[6] Heaton, ibid.

[7] Jones, Harry, "Tigers Slow Indians' Flag Drive, 5-3," *Cleveland Plain Dealer*, October 2, 1948.

[8] Feller, Bob and Gilbert, Bill, *Now Pitching, Bob Feller*, (New York, Citadel Press, 1990/2002). P. 158–159.

[9] Heaton, Charles, "Feller, Lemon Or Bearden May Get Boudreau's Call," *Cleveland Plain Dealer*, October 4, 1948.

## Chapter 19: One for All the Marbles

[1] Boudreau, Lou and Schneider, Russell, *Lou Boudreau: Covering All The Bases*, (Champaign, Illinois, Sagamore Publishing, 1993). P. 83.

[2] Boudreau and Schneider, ibid. P. 83.

[3] Boudreau and Schneider, ibid. P. 84.

[4] Boudreau and Schneider, ibid. P. 84–85.

[5] Linn, Ed, *Hitter: The Life And Turmoils Of Ted Williams*, (New York, Harcourt, Brace & Company, 1993). P. 207.

[6] "Veeck Gets Half A Wish," *Cleveland Press*, October 4, 1948.

[7] Ibid.

[8] Collier, Joe, "Ball Fans Go Beany In Boston," *Cleveland Press*, October 4, 1948.

[9] Boudreau and Schneider, ibid. P. 121.

[10] Boudreau and Schneider, ibid. P. 121.

[11] Cobbledick, Gordon, "Joins Speaker, Lajoie, Coveleski, Rookie Performs 'Impossible' Task," *Cleveland Plain Dealer*, October 5, 1948.

[12] Loveland, Roelif, "Hard-Way Victory Sends City Wacky," *Cleveland Plain Dealer*, October 5, 1948.

[13] Jones, Harry, "Indians Win First Pennant In 28 Years: Bearden Victor, 8–3," *Cleveland Plain Dealer*, October 5, 1948.

[14] Enright, James, "When Kickapoo Helped Injuns Win '48 Playoff," *Chicago American*, April 29, 1967.

[15] Enright, ibid.

## Chapter 20: The World Series at Last

[1] Skipper, John C., *Billy Southworth: A Biography Of The Hall Of Fame Manager And Ballplayer*, (Jefferson, North

Carolina, McFarland & Company, Inc., Publishers, 2013), P. 157.

2 Small, Jack, "Tribe Pennant Cheers Don Black In Hospital," *Cleveland Press*, October 5, 1948.

3 Staff Special, "Veeck Sets Record In Dash To Congratulate His Champions," *Cleveland Press*, October 5, 1948.

4 Fullerton, Hugh Jr., "Gene Protects Tattered Shirt," *Associated Press/Cleveland Plain Dealer*, October 6, 1948.

5 Heaton, Charles, "Bob Toils Long In First Drill At Braves Field," *Cleveland Plain Dealer*, October 5, 1948.

6 "Johnny Likes To Start And Finish," *Associated Press/Cleveland Plain Dealer*, October 6, 1948.

7 Feller, Bob and Gilbert, Bill, *Now Pitching, Bob Feller*, (New York, Citadel Press, 1990/2002). P. 163.

8 Feller and Gilbert, ibid. P. 164.

9 Feller and Gilbert, ibid. P. 165.

10 Gibbons, Frank, "Masi, 'Out' At 2nd, Scores Winning Run, *Cleveland Press*, October 6, 1948.

11 Holmes, Tommy, "Bob's Curve Has Braves Blinking," *International News Service/Cleveland Plain Dealer*, October 6, 1948.

12 Southworth, Billy, "Will Never Forget Sain's Pitching—Southworth," *Cleveland Press*, October 7, 1948.

13 Schoor, Gene, *The History Of The World Series*, (New York, William Morrow and Company, Inc., 1990). 1948 excerpt.

14 Holmes, Tommy, "Hero Of Opener Takes The Blame," *International News Service/Cleveland Plain Dealer*, October 7, 1948.

15 "Elliott Exhibits Bruises On Legs," *United Press*, October 7, 1948.

16 Boudreau, Lou and Schneider, Russell, *Lou Boudreau: Covering All The Bases*, (Champaign, Illinois, Sagamore Publishing, 1993). P. 132.

## Chapter 21: The Bright Lights in Cleveland

[1] McLaughlin, Richard, "He Will Live In A Tent At Gate E Till Bleacher Sale Begins Friday," *Cleveland Press*, October 6, 1948.

[2] McLaughlin, ibid.

[3] Earley, Joe, "Good Old Joe Earley Has Everything—Except Ticket To World Series," *Cleveland Press*, October 7, 1948.

[4] Dolgan, Bob, "Indians Hero Bearden Dies," *Cleveland Plain Dealer*, March 20, 2004.

[5] Holmes, Tommy, "Holmes Praises Stadium Field As One Of Best," *Cleveland Plain Dealer*, October 9, 1948.

[6] Heaton, Charles, "Doesn't Believe He'll Have To Go To Mound Again," *Cleveland Plain Dealer*, October 9, 1948.

[7] Gibbons, Frank, "Gromek Faces Sain As Tribe Seeks Three In Four," *Cleveland Press*, October 9, 1948.

[8] Dolgan, Bob, "A Racial Milestone," *Cleveland Plain Dealer*, April 26, 1998.

[9] Dolgan, ibid.

[10] Moore, Joseph Thomas, *Pride Against Prejudice: The Biography Of Larry Doby*, (New York, Praeger, 1988). P. 4.

[11] "Ex-Pitcher Steve Gromek Dies At 82," *Associated Press*, March 19, 2002.

## Chapter 22: Disappointment and Jubilation

[1] Feller, Bob and Gilbert, Bill, *Now Pitching, Bob Feller*, (New York, Citadel Press, 1990/2002). P. 170.

[2] Feller and Gilbert, ibid. P. 170.

[3] Ribowsky, Mark, *Don't Look Back: Satchel Paige In The Shadows Of Baseball*, (New York, Simon & Schuster, 1994), P. 272.

[4] Heaton, Charles, "'We're On Our Way,' Declares Braves' Elliott," *Cleveland Plain Dealer*, October 11, 1948.

[5] Heaton, Charles, "Bearden May Be Cast In New Hero's Role; Indians Heading Home," *Cleveland Plain Dealer*, October 11, 1948.

[6] Dolgan, Bob, "Indians Hero Bearden Dies," *Cleveland Plain Dealer*, March 20, 2004.

[7] Dolgan, Bob, "Bearden's One Shining Season," *Cleveland Plain Dealer*, June 14, 1948.

[8] Doyle, James E., "The Sport Trail: On Top By A Knuckle," *Cleveland Plain Dealer*, October 12, 1948.

[9] Boudreau, Lou and Schneider, Russell, *Lou Boudreau: Covering All The Bases*, (Champaign, Illinois, Sagamore Publishing, 1993). P. 135.

[10] Lewis, Franklin, "Parade Of Champions Is One Long Joy Ride," *Cleveland Press*, October 12, 1948.

# ABOUT THE AUTHOR

**L**EW FREEDMAN IS the author of more than 70 books about sports and Alaska. A veteran journalist, Freedman has won more than 250 awards and has worked on the staffs of such newspapers as the *Chicago Tribune*, the *Anchorage Daily News*, and the *Philadelphia Inquirer*.

In addition, he has written for various baseball web sites and his baseball books include biographies with Juan Marichal and Ferguson Jenkins. He has also written such baseball history books as the story of the first All-Star game, and the Chicago White Sox's 1959 pennant and the franchise's determination to erase the curse of the 1919 "Black Sox" Scandal.

Freedman and his wife Debra live in Indiana.